DESCARTES'S
GAMBIT

DESCARTES'S GAMBIT

Peter J. Markie

CORNELL UNIVERSITY PRESS

Ithaca and London

CORNELL UNIVERSITY PRESS GRATEFULLY ACKNOWLEDGES
A GRANT FROM THE ANDREW W. MELLON FOUNDATION
THAT AIDED IN BRINGING THIS BOOK TO PUBLICATION.

First published 1986 by Cornell University Press.

International Standard Book Number 0-8014-1906-9
Library of Congress Catalog Card Number 86-6241

Printed in the United States of America

Librarians: Library of Congress cataloging information
appears on the last page of the book.

The paper in this book is acid-free and meets the guidelines
for permanence and durability of the Committee on Production
Guidelines for Book Longevity of the Council on Library Resources.

To my parents:
Stanley Joseph Markie
Mary Frances Killeen Markie

CONTENTS

ACKNOWLEDGMENTS

I received a great deal of help in constructing my interpretation of Descartes's Gambit. Donald Sievert generously and constructively criticized almost all my early attempts. Fred Feldman's work on Descartes's theory of certainty inspired my own, and Fred made encouraging comments on my first attempt to understand Descartes's theory. Richard Feldman found problems in everything I sent him, and I sent him just about everything. Margaret Wilson, whose work on Descartes has taught me much, made insightful criticisms of one of my first interpretations of the *cogito*; so did Larry Hohm. Three anonymous readers for Cornell University Press showed me ways to tighten my interpretation.

Steven Cahn brought me together with Cornell University Press. John Ackerman at Cornell guided, encouraged, and never once deserted me in my efforts to produce a final draft. The University of Missouri gave me special financial support through research grants in the summer of 1978, the spring of 1984, and the summer of 1984.

Several editors have kindly permitted me to use material I originally published in their journals. Some of the material in Chapter 2 appeared in "Fred Feldman and the Cartesian Circle," *Philosophical Studies*, 31 (1977), copyright 1977 by D. Reidel Publishing Company, Dordrecht, Holland, and in "Clear and Distinct Perception and Metaphysical Certainty," *Mind*, 88 (January 1977). My papers "Dreams and Deceivers in Meditation One," *Philosophical Review*, 2 (April 1982), and "The *Cogito* Puzzle," *Philosophy and Phenomenological Research*, 43 (September 1982) contain some of the material I present in Chapters 2, 3, 4, and 5. A few of the points I consider in Chapter 6 are contained in "From Cartesian Epistemology to Cartesian Metaphysics," *Philosophical Topics*, 13 (1982).

Cambridge University Press has permitted me to use selections from *The Philosophical Works of Descartes*, vols. I–II, edited and translated by Elizabeth S. Haldane and G. R. T. Ross (Cambridge: Cambridge University Press, 1911–1912, corrected edition, 1931).

My greatest debts are to two indefatigible sources of emotional support:

The swimmers of the Columbia Missouri Masters Group endured my sometimes—they would say often—foul moods as I worked off my intellectual frustrations at the pool. I owe special thanks to Bob Frank, Jess Hartley, Al Hahn, and Donna Kuizenga.

Kate Markie, in the middle of a demanding legal career, accepted the burden of a husband whose mind was often on Descartes rather than her or the daily responsibilities of life. In large measure, this book is a product of her patience and understanding.

P. J. M.

NOTE ON REFERENCES

The standard edition of Descartes's works is *Oeuvres de Descartes*, vols. I–XII, edited by C. Adam and P. Tannery (Paris: Cerf, 1897–1913). The standard English translation of Descartes's works is *The Philosophical Works of Descartes*, vols. I–II, edited and translated by Elizabeth S. Haldane and G. R. T. Ross (Cambridge: Cambridge University Press, 1931). *Descartes, Philosophical Letters*, edited by Anthony Kenny (Oxford: Clarendon Press, 1970), contains translations of much of Descartes's correspondence, almost none of which is in the Haldane and Ross collection. Elizabeth Anscombe and Peter Geach also translate some of Descartes's correspondence in *Descartes: Philosophical Writings* (London: Nelson, 1954).

I usually give two references for each quote: the first is to Adam and Tannery, cited as AT, the second to Haldane and Ross, cited as HR, to Kenny, cited as KL, or to Anscombe and Geach, cited as AG, whichever is appropriate. If a passage is not translated by Haldane and Ross, Kenny, or Anscombe and Geach, I simply give a reference to the Adam and Tannery collection.

The fact that the Haldane and Ross translation is widely used by English-speaking students of Descartes is a strong point in favor of following it. That it mistranslates some philosophically important passages is a strong point against doing so. I have compromised. I follow

Haldane and Ross when they do not knock Descartes's philosophical thought out of joint and depart from them when they do. I indicate the passages where I depart even slightly from Haldane and Ross by placing an asterisk * after my reference to them. Whenever my departure from Haldane and Ross is crucial to my interpretation, I argue for the departure.

PETER J. MARKIE

Columbia, Missouri

DESCARTES'S
GAMBIT

Chapter 1

INTRODUCTION

Descartes's Gambit

Each of us has a mental life; we conceive, doubt, hope, believe, and so on. Do our mental traits belong to our physical body or to a nonphysical mind distinct from, but related to, our body? It is easy to formulate different theories on the issue but hard to show a particular theory is correct.

Consider Descartes's theory of the self. He formulates his main conclusions by using 'I' to refer to whatever has his mental traits, and he assumes each of us can truly say the same:

C1: I am a substance.
C2: I am essentially thinking.
C3: I am not essentially extended.
C4: I am not extended.
C5: I am not numerically identical with my body.
C6: My body and I are such that each can exist without the other.

Descartes's first conclusion is that he is the sort of thing that has properties but is itself neither a property nor a collection of properties. He is not just a bundle of thoughts, feelings, and perceptions. He is a thing to which such attributes belong. Descartes's second conclusion is that he has the property of thinking and it is logically impossible for

17

him to exist without it. The third says Descartes could, in terms of logical possibility, exist without being spatially extended and, so, without any physical traits that presuppose spatial extension. The fourth claim is that he is not spatially extended. The fifth conclusion draws out an implication of the fourth. Descartes must, if he is not extended, be diverse from, though in some way connected with, that thing which is his body. Descartes's last claim is that his connection with his body is not logically necessary; he and his body can exist without each other.

How can Descartes show he is right? He cannot do so by directing us to our physical senses. They would not provide evidence for the existence of a nonphysical mind, even if one existed. He cannot tell us to observe ourselves by introspection. When we introspect, we make and report discoveries in the first person, as in "I think"; we do not discover what sort of thing, if any, the 'I' in those reports designates. It may refer to a nonphysical self, as Descartes says, or it may refer to our body, as it seems to in "I am a handsome devil." Some philosophers have argued that 'I' is not a referring expression at all in such reports. Descartes cannot deduce his theory from premises true by definition. All he can deduce from such necessary truths are more necessary truths, and his claims are contingent (after all, he might not have existed). Descartes points out the futility of this procedure, which he associates with his Scholastic predecessors:

> Were I for example to ask Epistemon himself what a man is, and were he to reply, as is done in the Schools, that a man is a rational animal; and if, in addition, in order to explain these two terms which are not less obscure than the first, he were to conduct us by all the steps which are termed metaphysical, we should be dragged into a maze from which it would be impossible for us to emerge. As a matter of fact, from this question two others arise, the first is what is an animal? The second, what is reasonable? . . . You see that the question, like branches of a genealogical tree, would go increasing and multiplying; and finally all these wonderful questions would finish in pure tautology, which would clear up nothing, and would leave us in our original ignorance. [*The Search after Truth*: AT X, 515–516; HR I, 317; consider too: *Meditations*; AT VII, 25; HR I, 150]

Descartes can deduce his theory of the self from some of his general metaphysical principles and some contingent premises about himself. His metaphysics contains these principles:

MP1: Whatever thinks is a substance.

MP2: Whatever is extended is a substance.

MP3: Whatever thinks is essentially thinking but not essentially extended.

MP4: Whatever is extended is essentially extended but not essentially thinking.

MP5: If two things are substances other than God, then each can exist without the other.

These principles, plus the contingent facts that he thinks and that his body is extended, entail all six of Descartes's conclusions about himself. Yet no one will accept these metaphysical principles who does not already accept Descartes's conclusions. A materialist will scorn MP3 and MP4, in particular, as question begging. Those principles assume a dualistic picture of the world by dividing substances into the mutually exclusive categories of the thinking and the extended.

Sense experience, introspection, deductive reasoning from analytic truths or from general metaphysical principles all seem useless. If Descartes cannot defend his theory of the self in any of these ways, how can he defend it? Descartes thinks he can deduce his theory from contingent premises about his knowledge of himself. He nurtures this idea throughout his philosophical works.

We find this hint in the *Rules:*

Likewise many things are often necessarily united with one another, though most people, not noticing what their true relation is, reckons [*sic*] them among those that are contingently connected. As example, I give the following propositions: 'I exist, therefore God exists': also '*I know, therefore I have a mind distinct from my body.*' [XII; AT X, 421–422; HR I, 43; my emphasis]

Descartes is more explicit in *The Search after Truth:*

I am not a body; otherwise, doubting of my body I should at the same time doubt of myself, and this I cannot do; for I am absolutely convinced that I exist, and I am so much convinced of it, that I can in no wise doubt of it. [AT X, 518; HR I, 319]

That he is certain he exists but uncertain his body exists implies that he is not a body.

In the *Discourse on Method*, Descartes presents the premise that he is certain he exists and thinks but uncertain he has a body:

> Examining attentively that which I was, I saw that I could conceive that I had no body, and that there was no world nor place where I might be; but yet I could not for all that conceive that I was not. On the contrary, I saw from the very fact that I thought of doubting the truth of other things, it very evidently and certainly followed that I was; on the other hand if I had only ceased from thinking, even if all the rest of what I had ever imagined had really existed, I should have no reason for thinking that I had existed. [AT VI, 32–33; HR I, 101]

He then infers his theory of the self:

> From that I knew that I was a substance the whole essence or nature of which is to think, and that for its existence has no need of any place, nor does it depend on any material thing; so that this 'me', . . . is entirely distinct from body, . . . and even if body were not, the soul would not cease to be what it is. [AT VI, 32–33; HR I, 101]

Descartes indicates his intention to derive his theory of the self from premises about his self-knowledge in the preface to the *Meditations*:

> So far as I was aware, I knew nothing clearly as belonging to my essence, excepting that I was a thing that thinks, or a thing that has in itself the faculty of thinking. But I shall show hereafter how from the fact that I know no other thing which pertains to my essence, it follows that there is no other thing which really does belong to it. [AT VII, 7–8; HR I, 138]

In the *Principles*, Descartes reports his certainty that he thinks and exists and his uncertainty that he has a body:

> While we thus reject all that of which we can possibly doubt, and feign that it is false, it is easy to suppose that there is no God, nor heaven, nor bodies, and that we possess neither hands, nor feet, nor indeed any body; but we cannot in the same way conceive that we who doubt these things are not; for there is a contradiction in conceiving that what thinks does not at the same time as it thinks, exist. [I, vii; AT VIII, 7; HR I, 221]

He then asserts:

> This furnishes us with the distinction which exists between the soul and the body, or between that which thinks and that which is corporeal. [I, viii; AT VIII, 7; HR I, 221]

Descartes even remarks to Clovius that his views on self-knowledge are not as important for their own sake as they are for their implications regarding the nature of the self. His trademark dictum, "*Cogito, ergo sum,*" by which he reports his certainty that he thinks and exists, is "so simple and natural that it might have come from anybody's pen"; its real value is that it can be used to "establish that this conscious I is an immaterial substance with no corporeal element" [*Correspondence;* AT III, 247; KL, 84; AG, 263].[1]

Descartes's Gambit, then, is to deduce his theory of the self from premises about his self-knowledge. He states the premises in the first person to go with his main conclusions about the self:

P1: I am certain that I think.
P2: I am certain that I exist.
P3: I am uncertain that I have a body.

Each of us can truly say the same, according to Descartes, and so each of us has premises from which to deduce that we too fit his theory of the self.

Descartes is not the first philosopher to hit upon this strategy. Augustine argues:

> The mind knows itself, even when it seeks for itself, as we have already shown. But nothing is at all rightly said to be known while its substance is unknown. And therefore, when the mind knows itself, it knows its own substance; and when it is certain about itself it is certain about its own substance. But it is certain about itself, as those things which are said above prove convincingly; although it is not at all certain whether it is air, or fire, or body, or some function of body. Therefore it is not any of these. And to that whole which is bidden to know itself belongs this,

---

1. I follow Anscombe and Geach's translation here.

that it is certain that it is not any of those things of which it is uncertain, and is certain that it is that only, which only it is certain that it is.[2]

Nonetheless, Descartes's proposal of the strategy has a special, now well-known, historical significance. His suggestion is that a particular theory in metaphysics, which deals with the nature of reality (in this case, us), can be derived from a particular theory in epistemology, which deals with how we know reality (in this case, how we know ourselves). This brand of philosophical alchemy exemplifies Descartes's break with Scholastic philosophy; it is a defining trait of the early Modern period that begins with his work. Indeed, Descartes's Gambit is a precursor of the sort of philosophical transmutation often tried today: the attempt to get metaphysical conclusions about the nature of reality from linguistic theories about how we describe reality.[3]

Descartes's Gambit is promising. It is surely better than trying to establish his theory of the self on the basis of external sensation, introspection, or deductive reasoning from analytic or general metaphysical principles. He needs to find some non-question-begging premises from which to derive his theory; his best bet is to look beyond his metaphysics to other areas of his philosophy, and his claims about self-knowledge are natural candidates. He can defend them without assuming a dualistic picture of the world from the start, and since they

2. Augustine, *De Trinitate*, Book X, Chapter 10. Descartes misses this similarity between his position and Augustine's. He tells Clovius that what makes him different from Augustine is that he, Descartes, uses the premises about self-knowledge to argue for his theory of the self; consider the *Correspondence*; AT III, 247; KL, 84. I am indebted to two essays for bringing the similarity between Descartes's position and Augustine's to my attention: G. E. M. Anscombe's "The First Person," in *Mind and Language: Wolfson College Lectures 1974* (Oxford: Clarendon Press, 1975), pp. 45–65, and Harold Noonan's "Identity and the First Person," in *Intention and Intentionality: Essays in Honor of G. E. M. Anscombe*, eds. Cora Diamond and Jenny Teichman (Ithaca: Cornell University Press, 1979), pp. 55–70. I follow Noonan's translation of Augustine's remarks in *De Trinitate*. Edwin Curley's *Descartes against the Skeptics* (Cambridge: Harvard University Press, 1978) contains a fine discussion of the relations between Descartes's philosophy and Augustine's.

3. Consider, for example, Saul Kripke's attempt to derive Cartesian conclusions about the self using premises about proper names in "Naming and Necessity," in *Semantics of Natural Languages*, eds. Donald Davidson and Gilbert Harman (Dordrecht: Reidel, 1976). Descartes tries to derive C_1–C_6 from P_1–P_3 and in that way tries to derive a metaphysical theory from an epistemic one. He does not, however, make P_1–P_3 or any other epistemic claims the ultimate foundation of his metaphysics in the sense that all his metaphysical claims are to be derived from them.

describe how he knows himself, they are likely to have implications for what he is like.

Descartes never makes a clear, detailed attempt to implement his strategy. His works contain several obscure efforts in which he says just enough to leave us holding a bag of interpretive and evaluative questions. Let us look at the major questions.

The Theory of Self-Knowledge

We cannot appreciate Descartes's Gambit until we understand P1, P2, and P3, the premises about self-knowledge with which he begins. We cannot understand those premises until we know what he means by 'certain' and 'uncertain' in them.

Descartes describes certainty as an epistemic state, a degree of reasonable belief so high there is no reason to doubt what is believed:

> Inasmuch as reason already persuades me that I ought no less carefully to withhold my assent from matters which are not entirely certain [*certa*] and indubitable [*indubitata*] than from those which appear to me manifestly to be false, if I am to find in each one some reason to doubt [*rationem dubitandi*], this will suffice to justify my rejecting the whole. [*Meditations*; AT VII, 18; HR I, 145]

But what is it for a belief to be reasonable, and what is a reason for doubt? We need to know how Descartes relates the concept of certainty to such other concepts as truth and conviction. We can be uncertain of what is true; can we be certain of something that is not true? Is certainty the same as conviction? Descartes seems to equate certainty with unshakable conviction:

> We have assumed a conviction [*persuasionem*] so strong that nothing can remove it, and this persuasion [*persuasio*] is clearly the same as perfect certitude [*certitudo*]. [*Reply to the Second Objections*; AT VII, 144–145; HR II, 41]

Yet how can certainty be identical to both a degree of reasonable belief and a degree of conviction? If two people have the same evidence for the same belief, their beliefs must be equally reasonable, but they may have different degrees of conviction. Some are more gullible than others: while Descartes is not convinced there are bodies, a materialist might be.

Certainty, like any intentional attitude, has *de dicto, de re,* and *de se* forms, as represented by

    a. "Descartes is certain that someone thinks."   (*de dicto*)
    b. "Someone is such that Descartes is certain of her that she thinks."   (*de re*)
    c. "Descartes is certain that he himself thinks."   (*de se*)

P1, P2, and P3 concern *de se* certainty. We must determine what Descartes takes the content of his *de se* certainty or uncertainty to be. Of what is he certain when he is certain he thinks and exists? Of what is he uncertain when he is uncertain he has a body?

It is often assumed that Descartes is a proposition theorist. The proposition theory says the content of each form of certainty is a proposition; propositions are the primary bearers of truth value, whatever else they may be. When Descartes is certain *de dicto* that someone thinks, the content of his certainty is the proposition that someone thinks. When he is certain *de re* of someone that she thinks, the content is a proposition to the effect that that very person thinks. When he is certain *de se* that he himself thinks, the content is the proposition he would express in English by "I think." Certainty always involves a relation between a person and a proposition. The *de dicto* form is the primary one by which the other two are explained; we get *de dicto* certainty by being certain of propositions and *de re* and *de se* certainty by being certain of the right sorts of propositions. Different versions of the proposition theory give different accounts of what sorts of propositions are the "right sorts" for *de re* and for *de se* attitudes.[4]

---

    4. A recent statement of the proposition theory is Roderick Chisholm's *Person and Object* (London: George Allen and Unwin, 1976). Consider too Frege's "The Thought: A Logical Inquiry," *Mind,* 65 (July 1956), pp. 289–311. An alternative to the proposition theory is the property theory, in which the content of certainty is always a property. Recent statements of the property theory are Roderick Chisholm's *The First Person* (Minneapolis: University of Minnesota Press, 1981) and David Lewis's "Attitudes De Dicto and De Se," *Philosophical Review,* 88 (October 1979), pp. 513–543.

Descartes writes like a proposition theorist:

> I who have some little knowledge of the principles of geometry recog-
> nise quite clearly that three angles are equal to two right angles, and it is
> not possible for me not to believe this so long as I apply my mind to its
> demonstration; but so soon as I abstain from attending to the proof,
> although I still recollect having clearly comprehended it, it may easily
> occur that I come to doubt its truth, if I am ignorant of there being a
> God. [*Meditations*; AT VII, 69–70; HR I, 184]

What is known, believed, doubted, and clearly comprehended is a
thing capable of being demonstrated and possessing a truth value. It
appears, then, to be a proposition, in this case, that the three angles of
a triangle equal two right angles. Consider too Descartes's description
of our *de se* knowledge:

> Thus each individual can mentally have intuition of the fact that he
> exists, and that he thinks; that the triangle is bounded by three lines
> only, the sphere by a single superficies, and so on. [*Rules*, III; AT X,
> 368; HR I, 7]

What kind of proposition theorist is Descartes? How, in particular,
does he understand *de se* certainty in relation to *de dicto* certainty; what
sort of proposition does he think he must consider to have *de se* certainty rather than mere *de dicto* certainty? He sometimes writes as though
the content of his *de se* certainty is always a proposition to the effect
that he has or lacks a particular property. If he asserts "*Ego cogito*" to
himself with certainty, he uses 'ego' to refer to himself and so asserts
with certainty a proposition to the effect that he in particular thinks.
Consider again his remark in the *Rules*:

> Thus each individual can mentally have intuition of the fact that he
> exists, and that he thinks. [III; AT X, 368; HR I, 7]

Yet, Descartes also says:

> It is very manifest by the natural light which is in our souls, that no
> qualities or properties pertain to nothing; and that where some are
> perceived there must necessarily be some thing or substance on which

they depend. And the same light shows us that we know a thing or substance so much the better the more properties we observe in it. And we certainly observe many more qualities in our minds than in any other thing, inasmuch as there is nothing that excites us to knowledge of whatever kind, which does not even much more certainly compel us to a consciousness of our thought. [*Principles*, I, xi; AT VIII, 8–9; HR I, 223]

Some commentators take Descartes to be implying that we never apprehend a proposition to the effect that a particular thing has a particular property; we at best apprehend that a particular property exists and infer that some unspecified substance has it. These commentators find a similar implication in Descartes's remark that "We do not have immediate cognition of substances" [*Reply to the Fourth Objections*; AT VII, 222; HR II, 98].[5]

Once we understand P1, P2, and P3 by understanding Descartes's views on the nature and content of his certainty or uncertainty about himself, we still need to examine his arguments for the three premises themselves.

Descartes's remarks suggest at least three explanations of why he is certain he thinks and exists. First, his certainty that he thinks and that he exists stems from an intuition that he thinks and an intuition that he exists:

Intuition is the undoubting conception of an unclouded and attentive mind, and springs from the light of reason alone; it is more certain than deduction itself, in that it is simpler, though deduction, as we have noted above, cannot by us be erroneously conducted. Thus each individual can mentally have intuition of the fact that he exists, and that he thinks. [*Rules*, III; AT X, 368; HR I, 7]

Alternatively, his certainty that he thinks may stem from an act of intuition, but his certainty that he exists stems from an act of inference:

There is a contradiction in conceiving that what thinks does not at the same time as it thinks, exist. And hence this cognition, *I think, therefore*

---

5. Consider, for example, Donald Sievert's position in "Sellars and Descartes on the Fundamental Form of the Mental," *Philosophical Studies*, 37 (1980), pp. 251–257.

I am, is the first and most certain of all that occurs to one who philosophises in an orderly way. [*Principles*, I, vii; AT VIII, 6–7; HR I, 221*]

A third possibility is that his certainty that he thinks and exists results
from the fact that any attempt to cast doubt on these beliefs only
affirms them:

> But there is some deceiver or other, very powerful and very cunning,
> who ever employs his ingenuity in deceiving me. Then without doubt I
> exist also if he deceives me, and let him deceive me as much as he will,
> he can never cause me to be nothing so long as I think that I am
> something. [*Meditations*; AT VII, 25; HR I, 150]

> But it will be said that these phenomena are false and that I am dream-
> ing. Let it be so; still it is at least quite certain that it seems to me that I
> see light, that I hear noise and that I feel heat. That cannot be false;
> properly speaking it is what is in me called feeling; and used in this
> precise sense that is no other thing than thinking. [*Meditations*; AT
> VII, 29; HR I, 153]

Can we braid these different explanations into a single cogent one? If
we cannot, should we prefer one to the others?

Descartes's account of P3 is more straightforward: He is uncertain
whether he has a body because hypotheses such as that he is deceived by
a god give him a reason to doubt whether he has a body. Again, though,
what does he mean by a reason for doubt? Can he meet the objections
that have been raised to his claim to have a reason to doubt he has a
body, including the charge that his position is self-contradictory?[6]

The Theory of the Self

Descartes's theory of the self sounds simple enough at first. Each
person's self—that thing which is the subject of his mental attributes—
is a substance. It is essentially thinking; not essentially extended. It is
not extended, period. Each person's self and body are numerically

6. G. E. Moore, "Certainty," in *Philosophical Papers* (New York: Macmillan,
1959); David and Jean Beer Blumenfeld, "Can I Know that I Am Not Dreaming?" in
Descartes: Critical and Interpretive Essays, ed. Michael Hooker (Baltimore: Johns
Hopkins University Press, 1978).

distinct, and the connection between them is weaker than that between true lovers: each can exist without the other.

So what is a substance? Descartes sometimes writes as though it is anything with attributes:

> Everything in which there resides immediately, as in a subject, or by means of which there exists anything that we perceive, i.e. any property, quality, or attribute, of which we have a real idea, is called a *Substance*. [*Reply to the Second Objections*; AT VII, 161; HR II, 53]

He writes in the *Principles* as though a substance is anything that exists independently of all other things except God:

> By substance, we can understand nothing else than a thing which so exists that it needs no other thing in order to exist. And in fact only one single substance can be understood which clearly needs nothing else, namely, God. . . . Created substances, however, whether corporeal or thinking, may be conceived under this common concept; for they are things which need only the concurrence of God in order to exist. [I, li–lii; AT VIII, 24–25; HR I, 239–240]

These definitions do not seem equivalent. I appear to be a substance under the first, but I may not be one under the second, since, by Descartes's own account, I cannot exist unless the attribute of thought also exists. If my body and I are numerically distinct, our union is a substance according to the first definition but not according to the second. It has properties, but it cannot exist unless the substances that compose it—my body and my self—exist.

What is an essential attribute? Descartes says an attribute is essential to a thing only if the thing cannot exist without it: "For in my opinion nothing without which a thing can still exist is comprised in its essence" [*Reply to the Fourth Objections*; AT VII, 219; HR II, 97]. Essential attributes must meet some other condition as well, for Descartes does not include existence in his essence even though he cannot exist without it. We might take the extra condition to be that an essential attribute must be one some substance could exist without. This suits Descartes's claim that existence is not essential to him, but it contradicts his claim [*Meditations*; AT VII, 68; HR I, 182] that existence is essential to God.

Once we understand Descartes's theory of the self (C1–C6), we can consider his attempt to derive it from his theory of self-knowledge (P1–

P3). None of his metaphysical conclusions follows directly from his epistemic premises. Descartes sometimes tries to bridge the gap with premises about God:

> And first of all, because I know that all things which I understand clearly and distinctly can be created by God just as I understand them, it suffices that I am able to understand one thing apart from another clearly and distinctly in order to be certain that the one is different from the other, since they may be made to exist in separation at least by the omnipotence of God; and it does not matter by what power this separation is made for me to judge them to be different. Now just because I know certainly that I exist, and that meanwhile I do not remark that any other thing necessarily pertains to my nature or essence, except that I am a thinking thing, I rightly conclude that my essence consists solely in the fact that I am a thinking thing. And although possibly (or rather certainly, as I shall say in a moment) I possess a body with which I am very intimately conjoined, yet because, on the one side, I have a clear and distinct idea of myself inasmuch as I am only a thinking and unextended thing, and as, on the other, I possess a distinct idea of body, inasmuch as it is only an extended and unthinking thing, it is certain that I am really distinct from my body and can exist without it. [*Meditations*; AT VII, 78; HR I, 190*]

His attempts to establish God's existence are notoriously unsuccessful, so it is a relief when Descartes says we can establish his theory of the self without appealing to God:

> Consequently, if I had not been in search of a certitude greater than the vulgar, I should have been satisfied with showing in the Second Medita-tion that *Mind* was apprehended as a thing that subsists, although nothing belonging to the body be ascribed to it, and conversely that *Body* was understood to be something subsistent without anything being attributed to it that pertains to the mind. And I should have added nothing more in order to prove that there was a real distinction between mind and body: because commonly we judge that all things stand to each other in respect to their actual relations in the same way as they are related in our consciousness. But, since one of those hyperbolical doubts adduced in the First Meditation went so far as to prevent me from being sure of this very fact (viz. that things are in their true nature exactly as we perceive them to be), so long as I supposed that I had no knowledge of the author of my being, all that I have said about God and about truth in the Third, Fourth and Fifth Meditations serves to further the conclusion as to the real distinction between *mind* and *body*, which

is finally completed in Meditation VI. [*Reply to the Fourth Objections;*
AT VII, 226; HR II, 101]

We must appeal to God's existence to establish the theory of the self
with certainty. If we are willing to settle for less than certainty—at the
risk of being branded "vulgar"—we can leave God out of the argument. Descartes leaves God out in the *Discourse* [AT VI, 32–33; HR I,
101] and *The Search after Truth* [AT X, 518; HR I, 319].

Descartes's arguments are fast and loose with or without God. We
need to determine how he would tighten them to get a cogent argument for each of his conclusions about himself, or whether he can
even do so.

The Primacy of Certainty

Descartes's position on the nature and content of certainty is the
central element in his Gambit. It is the basis of his defense of his
premises about self-knowledge (P1, P2, and P3). It provides the principles that enable him to move from those premises to intermediate
conclusions about the logical possibility of his existing in some ways
and not others, from which he derives his theory of the self. Commentators who do not appreciate Descartes's Gambit—and there are
many—have not fully understood his position on the nature and content of certainty.[7]

It is not self-evident that Descartes's position on certainty is the
central element in his Gambit. No self-evident fact could have been so
long overlooked. When readers work their way through my discussion
of Descartes's position on the nature and content of certainty in Chapters 2 and 3, some will be puzzled as to how that material, especially
the parts dealing with such fine points as the contents of *de se* certainty,
can be central to Descartes's Gambit. I ask for patience and offer a

7. Two commentators who have seen that Descartes's position on the content of his
certainty is important to his Gambit strategy are Margaret Wilson, *Descartes* (London:
Routledge and Kegan Paul, 1978), pp. 67, 198–200, and James Van Cleve, "Conceivability and the Cartesian Argument for Dualism," *Pacific Philosophical Quarterly*,
64 (January 1983), pp. 35–45. Neither has devoted more than a few pages to this
important issue, however, and both have outlined positions considerably different
from the one I develop.

promise: The importance of Descartes's position on certainty gradually becomes clear in later chapters. In Chapters 4 and 5, I use it to interpret his theory of self-knowledge, and I display how Descartes's position on the nature and content of certainty plays a crucial role in his claim to be certain that he thinks and exists. In Chapters 6 and 7, I show how Descartes's position on the nature and content of certainty provides the crucial premises he needs to get from his theory of self-knowledge to his theory of the self.

As I present each part of my interpretation (my treatment of Descartes's position on certainty, my treatment of his theory of self-knowledge, and my treatment of his theory of the self), I argue for that part's textual and philosophical superiority to competing interpretations. The main strength of my interpretation lies in how the parts fit together to form an overall interpretation of Descartes's complex argument for mind–body dualism. My interpretation reveals that Descartes's argument is much stronger than has often been thought. Descartes has sound arguments for his three premises about self-knowledge and, so, a secure base from which to argue for his theory of the self. He has an interesting, non-question-begging argument for each of his six conclusions about himself, so his Gambit is a serious challenge to materialists.

Note on Accuracy and Intent

We must approach Descartes's philosophy as sympathetic, constructive critics in order to learn philosophy from him. We must not settle for just recounting the different parts of his position in general terms and noting which are straightforward and clear in their content and motivation and which are vague, ambiguous, or self-contradictory. We need to consider what he might have in mind when he is unclear or ambiguous and how he might have eliminated problems if they had been pointed out to him.

It is tempting, when taking this approach to the history of philosophy, to write as though one begins with an exclusive interpretation license granted by the historical figure and proceeds by way of a direct private line into his once-active head; "This is what Descartes meant, not that." We all know better. We begin with a hunch and proceed by guesses. My hunch is that Descartes is on the right track in attempting to derive his theory of the self from his theory of self-knowledge—significant parts of the latter can be strongly defended by appeal to the former—and we can appreciate this fact once we appreciate his position on the nature and content of certainty. My guesses concern what Descartes has in mind when he says puzzling things, and how he would clear away confusions and eliminate inconsistencies if they were pointed out to him. My guesses are not arbitrary; they are informed by Descartes's clear remarks and my own sense of what is philosophically plausible. The payoff is an increased knowledge of what Descartes might have thought and how he might have developed his position, an awareness of the extent to which his position, so developed, is correct, and a more profound understanding of the philosophical issues at hand. That is what I am out to gain.

Chapter 2

CERTAINTY

Descartes's Gambit is a double-lock box. The keys are the answers to two questions: What does Descartes mean by 'certainty'? What does he take the content of his certainty to be? I want to answer the first question now. Although, as we have seen, Descartes's remarks on certainty can be more confusing than clarifying, there is a cogent position behind them in which different kinds of certainty are defined and related to one another and to other important concepts. To present that position, I assume, for the moment, an answer to the second question; namely, that the content of certainty is always a proposition. I develop and defend this assumption in Chapter 3; for now, I present Descartes's different kinds of certainty as different kinds of relations between persons and propositions.

Epistemic and Psychological Varieties of Certainty

Descartes sometimes uses 'certainty' to designate a state he describes in psychological terms and sometimes uses it to designate a state he describes in epistemic terms. We might decide that he is confused over whether one thing, called 'certainty,' is a psychological or epistemic state, or we might decide that he considers one state to be both psychological and epistemic and alternately stresses one of its aspects to the exclusion of the other. Both options are too simplistic.

Descartes actually distinguishes, uses, and at times confuses three different kinds of certainty. Two are epistemic states, the third is psychological, and all three play important roles in his philosophy. The two epistemic states are metaphysical and moral certainty (his terms). The third is psychological certainty (my term for lack of one supplied by Descartes). The epistemic varieties of certainty are the most important for our purposes, since we are mainly interested in Descartes's theory of self-knowledge: he tells Gassendi explicitly that the basic claims of his theory (P1, P2, and P3) concern "metaphysical certitude" [*Reply to the Fifth Objections*; AT VII, 352; HR II, 207]. Nonetheless, we cannot fully appreciate metaphysical and moral certainty until we see how Descartes relates them to psychological certainty. I concentrate first on metaphysical and moral certainty, and then examine how Descartes relates them to psychological certainty, as well as to other concepts in his philosophy.

Metaphysical and Moral Certainty

Descartes distinguishes between metaphysical and moral certainty in the *Discourse*:[1]

> If there are finally any persons who are not sufficiently persuaded of the existence of God and of their soul by the reasons which I have brought forward, I wish that they should know that all other things of which they perhaps think themselves more assured (such as possessing a body, and that there are stars and an earth and so on) are less certain. For, although we have a moral assurance of these things which is such that it seems that it would be extravagant in us to doubt them, at the same time no one, unless he is devoid of reason, can deny, when a metaphysical certainty is in question, that there is sufficient cause for our not having complete assurance, by observing the fact that when asleep we may similarly imagine that we have another body, and that we see other stars

1. The material in this section is drawn from my "Dreams and Deceivers in Meditation One," *Philosophical Review*, 90 (April 1981), pp. 185–209, and "The *Cogito* Puzzle," *Philosophy and Phenomenological Research*, 43 (September 1982), pp. 59–81.

and another earth, without there being anything of the kind. [AT VI, 37–38; HR I, 104]

Descartes claims to be "less certain" that his body, the stars, and earth exist than that his soul and God exist. He has only moral assurance about his body, the stars, and earth; he has metaphysical certainty, or complete assurance, about his soul and God. But, even though moral certainty is of a lower grade than metaphysical certainty, it has some punch to it; Descartes calls it extravagant to doubt moral certainties.

The distinction between metaphysical and moral certainty is also present in the *Meditations*. Descartes describes the beliefs challenged by the Dream and Deceiver Arguments of Meditation One as "opinions in some measure doubtful . . . and at the same time highly probable, so that there is much more reason to believe in than to deny them" [AT VII, 22; HR I, 148]. He might have put his point differently: the beliefs he has considered are not metaphysical certainties (they are in some measure doubtful), but they are moral certainties (they are highly probable). Consider too Descartes's remark in Meditation Six:

> I easily understand, I say, that the imagination could be thus constituted if it is true that body exists; and because I can discover no other convenient mode of explaining it, I conjecture with probability that body does exist; but this is only with probability. [AT VII, 73; HR I, 186–187]

Again, Descartes might have put his point differently: since the proposition that he has a body gives the best explanation of the data about his imagination, it is a moral certainty (probable); that the proposition can explain the data does not make it a metaphysical certainty (it is only probable).

Descartes uses the distinction between metaphysical and moral certainty to answer his critics. Bourdin objects that Descartes contradicts himself in Meditation One in claiming to find nothing metaphysically certain and yet to know there is no peril in assuming an evil deceiver exists:

> What? 'I know'? Is that certain and beyond all doubt? And has our great shipwreck of truth left at least this driftwood floating? [*Seventh Objections and Replies*; AT VII, 471; HR II, 275]

Descartes punctures Bourdin's sarcasm with his distinction:

> I spoke only of the moral mode of knowing, which suffices for the regulation of life, and which I have often insisted is so vastly different from that Metaphysical mode of knowing which is here in question. [*Seventh Objections and Replies*; AT VII, 475; HR II, 278]

Moral and metaphysical certainty are different "modes of knowing." There is no contradiction in saying that a proposition is known in the first mode but not in the second.

Can we define moral and metaphysical certainty in a way that captures Descartes's remarks? Let us try moral certainty first.

Moral certainties have three important characteristics. It is "extravagant for us to doubt them" [*Discourse*; AT VI, 37–38; HR I, 104], we have "more reason to believe in than to deny them" [*Meditations*; AT VII, 22; HR I, 148], and there is "*much* more reason to believe in than to deny them" [*Meditations*; AT VII, 22; HR I, 148; my emphasis]. The first two traits are fairly easy to appreciate. We may adopt any of three epistemic attitudes toward a proposition: we may believe it, deny it, or doubt it (neither believe it nor deny it). The first trait of our moral certainties is that it is more reasonable for us to believe them than to doubt them. The second is that it is more reasonable for us to believe them than to deny them. The third trait (that there is *much* more reason to believe moral certainties than to deny them) is more difficult to understand. Descartes does not say how much is "much." I think the best interpretation of his view is that moral certainties are so reasonable to believe that metaphysical certainties are the only things, if any, more reasonable to believe. This interpretation has the implication that there is a void between moral and metaphysical certainty such that no moral certainty is more reasonable than another without being a metaphysical certainty, but that seems appropriate.[2]

---

2. There is another plausible way to understand Descartes's claim that, where moral certainties are concerned, belief is *much* more reasonable than denial. He may just mean that belief is more reasonable than denial and belief is so much more reasonable than denial that it is even more reasonable than doubt. If we interpret Descartes in this way, the third trait of moral certainties is included in the first two. This interpretation does not have the implication that there is a void between moral and metaphysical certainty. I shall stick with the interpretation I present in the text, though nothing in my position requires me to adopt it over this alternative.

What is the end in terms of which it is more reasonable to believe a moral certainty than to doubt or deny it? Descartes does not tell us. It surely is not the end of finding true metaphysical certainties, which he seems to adopt as part of his scientific method [*Discourse*; AT VI, 18; HR I, 92; *Meditations*; AT VII, 18; HR I, 145]. I presume moral certainties are defined by the end set by the standard epistemic imperative: Believe all and only what is true with regard to the matter under investigation. When Descartes says it is more reasonable to believe a moral certainty than to doubt it, he means that, from the perspective of believing all and only what is true, it is more reasonable to believe a moral certainty than to doubt it. When he says it is more reasonable to believe a moral certainty than to deny it, he means that, from the perspective of believing all and only what is true, it is more reasonable to believe a moral certainty than to deny it. When he says it is *much* more reasonable to believe a moral certainty than to deny it, he means that, from the perspective of believing all and only what is true, metaphysical certainties are the only things, if any, more reasonable to believe.

What I am suggesting is this:

> D1: *p* is a moral certainty for *S* = $_{df.}$ (1) believing *p* is more reasonable for *S* from the standard epistemic perspective than denying *p* or doubting *p* (neither believing nor denying *p*), and (2) believing some proposition *q* is more reasonable for *S* from the standard perspective than believing *p* only if *q* is a metaphysical certainty for *S*.

Some points should be noted about the definiens. To say that adopting epistemic attitude *A* to proposition *p* is more reasonable for *S* from the standard epistemic perspective than adopting attitude *B* to proposition *q* is roughly to say that adopting *A* to *p* is a better strategy for *S* for attaining the goal set by the standard epistemic imperative than adopting *B* to *q*. The evidence possessed by *S* regarding the truth values of the propositions determines which strategy is better. If *S* has strong evidence for *p* and none for not-*p*, believing *p* is a better strategy for her than either doubting or denying *p*. If *S* gradually loses her evidence for *p*, believing *p* ceases to be a better strategy for her than doubting *p* and then ceases to be a better strategy for her than denying *p*. Neither *S*'s degree of conviction nor the truth values of the propositions determines which strategy is better. When S has strong evidence for *p* and none for not-*p*, believing *p* is a better strategy for her than doubting or denying *p*, even if she is convinced that *p* is false and *p* is in fact false. There may be connections between a proposition's being a moral certainty for someone, on the one hand, and her believing it with a particular degree of conviction and its being true, on the other—I soon consider Descartes's position on the matter—but any such connections are not part of the definition of moral certainty. They are not due to its nature. They are due to contingent features of our nature as knowers.

One epistemic attitude can be more reasonable than another for a person from the standard epistemic perspective even if that person does not adopt the standard imperative. This fact allows propositions to be moral certainties for people who guide their epistemic attitudes by interests in things other than the truth. Congressional committees, university administrators, all of us are sometimes more concerned with believing what is expedient relative to some personal goal than with believing what is true. Even Descartes modifies the standard imperative to make way for a special interest in metaphysically certain truths as part of his scientific method [*Discourse*; AT VI, 18; HR I, 92; *Meditations*; AT VII, 18; HR I, 145].

A last point to note about the definiens is that I take the relation of being more reasonable than from the standard perspective to be transitive, irreflexive, and asymmetrical. If doubt is not more reasonable from that perspective than belief, then belief is more reasonable from that perspective than denial. The phrase 'than denying *p*' in the first clause of D1 is redundant given these restrictions. I include it for the sake of clarity.[3]

What about metaphysical certainty? It is a higher grade of certainty than moral certainty; it is "complete assurance." Descartes's point is again fairly clear. When a proposition is a metaphysical certainty, it is more reasonable from the standard perspective to believe it than to doubt or deny it: indeed, believing it is as reasonable as believing ever can be from that perspective:

---

3. Compare Roderick Chisholm, A *Theory of Knowledge* (2d ed., Englewood Cliffs, N.J.: Prentice-Hall, 1977), pp. 7–16. I rely heavily on Chisholm's insights throughout my discussion of certainty.

D2: p is a metaphysical certainty for S = $_{df.}$ (1) believing p is more reasonable for S from the standard epistemic perspective than doubting p or denying p, and (2) it could never be more reasonable for S to believe some proposition q than it is at present for S to believe p.

Descartes's metaphysical certainties are his best bets from the perspective of believing all and only what is true. As in the case of moral certainty, a proposition can be a metaphysical certainty for Descartes—can be a best bet for him from the standard epistemic perspective—even if he does not adopt the standard epistemic imperative.

My definitions capture Descartes's views about metaphysical and moral certainty. They make metaphysical certainty a higher grade of certainty than moral certainty by implying that all metaphysical certainties are moral certainties but not all moral certainties are metaphysical certainties. D1 reflects Descartes's remark that it is "unreasonable" and "extravagant" to doubt or deny a moral certainty; D2, his remark that metaphysical certainty is "complete assurance." We can understand Descartes's view that moral and metaphysical certainty are different "modes of knowing"; knowledge entails justification, and these are two degrees of justification.

My definitions avoid a serious mistake. Descartes's use of the terms 'moral' and 'metaphysical' suggests that moral and metaphysical certainty are different kinds of certainty distinguished by their objects—that moral certainty is the kind of certainty had about propositions regarding practical "moral" matters and metaphysical certainty the kind had about propositions regarding nonpractical, "metaphysical" matters. Not so. In Meditation One, Descartes takes some mathematical truths to be moral certainties; they are "highly probable so that there is much more reason to believe in than to deny them" [AT VII, 22; HR I, 148]. He includes these same propositions among his metaphysical certainties in Meditation Five [AT VII, 71; HR I, 185]. D1 and D2 present this position. D1 lets any proposition be a moral certainty: there just has to be enough evidence so that belief in it is more reasonable than denial or doubt from the standard perspective, and metaphysical certainties are the only things, if any, more reasonable to believe. D2 lets any proposition be a metaphysical certainty as long as the evidence is strong enough to make belief in it maximally reasonable from the standard perspective.

It is also a mistake to think of moral and metaphysical certainty as different kinds of certainty defined by different activities. One of Descartes's remarks can seduce the unwary into this trap:

> But we must note the distinction emphasized by me in various passages, between the practical activities of our life and an enquiry into truth; for, when it is a case of regulating our life, it would assuredly be stupid not to trust the senses, and those sceptics were quite ridiculous who so neglected human affairs that they had to be preserved by their friends from tumbling down precipices. It was for this reason that somewhere I announced *that no one in his sound mind seriously doubted about such matters*; but when we raise an enquiry into what is the surest knowledge which the human mind can obtain, it is clearly unreasonable to refuse to reject them as doubtful. [*Reply to the Fifth Objections*; AT VII, 350–351; HR II, 206]

This passage tempts us to define moral certainties as propositions more reasonable to believe than to doubt or deny when one is engaged in practical affairs and metaphysical certainties as those more reasonable to believe than to doubt or deny when one is engaged in an inquiry into truth. This is a temptation to resist. These definitions use the vague distinction between practical affairs and an inquiry into truth. What are these activities? What ends, if any, define them? If Descartes wonders whether his lover is unfaithful, is that a practical affair or an inquiry into truth? The definitions do not explain why all metaphysical certainties are moral certainties but not all moral certainties are metaphysical certainties. They turn Descartes's understanding of the relation between metaphysical certainty and an inquiry into truth topsyturvy. He does not understand metaphysical certainty in terms of an inquiry into truth; he understands an inquiry into truth in terms of metaphysical certainty. As he explains in the passage above, an inquiry into truth is an inquiry "into what is the surest knowledge the human mind can obtain."

We can appreciate the passage in terms of D1 and D2. When we engage in practical affairs, we should adopt the standard epistemic imperative and assent to both moral and metaphysical certainties. We engage in an inquiry into truth when we set out to construct a scientific theory and restrict the standard imperative, as Descartes does [*Discourse*; AT VI, 18; HR I, 92; *Meditations*; AT VII, 18; HR I, 145], to allow for a commitment to include in our scientific theory only what is both true and metaphysically certain. In such a case, we should not assent to mere moral certainties in the sense that we should not include them in our scientific theory. I say more on this point later in this chapter.

We can begin to appreciate Descartes's initial premises about his self-knowledge. He claims in P1 and P2 to be metaphysically certain he thinks and metaphysically certain he exists. His point is that that he thinks and that he exists are among his best bets from the standard epistemic perspective: (1) believing each is more reasonable for him from that perspective than denying or doubting it; (2) believing each is as reasonable for him from that perspective as believing ever can be. Descartes's claim in P3 is that even if he is morally certain he has a body, he is not metaphysically certain he has one. That he has a body may be a reasonable bet from the standard epistemic perspective, but it is not a best bet. It is more reasonable for him to believe he exists and thinks.

Reasons for Doubt

We can increase our appreciation of Descartes's initial epistemic premises by examining his criterion for separating metaphysical certainties from mere moral ones. A mere moral certainty, according to D1, is very reasonable, but not maximally reasonable, to believe. Belief is by far the most reasonable attitude to adopt toward it; it is just that a slight reason in favor of doubt keeps belief from being maximally reasonable. A metaphysical certainty, according to D2, is maximally reasonable to believe. Belief is again the most reasonable choice, and this time no, even slight, reason in favor of doubt keeps belief from being maximally reasonable. Metaphysical certainties, therefore, are just those moral certainties we lack even the slightest reason to doubt. Descartes accepts this implication of D1 and D2:

> The question was about only that supreme kind of doubt which, I have insisted, is metaphysical, hyperbolical and not to be transferred to the

sphere of the practical needs of life by any means. It was of this doubt also that I said the very least ground of suspicion was a sufficient reason for causing it. [*Seventh Objections and Replies*; AT VII, 459–460; HR II, 266]

If this conviction is so strong that we have no reason to doubt concerning that of the truth of which we have persuaded ourselves, there is nothing more to enquire about; . . . this persuasion is clearly the same as perfect certitude. [*Reply to the Second Objections*; AT VII, 144–145; HR II, 41]

Descartes adopts the epistemic principle:

> EP1: p is a metaphysical certainty for S if and only if p is a moral certainty for S and S has no reason to doubt p.

I refer to EP1 as the 'metaphysical certainty criterion.'

Descartes says little to clarify his concept of a reason for doubt, and some of what he does say is downright confusing: Reasons for doubt must be "powerful and maturely considered," yet the "very least ground of suspicion" is a reason for doubt [*Seventh Objections and Replies*; AT VII, 459–460; HR II, 266]. We can make a start at understanding EP1 by relying on his examples. He says that the hypotheses that he is dreaming (Dream Hypothesis) and that some god deceives him (Deceiver Hypothesis) give him reasons to doubt such sensory-evidenced beliefs as that he has a body and that there is a fire before him [*Meditations*; AT VII, 19–21; HR I, 145–147]. We can intuitively understand what he has in mind. Each hypothesis is a possibility he has not ruled out, and his failure to rule it out keeps his sensory beliefs from being maximally reasonable. More generally, proposition q gives us a reason to doubt proposition p just when (1) q is a possibility we have not ruled out and (2) our failure to rule out q keeps our belief in p from being maximally reasonable. We now need to know two things: How is a reason for doubt "a possibility we have not ruled out"? How does our not having ruled it out "keep our belief from being maximally reasonable"? Let us begin with the first question.

It will not do to say that reasons for doubt are possibilities we have not ruled out in the sense of being logical possibilities. We do not control what is logically possible, so we could never rule out a reason for doubt.

We do control some of our attitudes toward propositions. Commentators such as Edwin Curley think we should give a psychological account of how reasons for doubt are possible.[4] Curley notes that Descartes sometimes writes of assent-compelling propositions, and he explains:

> Some propositions compel our assent whenever we consider them (for instance, simple mathematical truths); when we consider them we cannot but assent to them; others (such as more complex mathematical truths) compel our assent because we see that they can be made the conclusion of an assent-compelling argument, that is, an argument whose premises compel our assent and whose conditionalization also compels our assent. (By the conditionalization of an argument I mean the conditional proposition which has the argument's conclusion as its consequent and the argument's premise, or the conjunction of its premises, as its antecedent.)[5]

Curley uses the concept of an assent-compelling proposition to explain what a reason for doubt is. On Curley's analysis,

> someone has a valid ground for doubting a proposition p if and only if he can think of some other proposition q such that (1) q is incompatible with p or with some principle r that provides the basis of his assent to p; (2) (a) if either p or r is not assent-compelling, then he can think of no assent-compelling proposition incompatible with q, and (b) if both p and r are assent-compelling, then so is q, and (3) q explains how he might have erroneously thought p.[6]

The second clause is Curley's account of how reasons for doubt are possible. In cases of metaphysical uncertainty in which our belief or our basis for belief does not compel assent, a reason for doubt is a possibility we have not ruled out in the sense that we have not thought of an assent-compelling proposition incompatible with it. We rule out our reason for doubt by thinking of such a proposition. Suppose our

---

4. Edwin Curley, *Descartes against the Skeptics* (Cambridge: Harvard University Press, 1978), p. 119. A less-developed version of the psychological approach is Alan Gewirth's in "The Cartesian Circle," *Philosophical Review*, 50 (October 1941), pp. 370–395.

5. Curley, p. 119.
6. Curley, p. 122.

sensory-evidenced belief that we have a body does not compel assent ·
and is metaphysically uncertain because the proposition that a god
deceives us gives us a reason to doubt it. We rule out this reason for
doubt by thinking of an assent-compelling proposition incompatible
with it; for example, that God exists and is not a deceiver. When our
belief and our basis for belief are both assent-compelling, a reason for
doubt is a possibility we have not ruled out in the sense that it too is
assent-compelling. There is no way to rule out such a reason for
doubt, if one ever exists.

Curley's interpretation has two problems common to all purely psychological accounts of how reasons for doubt are ruled out. It has no
textual support—Curley provides none, and I do not know of any—
and it chains Descartes to an incorrect position. It is silly to think that
by merely changing our psychological state we can change our epistemic position and so rule out a reason for doubt and make a mere
moral certainty into a metaphysical one. Suppose you have a reason to
doubt a morally certain, non-assent-compelling belief, and you want
to make your belief into a metaphysical certainty. Curley's Descartes
says: Just think of an assent-compelling proposition incompatible with
your reason for doubt. (Curley's principle actually requires even less;
you need only *be able* to think of a conflicting proposition that is assent
compelling. But this may be a misstatement.) Surely more is required.
You must increase your belief's reasonableness if you want to make it a
metaphysical certainty, and that entails finding evidence against your
reasons for doubt. Curley's Descartes might say that the assent-compelling propositions he has in mind will contain such evidence, but
even if that is so, it is the evidence's status *as evidence*, not its assent-
compelling nature, that causes your epistemic state to change.

We need an *epistemic* account of how reasons for doubt are possible.
We have two options. One is that each reason for doubt is a moral
possibility for us (we are not morally certain it is false); to rule out a
reason for doubt is to make it a moral impossibility (become morally
certain it is false). The other is that each reason for doubt is a metaphysical possibility for us (we are not metaphysically certain it is false);
to rule out a reason for doubt is to make it a metaphysical impossibility
(become metaphysically certain it is false). The first option makes it
harder for a proposition to qualify as a reason for doubt, since moral
possibility is a tougher requirement than metaphysical possibility. The

first option also makes it easier for us to rule out a reason for doubt: we need only become morally, not metaphysically, certain it is false.

The first option fails to reflect Descartes's examples. The hypothesis that he is dreaming is one of his main reasons for doubt in Meditation One [AT VII, 19; HR I, 145–146], but it is not a moral possibility for him. He is morally certain that he is not dreaming, just as he is morally certain of such sensory-evidenced beliefs as that he has a body. It is more reasonable, from the standard perspective, for him to believe he is not dreaming than it is for him to doubt or deny that fact; it is hard to see how anything short of a metaphysical certainty could be more reasonable for him to believe from that perspective. We also saddle Descartes with an implausible position if we decide reasons for doubt need only be moral possibilities. He would then be saying that we can make a moral certainty into a metaphysical certainty by ruling out each reason for doubt with moral certainty. That is not how things work. If we are just morally certain every reason for doubt is false, our belief remains a metaphysical uncertainty. It is not maximally reasonable, since we can increase its reasonableness by becoming *meta-physically* certain each reason for doubt is false.[7]

Each reason for doubt must be a metaphysical possibility. That is the only option left. It is consistent with the fact that ruling out a reason for doubt amounts to changing our epistemic state. It suits the major examples of reasons for doubt such as the Deceiver Hypothesis and the Dream Hypothesis; each is a moral impossibility for Descartes but each is also—at least prior to his proof of God's existence and goodness—a metaphysical possibility for him. He is not metaphysically certain no god deceives him; he is not metaphysically certain he is not dreaming. We capture Descartes's remark that even the least ground for suspicion can be a reason for doubt by letting metaphysical possibilities be reasons for doubt. The one remark we do not capture is that reasons for doubt must be "powerful." Metaphysical possibilities that are moral impossibilities are hardly powerful reasons for doubt. Having to ignore this

---

7. Fred Feldman says that reasons for doubt need only be moral possibilities in "Epistemic Appraisal and the Cartesian Circle," *Philosophical Studies*, 27 (1975), pp. 37–55; the objections I present against his position are also contained in my "Fred Feldman and the Cartesian Circle," *Philosophical Studies*, 31 (1977), pp. 429–432; see also James Van Cleve's "Foundationalism, Epistemic Principles and the Cartesian Circle," *Philosophical Review*, 88 (January 1979), pp. 55–91.

part of Descartes's position is not too high a price to pay for capturing the rest.

We still need to answer our second question about reasons for doubt. If a reason for doubt is a metaphysical possibility that detracts from our belief's reasonableness, what is the nature of this detraction relation? Let us again examine some answers that do not work to find and appreciate one that does.

What about logical inconsistency: A reason to doubt a belief is a metaphysical possibility that contradicts it? Descartes thinks that the hypothesis that some god deceives him into believing that he has a body gives him a reason to doubt his belief in his body [*Meditations*; AT VII, 21; HR I, 147]. The hypothesis and his belief are inconsistent. He does not have a body if some god deceives him into believing he has one.

This proposal has several instructive flaws. It does not work with some of Descartes's major examples, particularly his claim that the Dream Hypothesis gives him a reason to doubt such sensory-evidenced beliefs as that there is a fire before him. There is no logical contradiction between Descartes's dreaming, even his dreaming of a fire, and there actually being a fire in front of him. The proposal falsely implies that we can give someone a reason to doubt a proposition by just denying it. When Descartes believes there is a fire, we need only deny there is one to cite a metaphysical possibility inconsistent with his belief. Yet we surely do not give him a *reason* to doubt his belief, for we do not suggest or indicate to him how his belief might be false.

Another way to understand the relation between reasons for doubt and beliefs is suggested by one of Descartes's examples:

> That *an atheist can know clearly that the three angles of a triangle are equal to two right angles*, I do not deny, I merely affirm that, on the other hand, such knowledge on his part cannot constitute true science, because no knowledge that can be rendered doubtful should be called science. Since he is, as supposed, an Atheist, he cannot be sure that he is not deceived in the things that seem most evident to him, as has been sufficiently shown; and though perchance the doubt does not occur to him, nevertheless it may come up, if he examine the matter, or if another suggests it: and he can never be safe from it unless he first recognises the existence of a God.
> And it does not matter though he think he has demonstrations proving there is no God. Since they are by no means true, the errors in them

can always be pointed out to him, and when this takes place he will be driven from his opinion. [*Reply to the Second Objections*; AT VII, 141; HR II, 39]

Descartes seems to be saying the atheist has a reason to doubt his mathematical beliefs.[8] The atheist may never actually doubt them, but he has a reason to do so, and, if someone presents that reason to him, he will be forced to give up his opinion. Perhaps we should explain the concept of a reason for doubt in this way: the hypothesis q gives S a reason to doubt his belief p if and only if q is a metaphysical possibility for S and S would cease to believe p if he were to add q to his evidence for p.

This explanation lets the Dream Hypothesis give Descartes a reason to doubt his sensory-evidenced belief in the fire. If Descartes were to believe he is dreaming, his sensory evidence would no longer persuade him there is a fire before him. The proposal gives Descartes's evidence a role to play in determining when he has a reason to doubt. A hypothesis gives him a reason to doubt a belief only if his acceptance of the hypothesis would cause him to surrender his belief in the face of his evidence for it.

Nonetheless, the explanation has the first proposal's defect of allowing mere denials to be reasons for doubt. Since Descartes is dedicated to consistency in his beliefs, we need only deny that there is a fire before him to cite a metaphysical possibility his acceptance of which will cause him to cease believing in the fire. Suppose too that Descartes decides to model himself after Saint Augustine. He will dress like Augustine, walk like Augustine, talk like Augustine, even believe like Augustine. We need only cite the metaphysical possibility that Augustine did not believe a particular proposition to give Descartes a reason to doubt the proposition, according to the proposal. If Descartes were to accept the hypothesis that Augustine did not believe the proposition, his desire to be like Augustine would lead him to stop believing the proposition. The major flaw with this proposal is that it explains the detraction relation between beliefs and reasons for doubt in purely psychological terms. Whether a hypothesis gives us a reason to doubt a belief does not depend

8. There are other interpretations of what Descartes is saying, which I consider later. What is important here is that Descartes seems to be saying the atheist has a reason to doubt his mathematical beliefs, and what Descartes seems to be saying suggests a particular account of what constitutes a reason for doubt.

on whether our acceptance of the hypothesis would cause us to surrender the belief. It depends on how the hypothesis affects the reasonableness of our belief.

Some commentators have brought the idea of epistemic defeat into
play: A hypothesis q gives S a reason to doubt her morally certain belief
p if and only if q is a metaphysical possibility for S, and if S were to
become morally certain of q, her doing so would defeat her moral
certainty of p, thus making p a moral uncertainty for her.[9] A person
who recalls proving that the angles of a triangle equal two right angles
is morally, but not metaphysically, certain of the theorem. The metaphysical possibility that some god supplies her with false memories
gives her a reason to doubt. If she were to become morally certain
some god gives her false memories, her evidence for the theorem
would no longer suffice to make it morally certain. Her moral certainty
of the reason for doubt would "defeat" or "neutralize" her evidence—
her belief would no longer be morally certain.

The contrast between this proposal and the previous one should be
evident. That proposal makes the relation between reasons for doubt
and beliefs a causal relation between mental attitudes; a person's acceptance of the reason for doubt would cause her to doubt her belief.
This proposal makes the relation a causal relation between epistemic
states: the person's moral certainty of the reason for doubt would cause
her to be morally uncertain of the belief. The proposal needs to be
supplemented by rules of epistemic inference to explain which moral
certainties defeat which others, but, even incomplete, it is a clear
advance over the psychological approach.

It still retains a difficulty found in some of the other proposals,
however. It implies that we need only deny someone's belief to give
him a reason to doubt it. When Descartes's sensory evidence makes
him morally, but not metaphysically, certain he has a body, the hypothesis that he does not have a body is a metaphysical possibility for
him, and if he were to become morally certain of it, he would, by the
very definition of moral certainty (D1), cease to be morally certain of
his belief.

How then should we explain the detraction relation between reasons

9. See Feldman, p. 45; and Jeffrey Tlumak, "Certainty and Cartesian Method," in
Descartes: Critical and Interpretive Essays, ed. Michael Hooker (Baltimore: Johns
Hopkins University Press, 1978), pp. 40–73.

for doubt and beliefs? The best explanation is suggested by one of Descartes's examples [*Meditations*; AT VII, 20–21; HR I, 147]. Suppose Descartes believes a mathematical proposition on the evidence that he has mentally added two numbers and obtained a third. Descartes thinks that the metaphysical possibility that some god deceives him gives him a reason to doubt his belief, but the metaphysical possibility that his external senses deceive him does not. The difference ultimately lies in explanatory power. The Deceiver Hypothesis detracts from the reasonableness of Descartes's belief because it indicates how the belief might be false despite his evidence for it: some all-powerful god might be causing him to make addition errors. The Deceptive Senses Hypothesis does not detract from the reasonableness of Descartes's belief, because it does not indicate how the belief might be false despite his evidence: his evidence concerns his performance of a mental operation, not what he experiences through his senses.[10]

We might, then, try this: A reason to doubt a morally certain belief p is a metaphysical possibility q that indicates to the believer how p might be false despite the evidence for p. This still is not quite right. Suppose Descartes deduces a theorem from mathematical propositions evidenced by his recollection of having proved them. The hypothesis that all his mathematical recollections are false gives him a reason to doubt the conclusion of the proof, but, instead of indicating how the conclusion might be false despite the evidence for it (the mathematical premises from which he deduces it), it indicates how those premises might be false despite the evidence for them (despite his recollection of having proved them). We should adopt:

D3: q gives S a reason to doubt S's morally certain belief p if and only if (1) q is a metaphysical possibility for S, and (2) either q indicates to S how p might be false despite S's evidence for p, or q indicates to S how an essential part of S's evidence for p might be false despite S's evidence for that essential part.

10. It is important to distinguish between the case at hand and another. Suppose Descartes believes that two numbers equal a third on the evidence that there is one number of things to his left, another number of things to his right, and a third number of things about him overall. In this case, Descartes's evidence concerns what he experiences through his senses; the Deceptive Senses Hypothesis indicates how his belief might be false despite his evidence (his senses may deceive him when he sees n objects about him) and casts doubt on his belief.

The concepts of evidence and an essential part of evidence used in D3 need clarification. When a morally certain proposition is self-evident, S's evidence for it consists of his act of apprehending it; when a morally certain proposition is not self-evident, S's evidence consists of those morally certain propositions that are his reasons for believing it. An essential part of S's evidence for a moral certainty p is a morally certain proposition such that S would cease to be morally certain of p if he ceased to be morally certain of it.

D3 also employs the concept of indication. I make only a few remarks to clarify this concept here; in discussing Descartes's defense of his self-knowledge claims in Chapters 4 and 5, I present some epistemic principles that explain it further. Ultimately, those epistemic principles play crucial roles in Descartes's arguments for his self-knowledge claims and in his argument from those claims to his conclusions about his nature.

It is neither necessary nor sufficient that one proposition contradict another in order for the first to indicate how the second might be false. The Dream Hypothesis indicates how Descartes's sensory-evidenced belief in the fire might be false without contradicting it. The assertion that there is no fire contradicts Descartes's belief in a fire but does not indicate how it might be false.

It is neither necessary nor sufficient that our believing one proposition would cause us to doubt another for the first to indicate how the second might be false. Descartes might persist in his belief in the fire while believing the Dream Hypothesis: his adoption of the belief that there is no fire might cause him to give up his belief that there is one.

That Descartes's moral certainty of one proposition (there is no fire) would defeat his moral certainty of another (there is a fire) does not imply that the first indicates how the second might be false. Nonetheless, whenever one proposition indicates how another might be false, Descartes's moral certainty of the first would defeat his moral certainty of the second. Descartes's moral certainty of the Dream and Deceiver Hypotheses, if he could ever gain moral certainty of them, would defeat his moral certainty of his sensory-evidenced belief in the fire.

Now that we have examined the concept of a reason for doubt, let us take another look at the metaphysical certainty criterion, EP1. Just how plausible is it against the background of D1, D2, and D3 (the definitions of metaphysical certainty, moral certainty, and a reason for doubt)? Very plausible. EP1 says our metaphysical certainties are just those moral certainties we have no reason to doubt. On the one hand, as long as a metaphysically possible hypothesis indicates how our morally certain belief or an essential part of our evidence for it might be false, we are not metaphysically certain of our belief in the sense defined by D2. We can increase the reasonableness of our belief from the standard perspective by becoming metaphysically certain of the negation of every such hypothesis. On the other hand, once Descartes is metaphysically certain of the negation of every hypothesis, there is no metaphysically possible explanation of how his belief or an essential part of his evidence for it might be false. He can do nothing more to increase the reasonableness of his belief from the standard perspective. Any new evidence he might gain will do nothing to help rule out possibilities that question the reliability of his belief—there are no such possibilities—and so nothing to help increase the reasonableness of his belief.[11]

The metaphysical certainty criterion (EP1) sheds more light on Descartes's premises about self-knowledge. His claim in P1 has two parts: (1) he is morally certain that he thinks; (2) he has no reason to doubt his moral certainty that he thinks; that is, no metaphysically possible hypothesis indicates how his belief or an essential part of his evidence for it might be false. His claim in P2 is similarly complex: (1) he is morally certain that he exists; (2) he has no reason to doubt his morally certain belief; that is, no metaphysically possible hypothesis indicates how it or an essential part of his evidence for it might be false. Descartes's claim in P3 is that, even though he is morally certain he has a body, he has a reason to doubt his belief; some metaphysically possible hypothesis indicates how it might be false despite his evidence for it.

11. Some may see a problem for Descartes here: To become metaphysically certain of a proposition, we must first become metaphysically certain of the negations of all the reasons to doubt it, to become metaphysically certain of each of those negations, we must first become metaphysically certain of the negations of all the reasons to doubt it, and so on; we can never gain metaphysical certainty. Descartes avoids this problem by presenting some propositions that resist all reasons for doubt right from the start. I explain his position in detail in Chapter 5. Note that I say EP1 is very plausible when it is understood in terms of D1, D2, and D3. I do not dare say that it is clearly true. Some may question whether the absence of any metaphysically possible hypothesis indicating how Descartes's morally certain belief or evidence might be false really implies that Descartes's belief is maximally reasonable in the sense defined by D2. I must confess that I too am unsure of this point.

Truth and Psychological Certainty

I have defined metaphysical and moral certainty, examined Descartes's metaphysical certainty criterion, and used the results to clarify his initial epistemic premises. I now want to take our understanding of Descartes's views on certainty a step further. A network of epistemic principles ties Descartes's concepts of metaphysical and moral certainty to the rest of his epistemology. I want to consider the part that connects metaphysical and moral certainty to truth and psychological certainty.

I have defined moral and metaphysical certainty relative to an interest in truth. Moral certainties are propositions very reasonable to believe insofar as we have the end of believing all and only what is true. Metaphysical certainties are propositions maximally reasonable to believe insofar as we have that end. This way of connecting moral and metaphysical certainty to truth is my work. Descartes does not specify the end relative to which moral and metaphysical certainty are defined, and I have chosen the end of all and only true beliefs as the best way to fill the gap in his account.

The definitions of moral and metaphysical certainty do not make either a necessary condition for truth. They leave open the possibility that a true proposition is neither morally nor metaphysically certain for anyone. Descartes accepts this possibility with regard to human inquirers. He stresses to Bourdin—to whom he can never stress a point enough—that when he declares a proposition to be a metaphysical uncertainty for himself, he is not declaring it to be false:

> When I said that doubtful matters should sometimes be treated as though they were false, or rejected as if they were false, I clearly explained that I merely meant that, for the purpose of investigating the truths that are metaphysically certain, we should pay no more credence to doubtful matters than to what is plainly false. Thus surely no sane man can interpret my words otherwise, or attribute to me the opinion of wishing to believe the opposite of what is doubtful. [*Seventh Objections and Replies*; AT VII, 461; HR II, 266]

Divine knowers are a different story. Since God is necessarily existent and omniscient [*Principles*, I, xxii; AT VIII, 13; HR I, 228], no proposition can be true without being metaphysically, and so morally, certain for God.

A more interesting question is whether either degree of certainty is a sufficient condition for truth. Could a proposition be very, or even maximally, reasonable for us to believe when seeking the truth but not be true? The definitions of moral and metaphysical certainty allow for this possibility. Nothing in the nature of reasonable belief guarantees that what is maximally or very reasonable for us to believe is in fact true.

Descartes indicates that moral certainties can be false:

> It would certainly be desirable to have as high a degree of certitude in regard to the direction of life as is demanded when it is a question of attaining knowledge; but it is very easy to show that such certitude is not to be sought after nor to be expected. . . . Suppose a man chose to fast until he died because he was not certain that there was no poison in his food; suppose he thought that he was not obliged to eat, because it was not clear and manifest that there were to hand the means of sustaining life, and it would be better to abstain and wait for death to come than to kill himself by eating. Such a man would certainly be censured as a suicidal lunatic. *We may further suppose that the only food he can get is poisoned; even, that his constitution is such that starvation is conducive to his health; nevertheless, if the food does not appear to him to be poisoned but on the contrary thoroughly healthful, and if starvation seems likely to hurt him as much as other men, it will be his duty to take food, and thus to embrace what seems advantageous rather than what really is.* [*Correspondence*; AT III, 422; AG, 265; my emphasis][12]

The propositions evidenced by the man's senses (that his food is healthful and starvation not conducive to his health) are false, but they are moral certainties for him nonetheless; as Descartes puts it, the man has a "duty" to believe them and will be properly "censured as a lunatic" if he does not.

The relation between metaphysical certainty and truth is a different matter. Our nature as knowers ensures that all our metaphysical certainties are true. We can gain metaphysical certainty only by clear and distinct perception, and that faculty is locked onto the truth by our creator.

> The knowledge upon which a certain and incontrovertible judgment can be formed, should not alone be clear but also distinct. [*Principles*, I, xlv; AT VIII, 22; HR I, 237]

---

12. I have followed Anscombe and Geach's translation.

For every clear and distinct perception is without doubt something, and hence cannot derive its origin from what is nought, but must of necessity have God as its author—God, I say, who being supremely perfect, cannot be the cause of any error; and consequently we must conclude that it is true. [*Meditations*; AT VII, 62; HR I, 178*; consider too: *Principles*, I, xliii; AT VIII, 21; HR I, 236]

Descartes thus rules out the possibility of false metaphysical certainties:

EP2: A human S is metaphysically certain that p only if S clearly and distinctly perceives that p.

EP3: A human S clearly and distinctly perceives that p only if p is true.

Harry Frankfurt thinks Descartes does not really adopt EP3: "Descartes evidently recognizes that his position entails that from our knowing something with perfect certitude it does not follow that it is, 'speaking absolutely,' true. He explicitly concedes, in other words, that he has not proven that whatever is clearly and distinctly perceived is 'absolutely' true."[13] Frankfurt sets aside the passages in which Descartes clearly states EP3 on the basis of Descartes's remark to Mersenne:

To begin with, directly we think we rightly perceive something, we spontaneously persuade ourselves that it is true. Further, if this conviction is so strong that we have no reason to doubt concerning that of the truth of which we have persuaded ourselves, there is nothing more to enquire about; we have here all the certainty that can reasonably be desired. What is it to us, though perchance someone feigns that that, of the truth of which we are so firmly persuaded, appears false to God or to an Angel, and hence is, absolutely speaking, false? What heed do we pay to that absolute falsity, when we by no means believe that it exists or even suspect its existence? We have assumed a conviction so strong that nothing can remove it, and this persuasion is clearly the same as perfect certitude. [*Reply to the Second Objections*; AT VII, 144–145; HR II, 41]

According to Frankfurt, Descartes is saying we might clearly and distinctly perceive a proposition that appears false to God and is indeed false. Anthony Kenny and Bernard Williams have spotted where

13. Harry Frankfurt, *Demons, Dreamers and Madmen* (New York: Bobbs-Merrill, 1970), p. 179.

Frankfurt's train leaves the tracks.[14] Descartes is not describing a case in which a false proposition is clearly and distinctly perceived; he is describing one in which one person clearly and distinctly perceives a true proposition and another person feigns that that proposition is false. This interpretation of the passage lets us take Descartes's statements of EP3 seriously.

In all, then, Descartes relates moral and metaphysical certainty to truth relative to the epistemic abilities of knowers. Every truth is a metaphysical certainty, and so a moral certainty, for God. Since our senses can be both deceptive and a source of moral certainty, false propositions can be morally certain for us. Our only source of metaphysical certainty, the faculty of clear and distinct perception, is permanently targeted by our creator on the truth, so no falsehood can be a metaphysical certainty for us.

Descartes sometimes discusses a kind of certainty distinct from, but related to, moral and metaphysical certainty:

> I am of such a nature that as long as I understand anything very clearly and distinctly, I am naturally impelled to believe it to be true, . . . for example, when I consider the nature of a triangle, I, who have some little knowledge of the principles of geometry, recognise quite clearly that the three angles are equal to two right angles, and it is not possible for me not to believe this so long as I apply my mind to its demonstration. [*Meditations*; AT VII, 69–70; HR I, 183]

> And even although I had not demonstrated this [that all clear and distinct perceptions are true], the nature of my mind is such that I could not prevent myself from holding them [truths of mathematics] to be true so long as I conceive them clearly. [*Meditations*; AT VII, 65; HR I, 180]

Descartes says the nature of his mind is such that he must believe what he clearly and distinctly perceives. He does not say such beliefs are maximally or extremely reasonable; his claim is not about metaphysical or moral certainty. It is about his psychological compulsion to believe particular propositions, what I call his 'psychological certainty.'

---

14. Anthony Kenny, *Descartes: A Study of His Philosophy* (New York: Random House, 1968), p. 195; Bernard Williams, *Descartes: The Project of Pure Inquiry* (New York: Penguin Books, 1978), pp. 199–200.

D4: p is a psychological certainty for S $=$ $_{df.}$ S believes p and S is unable to doubt or deny p.

Do not miss the difference between moral and metaphysical certainty, on the one hand, and psychological certainty, on the other. Moral and metaphysical certainty are epistemic characteristics. A proposition must meet particular requirements defining reasonable belief from the standard epistemic perspective to be a moral or metaphysical certainty for someone. To tell someone a proposition is a moral or metaphysical certainty for her is to tell her that, from the standard epistemic perspective, she *ought* to believe it. Psychological certainty is not an epistemic concept. No standard of reasonable belief determines when a proposition is a psychological certainty; facts about the human mind do. To tell someone a proposition is a psychological certainty for her is to tell her she believes it and cannot do otherwise at present.

The definitions of the three kinds of certainty do not make either moral or metaphysical certainty a necessary condition for psychological certainty. They do not make either a sufficient condition for it. Nothing in the nature of compelled belief implies that what we are compelled to believe is reasonable to believe; nothing in the nature of reasonable belief implies that we are compelled to believe whatever is extremely or maximally reasonable to believe.

Descartes tends to conflate metaphysical and psychological certainty. Consider this:

> Directly we think we rightly perceive something, we spontaneously persuade ourselves that it is true. Further, if this conviction is so strong that we have no reason to doubt concerning that of the truth of which we have persuaded ourselves, there is nothing more to enquire about; we have here all the certainty that can reasonably be desired. [*Reply to the Second Objections*; AT VII, 144–145; HR II, 41]

Descartes's talk of persuasion suggests a concern with psychological certainty; his talk of reasons for doubt and all the certainty that can reasonably be desired makes it clear he is also concerned with metaphysical certainty. This tendency to conflate metaphysical and psychological certainty may stem from the fact that Descartes connects the two with a principle about our nature as knowers. Consider again part of his remarks on psychological certainty:

The nature of my mind is such that I could not prevent myself from holding them [truths of mathematics] to be true so long as I conceive them clearly. [*Meditations*; AT VII, 65; HR I, 180; my emphasis]

He accepts

> EP4: A human S clearly and distinctly perceives that p only if S is psychologically certain that p.

This principle combines with the principle that clear and distinct perception is our only source of metaphysical certainty (EP2) to imply that all our metaphysical certainties are psychological certainties; we cannot help but believe every proposition it is maximally reasonable for us to believe. Our creator has guaranteed this by making sure that the only faculty that gives us metaphysical certainty always gives us psychological certainty. As long as Descartes is metaphysically certain he thinks and exists, he clearly and distinctly perceives those facts, and as long as he clearly and distinctly perceives them, he is naturally compelled to believe them.

Descartes seems to be thinking of the connection between metaphysical certainty and psychological certainty by way of clear and distinct perception when he writes in the *Rules:*

> Whenever two men come to opposite decisions about the same matter one of them at least must be in the wrong, and apparently there is not even one of them who knows; for if the reasoning of the second was certain [*certa*] and clear [*evidens*] he would be able so to lay it before the other as finally to succeed in convincing *his* understanding also. [II; AT X, 363; HR I, 3*]

If, on the basis of the same evidence, I believe not-p and you believe p, neither of us has metaphysically certain knowledge. If you knew p with metaphysical certainty, you would have a clear and distinct perception and so psychological certainty of it. Then I, with the same evidence laid before me by you—the same clear and distinct perception— would be psychologically certain of p. I am not, for I deny p rather than believe it. Hence, you do not know p with metaphysical certainty. The same sort of reasoning shows that I am metaphysically uncertain of not-p.

Note what Descartes is *not* saying here. He is not saying that whenever two people disagree, neither has metaphysically certain knowledge. Descartes and an atheist disagree about God's existence, but Descartes, after the proof in Meditation Three, has metaphysical certainty of God's existence, or so he tells us [*Meditations*; AT VII, 53; HR I, 172]. Descartes is saying that whenever two people disagree *on the basis of the same evidence*, including the same clear and distinct perception, neither has metaphysically certain knowledge. Any evidence capable of producing metaphysical certainty in one is capable of producing psychological certainty, and so agreement, in both.

Descartes does not find an analogous link between *moral* certainty and psychological certainty. We can gain moral certainty by our senses, and the senses do not compel us to believe the way clear and distinct perception does. We can resist our "natural inclination" to believe what they tell us [*Meditations*; AT VII, 38; HR I, 160]. Descartes and a materialist might have the same sensory evidence for the existence of bodies and both be morally certain, yet Descartes might resist his natural inclination to believe in bodies while the materialist gives in to his. They may disagree in the face of the same sensory evidence.

Clear and distinct perception is the central element in Descartes's epistemic network. It ties metaphysical certainty to truth to psychological certainty. It is our only source of metaphysical certainty and a guaranteed source of truth and psychological certainty. Our nature as knowers thus ensures that we believe and are correct in believing whatever is maximally reasonable for us to believe. What, then, is clear and distinct perception, and does our clear and distinct perception of a proposition always make it a metaphysical certainty for us? I develop and defend my answers to these questions in Chapter 4 when I consider Descartes's account of how he gains metaphysical certainty of his thought and existence. Let me just sketch my position at this stage.

Descartes believes that some propositions about his mental state (e.g., that he thinks) and simple necessary truths (e.g., that two and three is five) are self-evident for him. He need only apprehend them when they are true to be morally certain of them. His moral certainty does not stem from evidence he has for them; his act of apprehension makes him morally certain of the propositions involved. One form of clear and distinct perception consists of Descartes's apprehension of such self-evident truths. I call this 'direct clear and distinct perception.'

Descartes acknowledges a second form of clear and distinct perception, which consists of his deduction of a proposition from self-evident propositions clearly and distinctly perceived directly. I call this 'deductive clear and distinct perception.' Whenever Descartes clearly and distinctly perceives a proposition in this way, it is a moral certainty for him. His evidence consists of the self-evident moral certainties from which he deduces it.

Descartes thinks some of his clear and distinct perceptions are metaphysically certain and some, metaphysically uncertain. Whenever he clearly and distinctly perceives a self-evident proposition about his mental state, it is a metaphysical certainty. Whenever he immediately deduces a proposition from such a metaphysical certainty, it too is a metaphysical certainty. Descartes's clear and distinct perceptions of simple necessary truths can be metaphysically uncertain. They are metaphysically uncertain until he rules out the Deceiver Hypothesis and becomes metaphysically certain that God makes all his clear and distinct perceptions true. The same goes for those clear and distinct perceptions that consist of his deduction of complex necessary truths from simple ones.

Clear and distinct perception is strikingly superior to sensation. Sense experience can give us moral certainty, but it does not always do so; clear and distinct perception always gives us moral certainty. Sense experience can give us a natural, but resistible, inclination to believe; clear and distinct perception gives us the irresistible inclination of psychological certainty. Sense experience can give us moral certainty of both true and false propositions; clear and distinct perception only shows us the truth. Sense experience never gives us metaphysical certainty; clear and distinct perception always gives us metaphysical certainty of our mental state and existence, and, once we rule out the Deceiver Hypothesis, it gives us metaphysical certainty of even more.

An Inquiry into Truth

One way to appreciate the strength of the interpretation I have developed so far is to see how it helps us understand two major parts of Descartes's philosophy: his conception of an inquiry into truth and his identification of science with propositions known with metaphysical certainty. I consider the former here.[15]

Consider again Descartes's remark to Gassendi:

> Note the distinction emphasized by me in various passages, between the practical activities of our life and an enquiry into truth; for, when it is a case of regulating our life, it would assuredly be stupid not to trust the senses, and those sceptics were quite ridiculous who so neglected human affairs that they had to be preserved by their friends from tumbling down precipices. It was for this reason that somewhere I announced *that no one in his sound mind seriously doubted about such matters*; but when we raise an enquiry into what is the surest knowledge which the human mind can obtain, it is clearly unreasonable to refuse to treat them as doubtful. [*Reply to the Fifth Objections*; AT VII, 351; HR II, 206]

My interpretation gives us a new and instructive way to understand what Descartes is saying here.

When we engage in practical affairs, we should adopt the standard imperative: Believe all and only what is true on the matter at hand. In practice, this obligation becomes one to assent to moral and metaphysical certainties, and in fact to any proposition it is more reasonable to believe than to doubt or deny. Some of those propositions, for example, some moral certainties evidenced by our senses, may in fact be false, but as long as it is reasonable for us to believe they are true, it is proper for us to assent to them in trying to honor our obligation to believe the truth.

To engage in an inquiry into truth is to set out to construct a scientific theory, and we must modify our belief policies accordingly. We must combine the standard imperative with the new Cartesian one: Place under the special heading of 'science' all and only what is metaphysically certain and true. Any proposition that is not a metaphysical certainty—even one that is morally certain and true—should be excluded from science and, in that way "treated as doubtful." The standard imperative still guides our beliefs. We still aim at believing the truth, and, in practice, we give our assent to propositions it is reasonable for us to think are true. The Cartesian imperative guides

---

15. Some of the material in this section is from my "Dreams and Deceivers in Meditation One."

our placement of beliefs under the heading 'science.' We try to place only metaphysically certain truths there. In practice, our obligation becomes one to place in that category only what it is reasonable for us to believe to be metaphysically certain and true. Some of these propositions may not be metaphysically certain and true, but as long as it is reasonable for us to think they are, it is proper for us to so place them in trying to honor our obligation.

Descartes's procedure in the *Meditations* is a perfect example. He sets out to construct a "firm and permanent structure in the sciences" [AT VII, 17; HR I, 144], and in First Philosophy (metaphysics) in particular. His first move is to supplement the standard epistemic imperative with the Cartesian one:

> Reason already persuades me that I ought no less carefully withhold my assent from matters which are not entirely certain and indubitable than from those which appear to me manifestly to be false. [AT VII, 18; HR I, 145]

Descartes's next move (Meditation One) is to reconsider his past beliefs to find some that meet the criteria for science. Several arguments lead him to the conclusion that at least most of his past beliefs are metaphysically uncertain. The arguments do not make him metaphysically certain that those past beliefs are metaphysically uncertain; he tells Bourdin the arguments themselves are "doubtful" [*Seventh Objections and Replies*; AT VII, 473; HR II, 277]. The arguments make him morally certain of that conclusion; he tells Bourdin that the conclusions drawn in Meditation One involve "only the moral mode of knowing, which suffices for the regulation of life" [*Seventh Objections and Replies*; AT VII, 475; HR II, 278]. Moral certainty is all Descartes needs. Since he is morally certain that his past beliefs are metaphysically uncertain, it is reasonable from the standard perspective for him to believe they are metaphysically uncertain. Since it is reasonable for him to believe that his past beliefs are metaphysically uncertain, and he has adopted the Cartesian imperative, it is reasonable for him to exclude those past beliefs from the category of science.

Here is how Descartes describes his situation:

> At the end I feel constrained to confess that there is nothing in all that I formerly believed to be true, of which I cannot in some measure doubt,

and that not merely through want of thought or through levity, but for reasons which are very powerful and maturely considered; so that henceforth I ought not the less carefully refrain from giving credence to those opinions than to that which is manifestly false, if I desire to arrive at any certainty in the sciences. [*Meditations*; AT IX, 17; HR I, 147–148][16]

I think Descartes has in mind that his moral certainty that his past beliefs are metaphysically uncertain ("I feel constrained to confess that there is nothing in all that I formerly believed to be true, of which I cannot in some measure doubt") and his decision to include in his scientific theory only what is metaphysically certain ("if I desire to arrive at any certainty in the sciences") make it reasonable for him to exclude his past beliefs from his scientific theory ("I ought not the less carefully to refrain from giving credence to these opinions than to that which is manifestly false").

In Meditation Two, Descartes examines his beliefs that he thinks and that he exists. Each is a true metaphysical certainty for him, and his examination makes him morally certain of that fact. Since it is reasonable from the standard perspective for him to believe each to be a true metaphysical certainty, and he adopts the Cartesian imperative, it is reasonable for him to include each in his science. This is the start of his First Philosophy, as he reports in the corresponding section of the *Principles*:

This cognition, *I think, therefore I am*, is the first and most certain of all that occurs to one who philosophises in an orderly way. [I, vii; AT VIII, 7; HR I, 221*; consider too: *Discourse*; AT VI, 32; HR I, 101]

Some may be reluctant to buy my account of what an inquiry into truth involves. I say that when Descartes becomes *morally* certain a proposition is a true metaphysical certainty, it is proper for him to include it under the heading of 'science.' Yet would not Descartes say that he must be *metaphysically* certain a proposition meets the requirements of the Cartesian imperative before it is proper for him to place it under that heading? I do not think he would. He claims in the *Discourse*

16. The final phrase, "in the sciences," occurs in the 1647 French translation approved by Descartes but not in the Latin original. This is one time the French edition amplifies Descartes's position in a way that better represents it.

[AT VI, 32; HR I, 101] and *Principles* [I, vii; AT VIII, 7; HR I, 221] that the proposition that he thinks and therefore exists is "the *first* and most certain" he finds. This suggests that when he adds that proposition to his science, no other proposition, including the one that he is metaphysically certain that he thinks and therefore exists, is a metaphysical certainty for him; such other propositions are at best moral certainties. This suggestion is reinforced by the fact that Descartes never claims to be metaphysically certain that he has metaphysical certainty of his thought and existence.[17]

Another aspect of my account of an inquiry into truth may be hard to accept. I say Descartes restricts his new Cartesian imperative to science; he continues to use the standard imperative to guide his beliefs, and so he never *really* doubts propositions that are morally certain but metaphysically uncertain. Descartes continues to believe such propositions, he just does not place them in his science. What justifies my reading the Cartesian imperative as "Place under the heading of 'science' all and only what is true and metaphysically certain" rather than as "Believe all and only what is true and metaphysically certain"? What justifies my view that Descartes excludes moral certainties that are not metaphysical certainties from science but never really doubts them? He sure seems to doubt them, and even to reject them as false, in the beginning of Meditation Two:

> The Meditation of yesterday filled my mind with so many doubts that it is no longer in my power to forget them. And yet I do not see in what manner I can resolve them; . . . I shall nevertheless make an effort and follow anew the same path as that on which I yesterday entered, i.e. I shall proceed by setting aside all that in which the least doubt could be supposed to exist, just as if I had discovered that it was absolutely false; . . . I suppose, then, that all the things that I see are false; I persuade myself that nothing has ever existed of all that my fallacious memory represents to me. [AT VII, 23–24; HR I, 149]

Descartes never explicitly adopts the Cartesian imperative without restriction, and he never explicitly restricts it to science. Several pas-

---

17. James Van Cleve disagrees in "Foundationalism, Epistemic Principles and the Cartesian Circle." Van Cleve bases his position on his belief that Descartes accepts the principle that all clear and distinct perceptions are always metaphysically certain. I have already stated my view that Descartes rejects that principle; I argue for this view in Chapter 5.

sages indirectly support my view, however. When Descartes presents the new imperative in Meditation One, he prefaces his statement of it with a biographical account showing the sciences are his concern:

> It is now some years since I detected how many were the false beliefs that I had from my earliest youth admitted as true, and how doubtful was everything I had since constructed on this basis; and from that time I was convinced that I must once for all seriously undertake to rid myself of all the opinions which I had formerly accepted, and commence to build anew from the foundation, if I wanted to establish any firm and permanent structure in the sciences. [AT VII, 17; HR I, 144]

Descartes makes explicit reference to the sciences when he cites his new imperative in the synopsis of the *Meditations:*

> In the first Meditation I set forth the reasons for which we may, generally speaking, doubt about all things and especially about material things, at least so long as we have no other foundations for the sciences than those which we have hitherto possessed. [AT VII, 12; HR I, 140]

In the dedication of the *Meditations,* he says the method he builds around his new imperative is one to be used in the sciences. He writes, with regard to establishing God's existence and the distinction between the human body and mind, that

> it was desired that I should undertake this task by many who were aware that I had cultivated a certain Method for the resolution of difficulties of every kind in the Sciences. [AT VII, 3; HR I, 134–135]

There is also good evidence that Descartes does not really deny or doubt moral certainties that are metaphysically uncertain but instead just excludes them from his science. He explains to Bourdin how he "denies" such propositions:

> When I said that doubtful matters should sometimes be treated as though they were false, or rejected as if they were false, I clearly explained that I merely meant that, for the purpose of investigating the truths that are metaphysically certain, we should pay no more credence to doubtful matters than to what is plainly false. [*Seventh Objections and Replies;* AT VII, 461; HR II, 266; consider too: *Notes against a Programme;* AT VIII-2, 366–367; HR I, 448–449]

Descartes does not really deny moral certainties that are metaphysical uncertainties. He treats them as if they were false in that he gives them no more credence than he gives to what is false. He does not give them credence, I suggest, in that he does not include them in his science, just as he does not include false propositions in his science.

Descartes explains to Gassendi how he "doubts" moral certainties that are metaphysically uncertain:

> Somewhere I announced *that no one in his sound mind seriously doubt-*
> *ed about such matters;* but when we raise an enquiry into what is the
> surest knowledge which the human mind can obtain, it is clearly unrea-
> sonable to refuse to treat them as doubtful, nay even to reject them as
> false, so as to allow us to become more aware that certain other things,
> which cannot be thus rejected, are for this very reason more certain,
> and in actual truth better known by us. [*Reply to the Fifth Objections;*
> AT VII, 351; HR II, 206]

Descartes says that, when we are engaged in an inquiry into truth, we should "treat as doubtful" and "reject as false" moral certainties that are metaphysically uncertain. We have just seen from his remark to Bour-din that rejecting such propositions as false does not amount to denying them. It amounts to excluding them from our science just as we exclude the false propositions we really do deny. So too, treating as doubtful moral certainties that are metaphysically uncertain does not amount to doubting them. It amounts to excluding them from our science just as we exclude the moral *uncertainties* we really do doubt. [18]

Metaphysical Certainty and Science

Why should we identify science with metaphysically certain knowledge? Descartes gives two reasons in the *Rules*:

> Science in its entirety is certain and evident cognition. He is no more
> learned who has doubts on many matters than the man who has never

18. I am not the first to claim that Descartes does not really doubt all the proposi-tions he finds metaphysically uncertain. Consider Harry Frankfurt's position in *De-mons, Dreamers and Madmen,* pp. 16–17. Frankfurt does not explain Descartes's position relative to the different imperatives guiding his inquiry, however.

thought of them; nay he appears to be less learned if he has formed wrong opinions on any particulars. Hence it were better not to study at all than to occupy one's self with objects of such difficulty, that, owing to our inability to distinguish true from false, we are forced to regard the doubtful as certain; for in those matters any hope of augmenting our knowledge is exceeded by the risk of diminishing it. Thus in accordance with the above maxim we reject all such merely probable knowledge and make it a rule to trust only what is completely known and incapable of being doubted. [II; AT X, 362; HR I, 3*]

Descartes's first reason, that a man who has doubts on a matter is no more learned than one who has never thought of it, is weak. Someone who is morally, but not metaphysically, certain of a truth is clearly in a better position with regard to the truth than one who has never thought of it. He has evidence that makes it very reasonable for him to accept it. Descartes later realizes the value of moral certainty [*Discourse*; AT VI, 37–38; HR I, 104; *Meditations*; AT VII, 22; HR I, 148; *Reply to the Fifth Objections*; AT VII, 351; HR II, 206]. Descartes's second reason deserves careful consideration:

It were better not to study at all than to occupy one's self with objects of such difficulty, that, owing to our inability to distinguish true from false, we are forced to regard the doubtful as certain; for in those matters any hope of augmenting our knowledge is exceeded by the risk of diminishing it.

If we accept mere morally certain truths into our science, we run a great risk when we try to extend our knowledge. When we try to add morally certain truths to our theory, we shall most likely lose some already in it. We shall diminish our knowledge in attempting to augment it. The only way to avoid this risk is to limit our science to true metaphysical certainties.

Descartes retains this position in the *Meditations*. He sets out to establish "a firm and permanent structure in the sciences" [AT VII, 17; HR I, 144] and decides that the only way to do so is to "no less carefully withhold [his] assent from matters which are not entirely certain and indubitable than from those which appear [to him] manifestly to be false" [AT VII, 18; HR I, 145]. Scientific knowledge must be metaphysically certain to be permanent.

Descartes is not the first or last philosopher to link a belief's degree of justification to its "permanence." Recall Plato's observation in the *Meno:* "True opinions are a fine thing and do all sorts of good so long as they stay in their place, but they will not stay long. They run away from a man's mind; so they are not worth much until you tether them by working out the reason. . . . Once they are tied down, they become knowledge, and are stable. That is why knowledge is something more valuable than right opinion. What distinguishes one from the other is the tether."[19] Plato thinks knowledge is true belief "tied down" by a justification; Descartes thinks the justification must yield metaphysical certainty for the belief to be tied down permanently. Risto Hilpinen has claimed more recently: "Knowledge cannot be 'lost' simply as a result of learning something new."[20] Jaakko Hintikka has expressed a similar sentiment: "If somebody says 'I know that *p*' in this strong sense of knowledge, he implicitly denies that any further information would have led him to alter his view. He commits himself to the view that he would still persist in saying that he knows *p* is true—or at the very least persist in saying that *p* is in fact true—even if he knew more than he now knows."[21] According to Descartes, Hilpinen and Hintikka are right only about metaphysically certain knowledge.

Let us see if we can better understand what Descartes has in mind. He adopts these epistemic principles:

EP5: If S knows that *p* with moral, but not metaphysical, certainty, then S's knowledge that *p* is impermanent.

EP6: If S knows that *p* with metaphysical certainty, S's knowledge that *p* is permanent.

From these he infers that we must limit science to metaphysically certain truths to ensure that our scientific knowledge is permanent. But what exactly is permanent knowledge? Some ways of understanding the concept of permanent knowledge make Descartes's position

19. Plato, *Meno*, 98a, translated by W. K. C. Guthrie in *Plato: Collected Dialogues*, edited by E. Hamilton and H. Cairns (Princeton: Princeton University Press, 1961).

20. Risto Hilpinen, "Knowledge and Justification," *Ajatus: Yearbook of the Philosophical Society of Finland*, 33 (1971), pp. 7–39.

21. Jaakko Hintikka, *Knowledge and Belief: An Introduction to the Logic of the Two Notions* (Ithaca: Cornell University Press, 1962), pp. 20–21. Marshall Swain presents an interesting discussion of what Hilpinen and Hintikka have in mind in "Epistemic Defeasibility," *American Philosophical Quarterly*, 11:1 (1974), pp. 15–25.

implausible. Suppose we say someone's knowledge is permanent just when there is no time in the future at which he fails to know the proposition with the same degree of certainty with which he knows it now.[22] If so, then, EP6, that metaphysically certain knowledge is permanent, is plainly false. Descartes can know a proposition with metaphysical certainty at one moment and not know it with metaphysical certainty at the next. He might forget his evidence; the proposition might change its truth value. A better way to understand permanent knowledge is this:

> D5: *S*'s knowledge that *p* with degree of certainty *C* is permanent = $_{df.}$
> (1) *S* knows that *p* with degree of certainty *C*, and (2) there is no proposition *q* such that (a) *q* is true, (b) *S* is not certain of *q* or of not-*q* to degree *C*, and (c) if *S* were to become certain of *q* to degree *C*, while retaining his evidence for *p*, *S* would cease to be certain of *p* to degree *C*.

Permanent knowledge is not knowledge we never lose. Permanent knowledge is knowledge we never lose as a result of extending our knowledge. When our knowledge that *p* is permanent, no true proposition to which we have yet to extend our certainty is such that our gaining certainty of it would cost us our certainty, and thereby our knowledge, of *p*. There is no chance that we shall, to use Descartes's phrase in the *Rules* passage above, "diminish" our knowledge in the process of "augmenting" it.[23]

What makes permanent knowledge, as I have defined it, so special? Descartes says it is more "firm," more "secure," than impermanent knowledge [*Meditations*; AT VII, 17; HR I, 144; *Discourse*; AT VI, 31; HR I, 100]. We must not read too much or too little into his remark.

22. This may be how Anthony Kenny, *Descartes*, p. 192, understands Descartes's position; for he writes: "It is not enough, for Cartesian certainty, that I should here and now unhesitatingly make a true judgment on the best possible grounds. It is necessary also that I should be in such a position that I will never hereafter have reason to withdraw that judgment." See my "Clear and Distinct Perception and Metaphysical Certainty," *Mind*, 88 (January 1979), pp. 97–104, and Fred Feldman and Arnold Levison's "Anthony Kenny and the Cartesian Circle," *Journal of the History of Philosophy*, 9 (October 1971), pp. 491–496 for more information about and arguments against Kenny's position.

23. Harry Frankfurt, *Demons, Dreamers and Madmen*, p. 27, understands the concept of permanent knowledge in a similar way. Frankfurt does not discuss the nature and importance of permanent knowledge and its connection with moral and metaphysical certainty in detail, however.

On the one hand, permanent knowledge can be overthrown into ignorance, just as impermanent knowledge can be. The world can change so that what we know with permanence today is false and hence not know by us tomorrow. Descartes may know with permanence today that he is in pain, but—if he is lucky—he will not know it tomorrow. We can lose our permanent knowledge by ceasing to have, even forgetting, the evidence that provides it. We do not escape all the natural limitations on our abilities as knowers by limiting science to permanent knowledge.

On the other hand, permanent knowledge is immune to one particular way of being overthrown to which impermanent knowledge is susceptible. It cannot happen that we know a proposition with permanence and then, while the features of the world we know remain unchanged and we retain our evidence for the proposition, we make some new discovery that defeats our justification and tosses us into ignorance. This can only happen when we know a proposition with impermanence. When we limit science to permanent knowledge, we thus guarantee that within the context of our natural limitations as knowers—a changing world, a weak memory, and the like—our knowledge will be secure as it can be. Once we know a proposition as part of our science, we can set it aside as secure and the question it answers as settled in the sense that no new discovery will defeat its certainty in the face of our evidence for it.

It is easy to establish EP5, that knowing a proposition with mere moral certainty is not sufficient for knowing it with permanence. Suppose Descartes is sitting before a fire, and his senses give him morally, but not metaphysically, certain knowledge of that fact. Suppose too that, unbeknownst to Descartes, Arnauld plans to deceive him this very day by making him believe there is a fire when there really is none (Arnauld does not implement his plan, however). Descartes's knowledge is impermanent in these circumstances. There is a fire and his senses make him morally certain of that fact, but his senses would not make him morally certain about the fire if he became morally certain that Arnauld planned to deceive him. His knowledge about Arnauld would cost him his knowledge about the fire.

There is a lesson behind EP5: when it comes to morally certain knowledge, even the truth can mislead us. Learning part of the truth (that Arnauld plans to deceive him) would cost Descartes his knowledge, even though learning the whole truth (that Arnauld plans to deceive him but does not) would not.

What about metaphysically certain knowledge? According to EP6, it is permanent. Suppose, then, that Descartes knows a proposition with metaphysical certainty. Perhaps it is a mathematical theorem he is deducing from axioms made metaphysically certain by his clear and distinct perception of them (he has ruled out the Deceiver Hypothesis). His knowledge is permanent if and only if no true metaphysical possibility of which he is ignorant is such that his gaining metaphysical certainty of it, while retaining his evidence for the theorem, would cost him his metaphysical certainty of the theorem. Let us try to find such a proposition.

Propositions inconsistent with the theorem are such that Descartes's metaphysical certainty of them would cost him his metaphysical certainty of the theorem. Yet, they are false. Propositions that indicate how the theorem or the axioms might be false, such as the Deceiver Hypothesis, may be such that Descartes's metaphysical certainty of them would cost him his metaphysical certainty of the theorem. Yet they are not metaphysical possibilities for Descartes. His evidence makes them metaphysical impossibilities; otherwise he would have a reason to doubt the theorem and would not be metaphysically certain of it. Some propositions that ordinarily support the theorem's negation are true metaphysical possibilities for Descartes; that Arnauld, who is generally reliable, asserts the theorem's negation, for example. Perhaps Descartes's metaphysical certainty of these propositions would cost him his metaphysical certainty of the theorem: if he became metaphysically certain of Arnauld's testimony for the theorem's negation, he would have some reason to believe the negation; the negation would be more reasonable, so the theorem would be less reasonable. Not so. When Descartes is metaphysically certain of the theorem, evidence that would otherwise support its negation fails to do so. In the present example, his metaphysical certainty of Arnauld's testimony would not increase the reasonableness of the theorem's negation and so decrease that of the theorem.

This last point is a subtle one; to appreciate it fully, consider the details of Descartes's situation. He starts by deducing the theorem from clearly and distinctly perceived axioms. His clear and distinct perception makes the axioms metaphysically certain; his deduction makes the theorem metaphysically certain. No even metaphysically possible hypothesis indicates how his axioms or the deduced theorem might be false. While he maintains his clear and distinct perception, he gains metaphysical certainty of another fact: Arnauld, who is generally reliable, asserts the theorem's negation. Does this new information increase the reasonableness of the negation and so decrease that of the theorem? No. It would do so only if there were a chance of the negation being true and the theorem false; that is, only if some metaphysical possibility gave Descartes a reason to doubt the theorem by indicating how it or his axioms might be false despite his clear and distinct perception. Descartes's evidence for the theorem excludes any such metaphysical possibility.

As far as I can tell, then, when Descartes, or anyone, knows a proposition with metaphysical certainty, no truth they have yet to discover is such that their knowing it with metaphysical certainty will cost them their original metaphysically certain knowledge. Their knowledge is permanent. EP6 is true.

Descartes thus has a persuasive rationale for his imperative to limit science to propositions known with metaphysical certainty. What undercuts his position is that his rationale presupposes our ability to gain metaphysical certainty in most, if not all, areas of scientific interest. Descartes has little patience with those who question our ability:

> No doubt men of education may persuade themselves that there is but little of such certain knowledge, because, forsooth, a common failing of human nature has made them deem it too easy and open to everyone, and so led them to neglect to think upon such truths; but I nevertheless announce that there are more of these than they think—truths which suffice to give a rigorous demonstration of innumerable propositions, the discussion of which they have hitherto been unable to free from the element of probability. [*Rules*, II; AT X, 362; HR I, 3]

Few who have studied Descartes's and others' attempts to find such metaphysically certain knowledge have been persuaded.[24]

24. In his own scientific work, Descartes sometimes seems willing to settle for less than metaphysical certainty, which makes one wonder how long he sustained his optimism regarding our ability to obtain knowledge with that high degree of certainty. An excellent discussion of this point is Daniel Garber's "Science and Certainty in Descartes," in *Descartes: Critical and Interpretive Essays*, ed. Michael Hooker (Baltimore: Johns Hopkins University Press, 1978).

Summary

Descartes's position on the nature of certainty contains a series of concepts: metaphysical certainty, moral certainty, rational doubt, truth, psychological certainty, clear and distinct perception, permanent knowledge, and impermanent knowledge. Descartes relates these concepts to one another with epistemic principles:

> EP1: p is a metaphysical certainty for S if and only if p is a moral certainty for S and S has no reason to doubt p.
>
> EP2: A human S is metaphysically certain that p only if S clearly and distinctly perceives that p.
>
> EP3: A human S clearly and distinctly perceives that p only if p is true.
>
> EP4: A human S clearly and distinctly perceives that p only if S is psychologically certain that p.
>
> EP5: If S knows that p with moral, but not metaphysical, certainty, S's knowledge that p is impermanent.
>
> EP6: If S knows that p with metaphysical certainty, S's knowledge that p is permanent.

A conception of our potential as inquirers lies behind the principles. God has given us sensation as a means to investigate the world. We have a natural but resistible inclination to believe what it reveals; what it reveals is often morally certain for us, but sometimes false nonetheless, and impermanent. God has provided us with the intellectual faculty of clear and distinct perception. What it reveals is always true and psychologically certain for us. It is our only source of metaphysical certainty and permanent knowledge. It enables us to engage in an inquiry into truth and to successfully construct science.

The picture of our intellectual abilities is as yet incomplete. I have not fully explained Descartes's concept of a reason for doubt. I have not explained in detail what clear and distinct perception is or how and under what conditions it is capable of making us metaphysically certain of propositions. I return to these points in Chapter 5 in a consideration of Descartes's account of how he gains metaphysical certainty that he thinks and exists. It is now time to consider the next thing we must understand to appreciate Descartes's Gambit: his position on the content of our certainty, especially our *de se* certainty.

Chapter 3

THE CONTENTS OF
SELF-KNOWLEDGE

One question stands between us and the ability to appreciate
Descartes's Gambit: What sorts of things, according to Descartes, are
the contents of his certainty? I have said propositions. I must now
defend my answer. It is also time to consider what sorts of propositions
Descartes takes the contents of his *de se* certainty to be. I must admit
that the relevance of these matters to Descartes's Gambit is not obvious; few commentators have paid careful attention to them.[1] Let me
renew the promise I made in Chapter 1: In later chapters we see that
Descartes's position on the contents of his certainty and, in particular,
on the contents of his *de se* certainty plays a crucial role in his defense
of his epistemic premises (P1, P2, and P3) and in his argument from
them to his conclusions about his nature (C1–C6).

Descartes as a Proposition Theorist

Certainty—be it metaphysical, moral, or psychological—has *de
dicto*, *de re*, and *de se* forms. Proposition theorists hold that in each

---

1. Two commentators who have taken note of the importance of Descartes's position on the contents of his *de se* certainty for his Gambit strategy are Margaret Wilson,
Descartes (London: Routledge and Kegan Paul, 1978), pp. 67, 198–200, and James
Van Cleve, "Conceivability and the Cartesian Argument for Dualism," *Pacific Philosophical Quarterly*, 64 (January 1983), pp. 35–45. Neither has examined the matter in
detail, however.

form the content of our certainty is always a proposition; propositions are the primary bearers of truth value, whatever else they may be. If Descartes is certain *de dicto* that someone is a philosopher, the content of his certainty is the proposition that someone is a philosopher. If he is certain *de re* of someone that she is a philosopher, the content is a proposition to the effect that that very person is a philosopher. If he is certain *de se* that he himself is a philosopher, the content of his certainty is the proposition he would express in English by "I am a philosopher." The *de dicto* form of each intentional attitude is primary; we get it by considering a proposition, and we get the *de re* and *de se* forms by considering the right sorts of propositions.

Descartes can adopt the proposition theory without subscribing to many of the views often associated with it. He need not take each proposition to be an eternally existant entity incapable of changing its truth value. He need not acknowledge that humans are capable of each type of intentional attitude dealt with by the theory; he might say we never apprehend a substance in the way required to have a *de re* attitude toward one. Descartes need not claim that every *de se* attitude is an instance of a *de re* attitude toward the self. He just has to say that whenever we have certainty or a related intentional attitude, the content of our attitude is a proposition, not some other sort of entity, such as a property.[2]

Descartes writes like a proposition theorist. Here is a typical remark about purely *de dicto* attitudes:

> I who have some little knowledge of the principles of geometry recognise quite clearly that the three angles are equal to two right angles, and it is not possible for me not to believe this so long as I apply my mind to its demonstration; but so long as I abstain from attending to the proof, although I still recollect having clearly comprehended it, it may easily occur that I come to doubt its truth, if I am ignorant of there being a God. [*Meditations; AT VII, 69–70; HR I, 184*]

What is known, believed, doubted, and clearly comprehended is a

2. David Lewis gives a version of property theory in "Attitudes *De Dicto* and *De Se*," *Philosophical Review*, 88 (October 1979), pp. 513–543, and Roderick Chisholm develops one in great detail in *The First Person* (Minneapolis: University of Minnesota Press, 1981). For some criticisms of Chisholm's theory see my "*De Dicto* and *De Se*," *Philosophical Studies*, 45 (1984), pp. 231–237.

thing capable of being demonstrated and possessing a truth value. It is a proposition: that the three angles of a triangle equal two right angles.

Descartes also writes like a proposition theorist in his most important and prominent descriptions of his *de se* attitudes. He presents their contents in the French and Latin equivalents of *that*-clauses; he describes the contents of his *de se* attitudes as truths, conclusions, or propositions. Here is what he says in the *Rules:*

> Each individual can mentally have intuition of the fact that he exists and that he thinks [*Ita unusquisque animo potest intueri, se existere, se cogitare*]; and that the triangle is bounded by three lines only, the sphere by a single superficies, and so on. [III; AT X, 368; HR I, 7]

In the *Discourse*, he tells us:

> Remarking that this truth [*cette vérité*] 'I think therefore I am', was so certain and so assured that all the most extravagant suppositions brought forward by the sceptics were incapable of shaking it, I came to the conclusion that I could receive it without scruple as the first principle of the Philosophy for which I was seeking. . . . from the very fact that I thought of doubting the truth of other things, it very evidently and certainly followed that I was [*de cela même que je pensais à doubter de la vérité des autres choses, il suivait très évidemment et très certainement que j'étais*]. [AT VI, 32; HR I, 101]

He announces his *de se* knowledge of his existence in Meditation Two:

> So that after having reflected well and carefully examined all things, we must come to the definite conclusion that this proposition: I am, I exist, is necessarily true each time that I pronounce it, or that I mentally conceive it [*Adeo ut, omnibus satis superque pensitatis, denique statuendum sit hoc pronuntiatum, Ego sum, ego existo, quoties a me profertur, vel mente concipitur, necessario esse verum*]. [AT VII, 25; HR I, 150][3]

3. The corresponding passage in the French text of the *Meditations* is also what we would expect of a proposition theorist: "De sorte qu' après y avoir bien pensé, et avoir soigneusement examiné toutes choses, enfin il faut conclure, et tenir pour constant que cette proposition: *Je suis, j'existe*, est nécessairement vraie, toutes les fois que je la prononce, ou que je la conçois en mon esprit"[AT IX, 19]. Examination reveals that Haldane and Ross follow the French text rather than the Latin in their translation; I stay with them since the differences between the two texts are philosophically unimportant in this case.

He gives a similar description of his self-knowledge at *Principles*, I, vii:

> And hence this cognition [*hæc cognitio*], I think, therefore I am is the
> first and most certain of all that occurs to one who philosophises in an
> orderly way. [AT VIII, 7; HR I, 221*]⁴

Descartes explains to Mersenne:

> *That everything that thinks is, or exists . . .* has rather been learned
> from the experience of the individual—that unless he exists, he cannot
> think. For our mind is so constituted by nature that general propositions
> [*generales propositiones*] are formed out of the knowledge of particular
> ones. [*Reply to the Second Objections*; AT VII, 140–141; HR II, 38*]

More important than the fact that Descartes writes like a proposition
theorist is that he assumes propositions are the contents of his *de se*
attitudes when he explains how he gains metaphysical certainty of his
existence. The passages I have just presented from the *Discourse* and
Principles make it clear that he thinks an inference is involved.⁵ That
from the *Rules* makes it clear that he also thinks intuition plays a role.
Descartes mentions both elements in a letter to the Marquis of Newcastle:

> You will surely admit that you are less assured of the presence of the
> objects you see than of the proposition [*cette proposition*] I experience,
> therefore I am? Now, this knowledge is no product of your reasoning,
> no lesson that your masters has taught you; it is something that your
> mind sees, feels, handles; and although your imagination, which insis-
> tently mixes itself up with your thoughts, reduces the clearness of this

4. The corresponding passage in the French text of the *Principles* is again what we
would expect of a proposition theorist: "nous ne saurions nous empêcher de croire que
cette conclusion: *Je pense, donc je suis*, ne soit vraie, et par conséquent la première et
la plus certaine qui se présente à celui qui conduit ses pensées par ordre" [AT IX-2,
27].

5. Some commentators have questioned whether Descartes thinks an inference is
involved in his *de se* metaphysical certainty that he exists. The most notable is Jaakko
Hintikka, "*Cogito, Ergo Sum*: Inference or Performance," *Philosophical Review*, 71
(January 1962), pp. 3–32. The difficulties in Hintikka's position are now well known
and are best displayed by Harry Frankfurt, "Descartes's Discussion of His Existence in
the Second Meditation," *Philosophical Review*, 75 (July 1966), pp. 329–356, and Fred
Feldman, "On the Performatory Interpretation of the *Cogito*," *Philosophical Review*,
82 (July 1973), pp. 345–363. In Chapter 5, I show how Descartes uses an inference to
gain metaphysical certainty of his existence.

knowledge, it is, nevertheless, proof of our soul's capacity for receiving from God an intuitive kind of knowledge (*une connaissance intuitive*). [AT V, 137; AG, 301][6]

I deal in Chapter 5 with the hard question of how Descartes's knowledge can be both inferential and intuitive. The point to see here is that each process can only be performed on propositions. We can only perform an inference on contents that have truth values (propositions). We can only intuit propositions; for Descartes tells us:

> Two things are requisite for mental intuition [*mentis intuitum*]. Firstly the proposition [*propositio*] intuited must be clear and distinct; secondly it must be grasped in its totality at the same time and not successively. [*Rules*, XI; AT X, 407; HR I, 33][7]

In all, we should interpret Descartes as a proposition theorist. He routinely and without qualification writes like one; his account of how he gains metaphysical certainty of his existence requires him to be one.

But what sort of proposition theorist is he? How, in particular, does he understand the difference between *de se* and non–*de se* attitudes? Descartes never explains the difference, but we must reach some conclusions about what he would say. As I have already promised, we see ultimately that how he understands his *de se* attitudes is crucial to the success or failure of his Gambit. Let us consider the basic questions he must answer to explain his *de se* attitudes and see if his statements on related matters provide any clues about how he would answer them.

De Se Attitudes

Suppose Descartes asserts to himself with metaphysical certainty, as he thinks he can, "*Ego cogito.*"[8] Does he use '*ego*' to refer to that

---

6. I have adopted Anscombe and Geach's translation.

7. To further appreciate how Descartes's position that he uses intuition and an inference to gain *de se* knowledge of his existence commits him to a proposition theory, consider how Roderick Chisholm, in adopting a nonproposition theory, is forced to explain our knowledge of our existence in noninferential and nonintuitive terms in *The First Person*, pp. 74–91.

8. Some of the material in this section is also contained in my paper "The *Cogito* Puzzle," *Philosophy and Phenomenological Research*, 43 (September 1982), pp. 59–81.

thing which is his self and thereby assert a proposition to the effect that it has the property of thought? Norman Malcolm thinks Descartes would say yes: "Descartes certainly believed that 'je', 'moi', 'ego', were used by him to refer to a certain thing."[9] Anthony Kenny thinks otherwise; according to Kenny, Descartes would say he asserts a proposition to the effect that a particular mental activity takes place, which could just as well be expressed by "This thinking takes place":

> [Descartes] would, I think, have agreed with Geach that "in soliloquy he could quite well have expressed himself without the first-person pronoun at all; he could have said, 'This is really a dreadful muddle,' where 'this' would refer back to his previous meditations."[10]

I suggest that Malcolm is headed in the right direction. More precisely, I think Descartes would accept three principles about *de dicto*, *de re*, and *de se* attitudes:

EP7: S is metaphysically certain (believes, doubts, conceives, etc.) *de se* that he himself is *F* only if there is a proposition *p* such that (1) S is metaphysically certain (believes, doubts, conceives, etc.) *de dicto* that *p*, and (2) *p* is a proposition to the effect that S is *F*.

EP8: S is metaphysically certain (believes, doubts, conceives, etc.) *de re* of *x* that it is *F* only if there is a proposition *p* such that (1) S is metaphysically certain (believes, doubts, conceives, etc.) *de dicto* that *p*, and (2) *p* is a proposition to the effect that *x* is *F*.

EP9: S is metaphysically certain (believes, doubts, conceives, etc.) *de se* that he himself is *F* only if S is metaphysically certain (believes, doubts, conceives, etc.) *de re* of S that it is *F*.

EP7 states two necessary conditions for *de se* attitudes: to have a *de se* attitude, Descartes must have the *de dicto* form of the attitude toward a proposition and the proposition must be about him; it must be the sort he would express by using an indexical, name, or definite description

9. Norman Malcolm, "Whether 'I' is a Referring Expression," in *Intention and Intentionality*, ed. Cora Diamond and Jenny Teichman (Ithaca: Cornell University Press, 1979), p. 15.

10. Anthony Kenny, *Descartes: A Study of His Philosophy* (New York: Random House, 1968), p. 59. Donald Sievert adopts a position similar to Kenny's in "Sellars and Descartes on the Fundamental Form of the Mental," *Philosophical Studies*, 37 (1980), pp. 251–257.

to refer to himself and a predicate expression to attribute a property to himself. EP8 presents similar necessary conditions for *de re* attitudes: to have a *de re* attitude toward a thing, Descartes must have the *de dicto* form of that attitude toward a proposition and the proposition must be about the thing; it must be the sort of proposition he would assert by using an indexical, name, or definite description to designate the thing and a predicate expression to attribute a property to it. EP9 says each *de se* attitude involves a *de re* attitude toward the self. When Descartes is metaphysically certain that he himself thinks, he is aware of himself in such a way as to be metaphysically certain of himself that he thinks. He does not simply direct his attention to some mental activity and gain metaphysical certainty that it occurs.[11]

None of these principles states sufficient conditions for *de se* or *de re* attitudes. Descartes clearly would not treat the two conditions in EP7 as jointly sufficient for a *de se* attitude. If he did, he would be committed to the false view that whenever he has a *de dicto* attitude about himself, he has a *de se* one as well. Surely Descartes might believe that the greatest philosopher is a mathematician without realizing that he himself is the greatest philosopher and so a mathematician.[12] I cannot tell whether Descartes would say the two conditions in EP8 are jointly sufficient for a *de re* attitude and side with those today known as "latitudinarian theorists," or deny that they are and side with "classical theorists."[13]

11. EP7 is redundant, since EP8 and EP9 entail it. I include it here for the sake of clarity.

12. Descartes can also believe *de re* of himself that he is a philosopher without believing *de se* that he himself is a philosopher. Consider Elizabeth Anscombe's "The First Person," in *Mind and Language: Wolfson College Lectures 1974*, ed. Samuel Guttenplan (Oxford: Clarendon Press, 1975), pp. 45–65, and Hector-Neri Castañeda's "He: A Study in the Logic of Self-Consciousness," *Ratio*, 8 (1966), pp. 130–157; "Indicators and Quasi-indicators," *American Philosophical Quarterly*, 4 (1967), pp. 85–100; "On the Logic of Attributions of Self-Knowledge to Others," *Journal of Philosophy*, 65 (1968), pp. 439–456; and "On the Phenomeno-Logic of the I," *Akten des XIV. Internationalen Kongress fur Philosophie*, 3 (University of Vienna, 1969), pp. 260–266.

13. The literature on the latitudinarian and classical approaches to *de re* attitudes is extensive; those unacquainted with the issues and interested in a short course might consider the discussions of *de re* attitudes in Chisholm's *Person and Object* (London: George Allen and Unwin, 1976), Richard Feldman's "Actions and *De Re* Beliefs," *Canadian Journal of Philosophy*, 8 (1978), pp. 577–581, Chisholm's *The First Person*, pp. 107–122, and Lynne Rudder Baker's "*De Re* Belief in Action," *Philosophical Review*, 91 (July 1982), pp. 363–387.

We have a strong reason to attribute EP7 in particular to Descartes. He indicates that he gains his *de se* mataphysical certainty that he exists by inferring his belief that he exists from his belief that he thinks, and we cannot give an adequate account of that inference unless we assume he refers to himself and considers a proposition to the effect that he thinks in his premise *"Ego cogito."* The best way to see this point is to consider what happens when we try to interpret Descartes's inference without assuming that he refers to himself in his premise. Kenny tries:

    i. This thinking is taking place.
    ii. This thinking is an attribute.
    iii. Every attribute is in some substance.
    iv. Therefore, this thinking is in some substance.[14]

This cannot be Descartes's inference. The conclusion is not equivalent to the fact that he exists, since he can exist when the particular thought it concerns does not. The argument uses the general premise that every attribute is in a substance, but Descartes indicates that he does not use any such premise:

> He who says, '*I think, hence, I am or exist,*' does not deduce existence from thought by a syllogism, but, by a simple act of mental vision, recognises it as if it were a thing known *per se*. This is evident from the fact that if it were syllogistically deduced, the major premise, *that everything that thinks is, or exists,* would have to be known previously; but yet that has rather been learned from the experience of the individual—that unless he exists, he cannot think. For our mind is so constituted by nature that general propositions [*generales propositiones*] are formed out of the knowledge of particular ones [*particularium*]. [*Reply to the Second Objections*; AT VII, 140–141; HR II, 38*]

We do not use general propositions like Kenny's (iii) to know particular ones like (iv), according to Descartes; we do just the opposite.[15]

Donald Sievert tries an approach similar to Kenny's. He reads Des-

---

14. Kenny, *Descartes*, p. 60.
15. Some may believe that Descartes takes back this point in the *Principles*, I, x [AT VIII, 8; HR I, 222]. I argue that he does not when I discuss his knowledge of his existence in detail in Chapter 5.

cartes's initial premise, *"Ego cogito,"* so that it concerns nothing in particular:

    i. Some thinking is taking place.
    ii. Every instance of thinking is an attribute.
    iii. Every attribute is in some substance.
    iv. Therefore, some substance thinks.[16]

The conclusion still is not equivalent to the fact that Descartes exists, and the inference still uses a general premise.

We avoid these problems if we attribute EP7 to Descartes and take his premise *"Ego cogito"* to be the proposition that he, in particular, thinks. That proposition immediately entails the conclusion that he, in particular, exists.[17]

The strongest support for EP7, EP8, and EP9 comes from two passages in the *Principles*, which, it is interesting to note, are frequently offered against them.

At *Principles*, I, xi, Descartes writes:

It is very manifest by the natural light which is in our souls, that no qualities or properties pertain to nothing; and that where some are perceived there must necessarily be some thing or substance on which they depend. And the same light shows us that we know a thing or substance so much the better the more properties we observe in it. And we certainly observe many more qualities in our minds than in any other thing, inasmuch as there is nothing that excites us to knowledge of whatever kind, which does not even much more certainly compel us to a consciousness of our thought. To take an example, if I persuade myself that there is an earth because I touch or see it, by the very same fact, and by yet stronger reason, I should be persuaded that my thought exists; because it may be that I think I touch the earth even though there is possibly no earth existing at all, but it is not possible that I who form this judgment and my mind which judges thus, should be non-existent; and so in other cases. [AT VIII, 8–9; HR I, 223]

16. Donald Sievert, "Sellars and Descartes on the Fundamental Form of the Mental," p. 255, and "Descartes's Self-Doubt," *Philosophical Review*, 84 (1975), pp. 51–69.

17. Some commentators argue that Descartes's inference is not immediate; I examine such arguments in detail and reply to them in Chapter 5. There are several propositions to the effect that Descartes thinks and exists. I am interested in the ones he would express by "I think" and "I exist."

Kenny and Sievert both interpret this passage as an implicit rejection of EP7, EP8, and EP9. They take Descartes to be saying we never apprehend that a particular substance has a particular quality; we only apprehend that a quality exists and infer, by the principle that every quality is in something, that something has the quality.[18]

That is not how I read the passage. Descartes does not explicitly say we never observe that a particular thing has a particular quality. His remark about observing qualities *in a substance* suggests he thinks we make such observations; so does the fact that he writes of a consciousness of *our* thought rather than just a consciousness of thought.[19]

Descartes is arguing that he knows himself better than he knows any other substance. He wants to establish that his *de re* knowledge of himself is superior to his *de re* knowledge of other substances. His argument is simple. First, he relates *de dicto* and *de re* knowledge: properties exist in substances, and the more propositions we know (*de dicto*) that predicate properties of a substance, the better we know (*de re*) the substance; as he puts it, "no qualities or properties pertain to nothing; . . . we know a thing or substance so much the better the more properties we observe in it." He applies this understanding of *de dicto* and *de re* knowledge to himself by treating his *de se* knowledge as a case of *de dicto* and *de re* knowledge. When he knows himself *de se*, when he knows, for example, that he himself thinks, he knows *de dicto* a proposition about himself and knows himself *de re*. He knows more propositions about himself in the course of his *de se* knowledge than he ever knows about any other substance. Hence, his *de re* knowledge of himself is more extensive, and so better, than his *de re* knowledge of any other thing.[20]

---

18. Kenny, *Descartes*, p. 60; Sievert, "Sellars and Descartes on the Fundamental Form of the Mental," p. 255.

19. The suggestions are in the French text as well: "Cette même luminère nous montre aussi que nous connaissons d'autant mieux une chose ou substance, que nous remarquons en elle davantage de propriétés. Or il est certain que nous en remarquons beaucoup plus en notre pensée qu'en aucune autre chose, d'autant qu'il n'y a rien qui nous excite à connaître quoi que ce soit, qui ne nous porte encore plus certainement à connaître notre pensée" [AT IX-2, 29].

20. Descartes's argument in the passage contains a serious error. He relies on the premise that our *de re* knowledge of *x* is superior to our *de re* knowledge of *y* if we know more properties of *x* than we know of *y*. He ignores the question of what sort of properties we know each to have. As Margaret Wilson has noted in *Descartes*, p. 96, "it is highly suprising to find Descartes espousing such a simplistically quantative conception of 'perfect comprehension.'"

My interpretation fits the title of the passage from the *Principles* ("How we may know our mind better than our body"), and it shows Descartes's use of EP7, EP8, and EP9: when he knows himself *de se*, he knows himself *de re*, and when he knows himself *de re*, he knows *de dicto* a proposition to the effect that he has or lacks some property. In another passage in the *Principles*, Descartes writes:

> Substance cannot be first discovered merely from the fact that it is a thing that exists, for that fact alone is not observed by us. We may, however, easily discover it by means of any one of its attributes because it is a common notion that nothing is possessed of no attributes, properties, or qualities. For this reason, when we perceive any attribute, we therefore conclude that some existing thing or substance to which it may be attributed, is necessarily present. [I, lii; AT VIII, 24–25; HR I, 240]

Sievert believes Descartes to be saying we never apprehend that a particular thing has a particular quality; we apprehend only that a quality exists and infer that something has it, by the principle that every attribute is in something.[21] But we must read a great deal into the passage to extract this message. All Descartes says in the first sentence is that we never observe that a particular thing exists without observing other facts about it. Next, he presents the principle that nothing is without attributes. He never presents the principle that every attribute is in something.

I suggest that here Descartes is again concerned with the relation between *de re* knowledge of substances and *de dicto* knowledge of propositions about them. His first point—"Substance cannot be first discovered merely from the fact that it is a thing that exists, for that fact alone is not observed by us"—is that we cannot gain *de re* knowledge of a substance *solely* by knowing *de dicto* a proposition to the effect that it exists, for we cannot know such a proposition independently of knowing other propositions about the substance, such as that it thinks or that it is extended. His second point—"We may, however, easily discover it by means of any one of its attributes because it is a common notion that nothing is possessed of no attributes, properties or qualities"—is that we can easily obtain *de re* knowledge of substances, since each has some

21. Sievert, "Sellars and Descartes on the Fundamental Form of the Mental," p. 257.

attribute, such as thought or extension, which we can *de dicto* know it to have. Descartes's last point—"When we perceive any attribute we therefore conclude that some existing thing or substance to which it may be attributed is necessarily present"—is that our *de dicto* knowledge of a proposition predicating an attribute like thought or extension to a thing is also the source of our knowledge that the thing exists. [22] My interpretation reveals one of Descartes's most important, and most ignored, insights. No one can know the fact that a particular thing exists without also knowing other facts about the thing. The property of existence lacks the kind of content that would allow us to know noninferentially the fact of its presence in an object. The best we can do is know, by intuition or sense perception, the fact that a particular thing has a property like thought or extension and infer from that that the thing exists. [23]

Let me sum up the position I think Descartes presents in these two passages from the *Principles*. Whenever we have *de se* knowledge, we have *de re* knowledge about the self, and we get both by knowing *de dicto* a proposition to the effect that it has or lacks some property. We have so much *de se* knowledge that our *de re* knowledge of the self is more extensive, and in that way better, than our *de re* knowledge of any other thing. While we obtain *de re* knowledge of a thing by knowing *de dicto* propositions to the effect that it has or lacks some property, we never obtain *de re* knowledge just by knowing a proposition to the effect that the thing exists. We can only know that a particular thing exists by inferring that fact from the premise that it has some other quality, like thought or extension. Descartes accepts EP7, EP8, and EP9 rather than rejecting them.

If we interpret Descartes in this way, how are we to understand his remarks about our inability to apprehend substances in his replies to the objections of Hobbes and Arnauld? Take a look at what he says. He writes in reply to Hobbes's objections:

> It is certain that no thought can exist apart from a thing that thinks; no activity, no accident can be without a substance in which to exist.

---

22. Some may wonder whether Descartes's remarks in the passage at hand can be plausibly interpreted so they *only* concern *de re* knowledge of substances. I think not. In the last sentence of the passage, Descartes clearly tells us the knowledge is inferential, and, since we only perform inferences on propositions, the knowledge must at least be *de dicto*.

23. Stephen Schiffer also makes this point in "Descartes on His Essence," *Philosophical Review*, 85 (January 1976), p. 23.

Moreover, since we do not apprehend the substance itself immediately though itself [*cùm autem ipsam substantiam non immediate per ipsam cognoscamus*], but by means only of the fact that it is the subject of certain activities [*sed per hoc tantùm quòd sit subjectum quorundam actuum*], it is highly rational, and a requirement forced on us by custom, to give diverse names to those substances that we recognize to be the subjects of clearly diverse activities or accidents, and afterwards to inquire whether those diverse names refer to one and the same or to diverse things. [*Third Objections and Replies*; AT VII, 175–176; HR II, 64]

Descartes says that we never apprehend a substance "itself immediately through itself," but only by means of the "fact that it is the subject of certain activities."[24] He is here making two points consistent with EP7, EP8, and EP9.

The first is that we never apprehend a substance, even the self, in such a way that it alone is the content of our thought; the content of our thought is always a proposition to the effect that the substance has or lacks some property. This is Descartes's point when he says we always apprehend a substance by means of "the fact that it is the subject of certain activities." This can be stated as

> EP10: *S* apprehends *x* only if there is some proposition *p* such that (1) *S* considers *de dicto* that *p*, and (2) *p* is a proposition to the effect that *x* has (lacks) some property.[25]

I do not know whether Descartes would say that the conditions in EP10 are sufficient for the apprehension of a substance. I suspect he would treat apprehending a substance as equivalent to having a *de re* attitude toward one, and, as I have noted already, I am not sure what he would take the sufficient conditions for a *de re* attitude to be. It is easy to appreciate EP10, however: just try to focus your attention on a thing, even yourself, without attending to its modifications.

Descartes's second point is captured by

> EP11: *S* apprehends *x* only if there is some property *C* such that (1) *C* is an individual concept of *x* (*x* has *C* and it is impossible that more than one thing has *C*), and (2) *S* conceives *C*.

---

24. The French text is: "Mais, d'autant que nous ne connaissons pas la substance immédiatement par elle-même, mais seulement parce qu'elle est le sujet de quelques actes" [AT IX, 136].

25. Margaret Wilson briefly considers a similar way of understanding Descartes in *Descartes*, pp. 67, 198–200.

When we apprehend a substance, the proposition we consider consists of an individual concept of the substance and some other property we believe the substance to have. The substance itself is not part of the propositional content of our thought. I think EP11 is what Descartes is aiming at when he says we never apprehend a substance "itself immediately through itself." Other passages suggest EP11 as well. Descartes writes in the *Meditations* of our conceiving substances through conceiving ideas of them:

> There is no doubt that those [ideas] which represent to me substances are something more, and contain so to speak more objective reality within them than those that simply represent modes or accidents. [AT VII, 40; HR I, 162]

He says in *Reply to the Second Objections* that

> existence is contained in the idea or concept of everything, because we can conceive nothing except as existent, with this difference, that possible or contingent existence is contained in the concept of a limited thing, but necessary and perfect existence in the concept of a supremely perfect being. [AT VII, 166; HR II, 57]

We conceive substances through concepts, each of which contains either contingent or necessary existence. When Descartes lists the things of which we can be directly aware, substances are conspicuously absent:

> *Thought* is a word that covers everything that exists in us in such a way that we are immediately conscious of it. Thus all the operations of will, intellect, imagination, and of the senses are thoughts. [*Reply to the Second Objections*; AT VII, 160; HR I, 52][26]

EP10 and EP11 are the key to understanding what Descartes has in mind when he tells Hobbes (above) that "it is highly rational, and a

---

26. Others have disagreed with Descartes's position that a substance cannot be part of the immediate content of our thought. Consider Russell's position in *The Problems of Philosophy* (Oxford: Oxford University Press, 1977), Chapter 5, especially p. 51.

requirement forced on us by custom, to give diverse names to those substances that we recognize to be the subjects of clearly diverse activities or accidents, *and afterwards to inquire whether those diverse names refer to one and the same or to diverse things"* (my emphasis). Suppose Descartes apprehends substance *x* and substance *y* in such a way that he recognizes them "to be subjects of clearly diverse activities"; that is, in terms of EP10 and EP11, the individual concept by which he conceives *x* and the property he considers it to have are different from the individual concept by which he conceives *y* and the property he considers it to have. Descartes's point to Hobbes is that it does not automatically follow that *x* and *y* are nonidentical. One substance can satisfy several individual concepts (Arnauld can be both the greatest seventeenth-century philosopher and the greatest seventeenth-century logician) and have several properties (being such as to develop theories in metaphysics, being such as to develop theories in logic). Descartes might first apprehend a substance by considering a proposition that contains one of its individual concepts and properties (that the greatest seventeenth-century philosopher develops theories in metaphysics) and then apprehend the substance by considering another proposition that involves a different individual concept and property (that the greatest seventeenth-century logician develops theories in logic).

Here again we have one of Descartes's most important ideas: he can apprehend substance *x* and substance *y* but be unable to determine by inspecting the content of his thought whether *x* is diverse from *y*. Neither *x* nor *y* is part of the content of his thought. The contents are propositions. The fact that he finds the propositions and the concepts they involve to be nonidentical does not justify him in concluding that the substances are nonidentical.[27]

EP10 and EP11 are consistent with EP7, EP8, and EP9. Those three principles say that when Descartes has a *de se* attitude, he has a *de re* attitude toward himself by having a *de dicto* attitude toward a proposition to the effect that he has or lacks some property. EP10 and EP11 just add that when Descartes apprehends himself in a *de se* attitude, the content of his apprehension is a proposition containing an

---

27. Some charge that Descartes ignores this point in his attempt to show that he and his body are nonidentical. I show in Chapter 7 that he does not.

individual concept of himself and some other property he considers himself to have or lack.[28]

Descartes also discusses our apprehension of substances in reply to Arnauld's objections:

> We do not have immediate cognition of substances, as has been else-where noted; rather from the mere fact that we perceive certain forms or attributes which must inhere in something in order to have existence, we name the thing in which they exist a *substance*. [*Reply to the Fourth Objections*; AT VII, 222; HR II, 98]

There are several ways to slide Descartes's remark under my interpretation. His point may be that we never apprehend a substance except as modified in some way (EP10), and/or that we never apprehend a substance except through conceiving some concept of it (EP11). He may even have another point in mind. The context makes it clear that he is concerned with how we might know of a substance that it is a substance, for in the preceeding lines of the passage he says each substance has "forms or attributes which suffice to let [him] recognise that it is a substance."[29] So when he says, "from the mere fact that we perceive certain forms or attributes that must inhere in something in order to have existence, we name the thing in which they exist a substance," he may be making the same point about being a substance that we have already found him to make about existence [*Principles*, I, lii; AT VIII, 24–25; HR I, 240]: we never just know of a thing that it is a substance; we know it to have some other properties, like thought or extension, and infer from that information that it is a substance.

In all, I think Descartes would tell us that when he says to himself with metaphysical certainty, "*Ego cogito*," he uses '*ego*' to refer to

---

28. We can use the notion of an individual concept to explain the talk in EP7, EP8, and EP10 about a proposition *to the effect that a particular thing has a particular quality*: p is a proposition to the effect that x has $F =_{df}$ there is a property G such that (1) G is an individual concept, (2) p contains the conjunction of G and F, and (3) x has G. Proposition p contains the property of being $F =_{df}$ p is necessarily such that (1) if p is true, something has the property of being F, and (2) whoever accepts p believes that something is F. These two definitions are modeled on the similar ones given by Chisholm in *Person and Object*, Chapter 1.

29. Consider the French text as well: "Je n'entends autre chose qu'une substance revêtue des formes, ou attributs, qui suffisent pour me faire connaître qu'elle est une substance" [AT IX, 172].

himself, and the content of his *de se* metaphysical certainty is a proposition to the effect that he has the property of thought. He is metaphysically certain *de re* of himself that he thinks; he apprehends himself, although he is not part of the immediate content of his thought. The content of his thought is a proposition that contains an individual concept of himself and the property of thought.

Self-Individuation in *De Se* Attitudes

By what individual concept does Descartes direct his attention to himself, individuate himself from other things, when he has a *de se* attitude? Not just any individual concept of him will do. Suppose Descartes believes *de dicto* that the person in the mirror is a philosopher and *de re* of that person that he is a philosopher, but he does not believe *de se* that he himself is a philosopher, even though, unbeknownst to him, he is the person in the mirror. He distinguishes himself from other things by conceiving one of his individual concepts, being the person in the mirror. He apprehends himself and forms a *de re* belief of himself. Yet he does not believe *de se* that he himself is a philosopher, and he does not individuate himself *as himself*. What individual concept must he conceive to do that?

Descartes must answer this question in one of two ways: (1) when he has a *de se* attitude, he individuates himself *per se* (without relating himself to any other thing); or (2) when he has a *de se* attitude, he individuates himself relative to some other thing he individuates *per se*. Let us start with the second option.

Perhaps Descartes would say that when he has a *de se* attitude, he is directly aware of one of his mental attributes and conceives of himself as the thing that has it. He individuates the attribute *per se* and himself relative to the attribute. When he asserts "*Ego cogito*," he asserts the same proposition he would by "the thing with this thinks" if he used 'this' to demonstrate one of his mental traits.[30] This proposal differs from the one championed by Kenny which I discarded in the last

---

30. James Van Cleve, "Conceivability and the Cartesian Argument for Dualism," takes the content of Descartes's *de se* claim to be unextended to be the proposition he would express in English by "The thinker of this thought is unextended."

section. The proposal here is that for Descartes "*Ego cogito*" expresses a proposition about himself by virtue of containing an individual concept he satisfies, being the thing with a particular mental trait. He would express that proposition in English by "The thing with this thinks" if he used 'this' to demonstrate that trait. Kenny's view is that for Descartes "*Ego cogito*" does not express a proposition about himself at all; it expresses a proposition about a particular mental event to the effect that it takes place. Descartes would express that proposition in English by "This thinking is taking place" if he used 'this' to demonstrate that mental attribute.

Descartes sometimes seems to believe he individuates himself relative to his mental traits in his *de se* attitudes. He says he can be immediately aware of his mental attributes, which suggests he can individuate them *per se*:

> *Thought* is a word that covers everything that exists in us in such a way that we are immediately [*immediate*] conscious of it. [*Reply to the Second Objections*; AT VII, 160; HR II, 52]

He describes himself relative to his thoughts in the *Discourse*:

> But immediately afterwards I noticed that whilst I thus wished to think all things false, it was absolutely essential that *the I, who thought this*, should be somewhat, and remarking that this truth 'I think, therefore I am' was so certain and so assured that all the most extravagant suppositions brought forward by the sceptics were incapable of shaking it, I came to the conclusion that I could receive it without scruple as the first principle of the Philosophy for which I was seeking. [AT VI, 32; HR I, 101; my emphasis]

He gives a similar description in the *Principles*:

> It is easy to suppose that there is no God, nor heaven, nor bodies, and that we possess neither hands, nor feet, nor indeed any body; but we cannot in the same way conceive that *we, who think these things*, are not; for there is a contradiction in conceiving that what thinks does not at the same time as it thinks, exist. [I, vii; AT VIII, 7; HR I, 221; my emphasis; cf. *Meditations*; AT VII, 25; HR I, 150*]

Note that Descartes says, "There is a contradiction in conceiving that what thinks does not at the same time as it thinks, exist"; perhaps his point is that, since he individuates himself relative to his thoughts, the proposition he would express by "I do not exist" is identical with the contradiction he would express by "The thing with these does not exist," where 'these' refers to his thoughts.[31]

These passages are misleading. Several points make it clear Descartes neither would nor should say he individuates himself relative to his mental traits in his *de se* attitudes. If Descartes individuates himself relative to his thoughts, how does he gain metaphysical certainty that he thinks? He must discover a mental attribute, determine that it is a thought, decide that one and only one thing has it, and then conclude "The thing with this thinks" ("*Ego cogito*"). Yet Descartes says he knows that he thinks by an act of intuition: "Thus each individual can mentally have intuition of the fact that he exists, and that he thinks" [*Rules*, III; AT X, 368; HR I, 7]. Although he indicates in later works that his knowledge of his existence involves both an intuition and an inference, Descartes never indicates that an inference is involved in his knowledge that he thinks.

Strange things follow from the view that Descartes individuates his thoughts *per se* and himself relative to his thoughts. It implies that when he is metaphysically certain he thinks, he is metaphysically certain of the proposition he would express by "The thing with this thinks," where 'this' demonstrates a particular one of his thoughts. Yet that proposition is not equivalent to the fact that he thinks, for he can think when the particular thought it concerns does not exist. The same is true of Descartes's *de se* knowledge that he exists. If he individuates himself relative to his thoughts, the content of his metaphysical certainty is the proposition he would express by "The thing with this exists," where 'this' demonstrates a thought, but he can exist when that thought does not.

If Descartes claims to individuate himself relative to his thoughts in his *de se* attitudes, he cannot explain the difference between some of his non-*de se* attitudes toward himself and his *de se* attitudes. Here is an example. Descartes considers one of his ideas, does not realize that he has created it, and wonders whether he or some other being has caused it

31. The sentence "The thing with these does not exist" is, of course, ambiguous. It may be taken to express the same self-contradictory proposition as "There exists one and only one thing that has these and it does not exist," or it may be taken to express the same proposition as "Nothing is the one and only thing that has these," which is not self-contradictory.

to exist in his mind. He says to himself, "The thing that produced this is perfect," using 'this' to demonstrate the idea. He then decides he is the source of the idea and concludes, "I am perfect." Descartes expresses different propositions by "The thing that produced this is perfect" and "I am perfect." He does not form a *de se* belief when he believes the first; he does when he believes the second. If Descartes really does individuate himself relative to his thoughts in his *de se* attitudes, there is little difference between his two beliefs. When he has his non–*de se* belief, he believes the proposition he expresses by "The thing that caused this is perfect," and when he has his *de se* belief, he believes the proposition he expresses by "The thing that has this is perfect"; in each case 'this' refers to the same idea, so the only difference between his two belief states is that in one he individuates himself as the cause of the idea, and in the other he individuates himself as the thing that has it. That cannot be. Descartes gains a new kind of self-awareness when he moves from his non–*de se* belief about himself to his *de se* belief. He shifts from individuating himself to individuating himself as himself. Whatever this change involves, it involves more than a shift from individuating himself as the producer of an idea to individuating himself as its owner.

A final problem for the view that Descartes individuates himself relative to his thoughts is raised by Elizabeth Anscombe's question "How do I know that 'I' is not ten thinkers thinking in unison?"[32] Descartes takes note of his pain and asserts to himself, "I am in pain." He takes note of his sadness and asserts to himself, "I am sad." He is justified in both beliefs, and, on the basis of them, he forms the third justified belief, "I am in pain and sad." He cannot explain why his third belief is justified if he says he individuates himself relative to his thoughts. If that is how he individuates himself, his inference runs as follows:

    i. The thing with this^a is in pain.
    ii. The thing with this^b is sad.
    iii. Before, the thing with this^c is in pain and sad.

The demonstratives refer to his pain (^{a}), his sadness (^{b}) and their combination (^{c}). He is justified in believing (iii) on the basis of (i) and (ii) only if he is justified in believing

32. Elizabeth Anscombe, "The First Person," p. 58.

ii′. The thing with this^a is identical to the thing with this^b.

(ii′) is not justified for him. If all he is immediately aware of are a sensation of pain and a sensation of sadness, he has no reason to believe that the subject of one is identical to the subject of the other.[33]

We should not saddle Descartes with the view that he individuates himself relative to his mental traits in his *de se* attitudes. That view of self-individuation conflicts with his account of how he gains *de se* knowledge that he thinks. It contains strange implications and serious problems he is better off without.

We can rule out two other possibilities as well. Descartes would deny that he individuates himself relative to one of his physical attributes when he has a *de se* attitude. He says he has no physical attributes. He would deny that he individuates himself relative to some other substance, such as God or his body, for he believes he can be metaphysically certain *de se* that he thinks and exists without being metaphysically certain of the existence of any other substance.

Descartes is right to deny that he individuates himself relative to his physical traits. Even if he has such properties, the view that he individuates himself relative to them in his *de se* attitudes is just as misguided as the view that he individuates himself relative to his thoughts. Inspection will reveal that it has all the same problems: it has anomalous implications for the contents of Descartes's *de se* knowledge that he thinks and exists, it fails to distinguish between his *de se* and non–*de se* attitudes about himself, and it does not allow for the unity of consciousness.

Descartes is also right to avoid the idea that he individuates himself relative to some other substance in his *de se* attitudes. He can quite coherently assert to himself, "I exist and nothing else does." His assertion is not anything like the incoherent one he would make by "The

---

33. Those sympathetic to the view that we individuate ourselves relative to our thoughts may try to meet this objection by claiming that Descartes always individuates himself relative to the entire contents of his consciousness, so the demonstratives in his premises refer to the same thing in this case. This move just trades one problem for another. How is Descartes justified in even believing what he expresses by "The thing with this is in pain" where 'this' demonstrates the entire contents of his consciousness? What justifies him in thinking that there is one and only one thing that has all the contents of his consciousness? These points have been made before. Consider Sidney Shoemaker's discussion in *Self-Knowledge and Self-Identity* (Ithaca: Cornell University Press, 1963), pp. 102–106.

thing that is not identical to this but directs it by its will exists, but nothing other than it does," where 'this' refers to another substance, say his body, which he individuates *per se*.

So how does Descartes think he individuates himself in his *de se* attitudes? There is only one option left, given that he thinks he individuates himself by conceiving a concept of himself but does not think he individuates himself relative to a mental attribute, physical attribute, or other substance he individuates *per se*. He thinks he individuates himself by conceiving an individual concept that distinguishes him from all other entities—substances and attributes—without relating him to any. He apprehends himself indirectly by conceiving a concept of himself— but *per se*; the concept does not relate him to any other thing.

Descartes never indicates what this individual concept might be, and few concepts qualify. Those by which he might individuate himself *per se* under special circumstances, such as being the philosopher (in that case in which he is the only philosopher), do not in fact apply to him or are not part of the content of his *de se* attitudes. Even if he is the only philosopher, the content of his metaphysical certainty, when he is metaphysically certain he himself thinks and exists, is not that the philosopher thinks and exists. The most promising candidate is Descartes's property of being identical to himself. It distinguishes him from all other things (he must have it and only he can have it) without relating him to any. It is plausible to believe it is part of the content of his *de se* attitudes, so that when he affirms "*Ego cogito*," he believes the proposition he would express by "That which is identical to me thinks."[34] I shall call this account of self-individuation in *de se* attitudes the 'Self-Identity Theory.' It does not land Descartes in the philosophical brambles associated with the other options.

The Self-Identity Theory is consistent with Descartes's belief that he gains *de se* metaphysical certainty that he thinks by an act of intuition rather than an inference. If the proposition he expresses by "*Ego cogito*" contains the property of being identical to him, he individuates himself *per se* when he apprehends it. He does not first individuate one of his mental attributes, then conclude that something has it, and finally individuate himself as the thing that has it.

34. Roderick Chisholm develops this view of the content of *de se* attitudes in *Person and Object*, Chapter 1.

The Self-Identity Theory makes the content of Descartes's *de se* certainty that he thinks no more and no less than we expect it to be. He is metaphysically certain of a proposition that must be true when and only when he, in particular, thinks. When he is metaphysically certain he exists, he is certain of a proposition that must be true when and only when he, in particular, exists.

It is easy to appreciate the difference between Descartes's *de se* and non–*de se* beliefs about himself in terms of the Self-Identity Theory. Suppose Descartes contemplates an idea he has produced in himself, affirms, "The thing that produced this is perfect," but does not realize he is that thing; he later realizes he is the cause of the idea and asserts to himself, "I am perfect." He initially individuates himself by conceiving the individual concept he expresses by "The thing that produced this," where 'this' refers to an idea of which he is directly aware. He individuates himself relative to a mental attribute rather than *per se*, and he does not individuate himself as himself. Then he individuates himself by conceiving the individual concept of being identical to him, which he expresses by 'I.' He individuates himself *per se* and is aware of himself as himself. He moves from a non–*de se* to a *de se* belief.

The Self-Identity Theory does not threaten to divide each of us into a host of thinkers thinking in unison. It lets us say that if Descartes is justified in believing that he is in pain and that he is sad, he is also justified in believing that he is in pain and sad. His inference runs:

  i. I am in pain.
  ii. I am sad.
  iii. Therefore, I am in pain and sad.

The term 'I' in each line refers to Descartes and expresses the property of being identical to him. The premises entail the conclusion, and Descartes is justified in believing it, since he is justified in believing them. Some may demand that Descartes's premises include

  ii'. I am identical to I.

Descartes is justified in believing this. It simply says that what has the property of being identical to him is identical to what has the property of being identical to him.

Does the Self-Identity Theory conflict with any of Descartes's explicit philosophical commitments? I see only one potential trouble spot. Descartes says that thought is his only essential property [*Principles*, I, liii; AT VIII, 25; HR I, 240], but if he has the property of being identical to him, he cannot exist without it, so it looks like that property is essential to him, too.

This conflict is only apparent. That Descartes cannot exist without being identical to himself does not imply that he is essentially identical to himself. Descartes so understands the concept of an essence that several properties he must have are not essential to him. Two of the most notable are being a substance and having duration. Descartes knows he cannot exist without them [*Principles*, I, xlviii; AT VIII, 22–23; HR I, 238], but he excludes them from his essence, and at least part of his reason seems to be that, since every substance must have them, they do not help define him as a particular kind of thing.[35] So too, his property of being identical to himself, which no other substance can have, does not define him as a particular kind of thing—except for the overly restrictive kind of which he is the only specimen—and may be properly excluded from his essence. (I explain Descartes's concept of essence in greater detail in Chapter 6.)

In all, even though Descartes does not say how he individuates himself in his *de se* attitudes, we may draw some conclusions about what he would and should say. He individuates himself indirectly by conceiving an individual concept of himself—yet *per se*; the concept does not relate him to any mental attribute, physical attribute, or other substance he individuates *per se*. The Self-Identity Theory is one plausible way, perhaps the only plausible way, he might have developed this view.

The Privacy of *De Se* Attitudes

Proposition theorists often claim that the contents of *de se* attitudes are private. Frege says:

> Everyone is presented to himself in a particular and primitive way, in which he is presented to no-one else. So, when Dr. Lueben thinks that

---

35. Compare Stephen Schiffer's discussion in "Descartes on His Essence," pp. 22–26.

he has been wounded, he will probably take as a basis this primitive way in which he is presented to himself. And only Dr. Leuben himself can grasp thoughts determined in this way. But now he may want to communicate with others. He cannot communicate a thought which he alone can grasp. Therefore, if he now says, "I have been wounded", he must use the "I" in a sense which can be grasped by others, perhaps in the sense of "he who is speaking to you at this moment."[36]

Hector-Neri Castañeda says it is a "truth of great importance" that "propositions about a given I can be the full objects of belief (knowledge, assumption, assertion, etc.), only if the belief (knowledge, etc.) in question belongs to the same I."[37]

What is Descartes's position? It is often assumed he adopts some sort of privacy thesis about *de se* attitudes, but, insofar as I know, there are no passages in which he deals with the issue.[38] Once again, we face the question of what he would say if he were to confront it.

There is reason to think Descartes would side with Frege and Castañeda and adopt

> EP12: If S conceives *de se* that he himself is F and p is the propositional content of S's conception, then no one other than S can conceive that p.

According to EP12, no one has access to the propositions that are the contents of someone else's *de se* attitudes. Arnauld cannot apprehend Descartes's, and you cannot apprehend mine.

EP12 follows from three plausible assumptions Descartes might combine with his proposition theory. First, propositions that differ in

36. Frege, "The Thought: A Logical Inquiry," *Mind*, 65 (July 1956), p. 298.

37. Hector-Neri Castañeda, "On the Phenomeno-Logic of the I," p. 263. Chisholm also affirms the privacy of the contents of *de se* attitudes in *Person and Object*, p. 36. Some, of course, deny that there can be a private language; Anthony Kenny, "The First Person," in *Intention and Intentionality*, eds. Diamond and Teichman, p. 11, writes: "Thoughts may be kept to oneself; but even the most secret thought must be capable of being made public, and the sense of the thought expressed in public must be the same as the sense of the thought entertained in private—otherwise we could not speak of the 'expression' of the thought." Castañeda gives a fine summary of the issues involved here in "The Private Language Problem," in *The Encyclopedia of Philosophy*, ed. Paul Edwards (Glencoe: Free Press, 1977).

38. Consider Edwin Curley's discussion of how much of what is often taken to be Descartes's position on this and related matters is actually presented by Descartes, *Descartes against the Skeptics* (Cambridge: Harvard University Press, 1978), pp. 170–193.

truth value are numerically diverse. This is an instance of the principle of the indiscernibility of identicals. Second, if two people have the same intentional attitude toward the same (numerically identical) proposition, they are in what counts as the same mental state for the purpose of explaining their behavior. This, I think, is a fairly obvious principle of individuation for mental states. Third, if one person's mental state causes him to behave one way and another's causes her to exhibit what counts as different behavior, then, all other things being equal, they are in different mental states. We can put the point this way: All other things being equal, people in the same mental state behave in the same way. This is a principle of individuation necessary to any attempt to explain the mental causes of behavior.

To see how Descartes might reason from these plausible assumptions to EP12, consider a simple case. He believes *de se* that he is the author of the *Meditations*. Can Arnauld believe the very same proposition? Arnauld cannot believe it by affirming to himself with regard to Descartes, "He is the author of the *Meditations*." If Arnauld believed the very same proposition, he would be in the same mental state and exhibit the same behavior in the same circumstances; but he behaves differently. When each is asked to identify the author of the *Meditations*, Descartes points to Descartes and to himself; Arnauld only points to Descartes. Arnauld cannot believe the very same proposition as Descartes by affirming to himself, "I am the author of the *Meditations*." He believes a proposition that is false, while Descartes believes one that is true. Arnauld, it seems, cannot believe the proposition Descartes believes. The best explanation is that he cannot conceive it.

Some may object that the case I have described is special. It involves a property that is true of Descartes but not of Arnauld (being the author of the *Meditations*), and that is why Descartes and Arnauld must apprehend different propositions when each says to himself, "I am the author of the *Meditations*." If we pick a property each has, such as being human, we can say that each apprehends the same (identical) proposition when he says to himself, "I am human." This objection misses the point. That Descartes apprehends a true proposition and Arnauld a false one in my example helps us see that the propositions are diverse, but it is not what makes them diverse. What makes the propositions diverse is that Descartes's is about Descartes and not about Arnauld (that is why it is true) and Arnauld's is about Arnauld and not about Descartes (that is why it is false). This feature of the case will be duplicated in any instance in which we have two people each asserting a belief in the first person. I do not claim that Descartes ever gives this argument for EP12. He does not. My point is that it shows how EP12 follows from his proposition theory by some plausible assumptions.

Objections to Descartes's Proposition Theory

Some philosophers deny that propositions are the contents of intentional attitudes like knowledge, belief, and metaphysical certainty, and their most recent arguments challenge claims central to Descartes's position. David Lewis asks us to consider the case of Heimson and Hume. Each affirms to himself, "I am Hume," and, according to Lewis, "Heimson's belief and Hume's belief have the same object, but Heimson is wrong and Hume is right. Thus the object of their shared belief is not a proposition."[39] Lewis's argument, in a somewhat expanded form, is:

1. The content of Heimson's belief is identical to the content of Hume's.
2. If the content of Heimson's belief is identical to the content of Hume's, then if the content of each belief is a proposition, Hume's belief is true if and only if Heimson's belief is true.
3. If the content of each belief is a proposition, Hume's belief is true if and only if Heimson's belief is true.   [from 1 and 2]
4. Hume's belief is true and Heimson's is false.
5. Therefore, the content of each belief is not a proposition.   [from 3 and 4]

Why accept the first premise? We might say—indeed the most direct way for a proposition theorist to meet this objection is to say—Heimson's and Hume's beliefs are nonidentical, though similar, in content. Heimson believes a proposition he would express by "I am Hume"; Hume believes a proposition he would express by "I am Hume." The propositions are numerically diverse, since the first is

39. David Lewis, "Attitudes *De Dicto* and *De Se*," p. 526.

false while the second is true, and, if the Self-Identity Theory is right, the first involves Heimson's property of being identical to himself while the second involves Hume's property of being identical to himself. The propositions are similar, since each involves the property of being Hume and, if the Self-Identity Theory is right, someone's property of being identical to himself.

Lewis defends his first premise:

> Heimson may have got his head into a perfect match with Hume's in every way that is at all relevant to what he believes. If nevertheless Heimson and Hume do not believe alike, then beliefs *ain't in the head!* They depend partly on something else, so that if your head is in a certain state and you're Hume you believe one thing, but if your head is in the same state and you're Heimson you believe something else. Not good. The main purpose of assigning objects of attitudes is, I take it, to characterize states of the head; to specify their causal role with respect to behavior, stimuli, and one another. If the assignment of objects depends partly on something besides the state of the head, it will not serve this purpose. The states it characterizes will not be the occupants of the causal roles.[40]

I think Lewis's argument is this:

1. Hume and Heimson are in the same mental state.
2. If Hume and Heimson are in the same mental state, then the causal roles of their states are the same.
3. If Hume's mental state has the same causal roles as Heimson's, then their contents are identical.
4. Therefore, the content of Heimson's belief is identical to the content of Hume's.

Consider how we must understand the word 'same' in its various occurrences here. We must read it in premise (1) as equivalent to 'similar' or 'type identical' rather than 'numerically identical.' The example contains *two* cases of *de se* belief, Heimson's and Hume's. We must interpret 'same' as 'similar' or 'type identical' in premise (2) as well. All other things being equal, Hume's belief will lead Hume to exhibit the same type of behavior as Heimson's belief will lead Heim-

---

40. David Lewis, "Attitudes *De Dicto* and *De Se*," pp. 525–526.

son to exhibit; each will point to himself when asked who Hume is, and the world will be richer by two distinct, though similar, actions. Because we must read 'same' as 'similar' or 'type identical' in premises (1) and (2), we must also read it that way in the antecedent of (3). We must read 'identical' in the consequent of (3) as 'numerically identical' to get the conclusion Lewis needs. Premise (3) thus turns out to be the unwarranted claim that if Hume's and Heimson's mental states have similar causal roles, they have numerically identical contents. There is no need for their contents to be identical. The contents need only be similar. I have already described how the contents can be similar, though numerically diverse, propositions.

There is an advantage to assigning nonidentical contents to Hume's and Heimson's states. Hume and Heimson behave in the same way in that each points to himself when asked who Hume is, but they also behave differently: Hume points to Hume, not Heimson, and Heimson points to Heimson, not Hume. We can easily explain this difference in their behavior if we assign different contents to their states. Hume points to Hume because he believes him to be Hume, and he believes him to be Hume because he believes a proposition about him to the effect that he is Hume. Heimson points to Heimson because he believes him to be Hume, and he believes him to be Hume because he believes a proposition about him to the effect that he is Hume. That the proposition theory assigns different contents to Hume's and Heimson's beliefs is one of its strengths.[41]

Roderick Chisholm attacks the self-identity version of the proposition theory in an argument that might also be aimed at Descartes's position. Descartes is committed to the view that he individuates himself in his *de se* attitudes by conceiving a concept that does not relate him to any other substance or to any physical or mental attribute he individuates *per se*. The most plausible candidate, perhaps the only

---

41. See Richard Feldman's "Actions and *De Re* Belief" and Lynne Rudder Baker's "*De Re* Belief in Action" for more on the role of *de re* attitudes in the explanation of actions. Feldman assumes that *de re* attitudes play an important role in action explanation and argues that only a classical theory of *de re* attitudes can account for that fact; Baker argues that a particular *de re* explanation schema is incorrect and concludes that *de re* attitudes do not have a role to play in action explanations. Although I cannot argue the point here, I think other *de re* explanation schemas easily avoid Baker's objection, though they do not support Feldman's argument for a classical theory of *de re* attitudes.

plausible candidate, for such a concept is Descartes's property of being identical to himself. Chisholm argues:

> If I can grasp my individual essence, then I ought also to be able to single out in it those features that are unique to it. If *being identical with me* is my individual essence and *being identical with you* is yours, then, presumably, each analyses into personhood and something else as well—one something else in my case and another in yours—but I haven't the faintest idea what this something else might be.[42]

Chisholm's argument, as I understand it, is this:

1. A person has and can grasp the property of being identical to himself only if he can analyze that property into a set of properties the conjunction of at least some of which is not contained in any other person's property of being identical to himself.
2. I cannot so analyze the property of being identical to myself.
3. Therefore, it is not the case that I have and can grasp the property of being identical to myself.
4. Therefore, no one has and can grasp the property of being identical to himself.

Premise (1) is unwarranted. Why should we believe that a person can grasp his property of being identical to himself only if he can analyze it? Perhaps each person's property of being identical to himself is unanalyzable. That each person's property of being identical to himself entails other properties, like existence and, perhaps, being a person, does not imply that each person's property of self-identity is analyzable. Being red entails being colored, but several philosophers, including Chisholm, have claimed it to be unanalyzable.[43] We capture some interesting philosophical insights if we adopt the Self-Identity Theory and say that each person's property of being identical to himself is unanalyzable. There is Frege's claim that "everyone is presented to himself in a particular and *primitive* way" (my emphasis).[44] We also capture the idea that much of our self-knowledge is synthetic.

42. Roderick Chisholm, *The First Person*, p. 16.
43. Roderick Chisholm, *A Theory of Knowledge*, 2d ed. (Englewood Cliffs, N.J.: Prentice-Hall, 1977), p. 59; see too G. E. Moore, *Principia Ethica* (Cambridge: Cambridge University Press, 1903), p. 7.
44. Frege, "The Thought," p. 298.

When Descartes is metaphysically certain *de se* that he thinks, he knows a proposition in which the predicate is not part of the analysis of the subject.

Conclusion

Descartes thinks that propositions are the contents of his metaphysical certainty and related intentional attitudes. He gets the *de dicto* variety of an attitude by adopting the attitude toward a proposition and the *de re* and *de se* varieties by adopting the attitude toward the right sort of proposition. Descartes never explains what sorts of propositions are the contents of his *de se* attitudes, how they are about him, and how they are about him in a way different from those that are the contents of his non–*de se* attitudes toward himself. Nonetheless, we have good reason to think he would accept this particular line of explanation: The contents of his *de se* attitudes are propositions about him, not just about a mental event or indefinite thing. Each of his *de se* attitudes is an instance of a *de re* attitude toward himself, although he never apprehends a substance, even himself, directly and unmodified. He apprehends a substance by conceiving an individual concept of it and as modified by some property he believes it to have. He individuates himself *per se* in his *de se* attitudes. The Self-Identity Theory is one plausible way he can combine his claim that he can only apprehend himself by conceiving an individual concept of himself with his view that he individuates himself *per se*. The concept by which he does both is the property of being identical to himself, which he must have and only he can have.

This is Descartes's position on the contents of certainty. Parts are vague and incomplete, and much is controversial, but it combines with his understanding of metaphysical, moral, and psychological certainty to form a view that is coherent and strong in its major claims. Now that we have it before us, we can examine Descartes's defense of P1, P2, and P3, the initial premises in his Gambit.

Chapter 4

THE BODY, SENSES, AND UNCERTAINTY

Descartes opens his Gambit with a defense of P3, that he is metaphysically uncertain he has a body. He makes his move with varying degrees of style and success in *The Search after Truth, Discourse, Meditations,* and *Principles,* and, since his arguments in Meditation One are the most promising, I concentrate on them. In this chapter I give a new interpretation of Descartes's defense and argue that, despite temporary setbacks, his opening move succeeds.

Preliminaries

Descartes's claim in P3 is that he is metaphysically uncertain he has a body. The content of his metaphysical uncertainty is the proposition he would express in English by "I have a body" if he used 'I' to refer to himself and assigned 'I' the individual concept of being him, which differentiates him from all things without relating him to any, as its meaning. This proposition is actually a disjunction: Either he is spatially extended, or something else is spatially extended and related to him as his body. Descartes's position is that, for all he is metaphysically certain, the entire disjunction is false: he is not extended and nothing else is extended and related to him as his body.

Descartes makes this claim in Meditation One only to reject it in Meditation Six by saying he is metaphysically certain something else is extended and related to him as his body [AT VII, 78–81; HR I, 190–192]. There is no contradiction here. Descartes's position in Meditation One is that *the evidence available to him at that time* does not make him metaphysically certain he has a body; it at best makes him morally certain. His belief in his body is among those opinions "in some measure doubtful . . . and at the same time highly probable, so that there is much more reason to believe in than to deny them" [*Meditations*; AT VII, 22; HR I, 148; consider too: *Discourse*; AT VI, 37–38; HR I, 104]. His position in Meditation Six is that *new evidence* makes him metaphysically certain he has a body.

What evidence fails to make Descartes metaphysically certain of his body in Meditation One? All the evidence he can get on the basis of sensation alone. He starts Meditation One by assuming for the sake of argument that "all that up to the present time I have accepted as most true I have learned either from the senses or through the senses" [*Meditations*; AT VII, 18; HR I, 145*].[1] We have seen Descartes thinks sensation can make him morally certain of propositions without yielding psychological or metaphysical certainty. He does not mention his other source of evidence, clear and distinct perception, anywhere in Meditation One, including his defense of P3. P3 takes on a new shape relative to these discoveries:

> P3(a): That I have a body (either I am spatially extended or something else is spatially extended and related to me as my body) is a metaphysical uncertainty for me (even if it is a moral certainty for me, I have a reason to doubt it), as long as all my evidence for it ultimately consists solely of sensation reports.

1. Harry Frankfurt, *Demons, Dreamers and Madmen* (New York: Bobbs-Merrill, 1970), pp. 62, 64, and Alan Gewirth, "The Cartesian Circle Reconsidered," *Journal of Philosophy*, 67 (October 8, 1970), p. 670, cite other passages to show Descartes takes sensation to be his only source of evidence in Meditation One: *Conversation with Burman*, AT V, 146 and *Seventh Objections and Replies*, AT VII, 459–460, 476–477, 481; HR II, 266, 279, 282. The content of these passages is unclear; see Anthony Kenny, "The Cartesian Circle and the Eternal Truths," *Journal of Philosophy*, 67 (October 8, 1970), p. 691. Kenny cites two passages from outside Meditation One in an attempt to show that Descartes really does not assume sensation is his only source of evidence at that point: *Meditations*; AT VII, 65; HR I, 180 and *Reply to the Sixth Objections*; AT VII, 445; HR II, 257. Neither passage supports Kenny's position, however; I shall discuss them shortly.

We can learn more from Descartes's remarks on sensation. He distinguishes between beliefs learned "from" the senses and beliefs learned "through" the senses in the passage just quoted, and he explains elsewhere that a belief learned "from" the senses is evidenced by our sense perception of the object, whereas one learned "through" the senses is evidenced by our sense perception of someone else's description of the object [*Conversation with Burman*; AT V, 146]. The difference seems irrelevant to his purpose in Meditation One, and I am not sure why he mentions it, but he combines it with a more helpful characterization of sensation in the *Rules*:

> Matter of experience consists of what we perceive by sense, what we hear from the lips of others, *and generally whatever reaches our understanding either from external sources or from that contemplation which our mind directs backwards on itself.* [XII; AT X, 422–423; HR I, 43–44; my emphasis]

There are two basic kinds of sensation reports. Some are first-person reports of what we seem to experience by external sensation; for example, Descartes's report, "It seems to me that I see light, that I hear noise and that I feel heat" [*Meditations*; AT VII, 29; HR I, 153]. The rest are first-person reports of what we find when we direct our mind "backwards upon itself"; that we think, that we recall proving God's existence, that we add two and three and get five. We might call these reports of "internal sensation."[2]

Sensation is related to clear and distinct perception in two important ways. First, beliefs about the external world evidenced *solely* by sensation are not perceived clearly and distinctly. When Descartes believes there is a fire before him because he seems to see light, hear noise, and feel heat, he does not clearly and distinctly perceive that there is a fire. He does not do so directly. His direct clear and distinct perceptions are limited to simple necessary truths and propositions about his mental state; that there is a fire is a contingent truth about the external world. He also does not do so deductively, since the proposition that there is a fire is only inductively related to his evidence. Second, propositions

---

2. Descartes's two kinds of sensation reports roughly correspond to Locke's two kinds of experience: sensation and reflection. See Book II, Chapter I, Section 2 of *Essay Concerning Human Understanding*.

perceived clearly and distinctly may or may not be essentially evidenced by sensation. Descartes does not rely on sensation to perceive clearly and distinctly that the angles of a triangle equal two right angles. He deduces that conclusion from simple mathematical axioms he clearly and distinctly perceives directly; the axioms are not sensation reports, and, as self-evident propositions, they are not essentially evidenced by any.[3] Yet Descartes can clearly and distinctly perceive his sensation reports directly, and any proposition he deduces from one will be both clearly and distinctly perceived and essentially evidenced by sensation. He can deduce that he exists from the sensation report that he seems to see light. He says he clearly and distinctly perceives that God exists by deducing God's existence from premises that include the sensation report that he has an idea of God [*Meditations*; AT VII, 51–52; HR I, 171].

Descartes's idea in P3 is that, as long as his evidence is ultimately limited to sensation reports, he does not clearly and distinctly perceive that he has a body. He does not do so directly; that he has a body is contingent and about the external world. He does not do so deductively, since the relation between his belief in his body and his sensation reports is inductive. As long as he lacks a clear and distinct perception, he lacks metaphysical certainty. Recall EP2: a human is metaphysically certain of a proposition only if he clearly and distinctly perceives it. When Descartes claims to be metaphysically certain he has a body in Meditation Six, he thinks he clearly and distinctly perceives he has one. He gains that clear and distinct perception by combining his sensation reports with premises about God's existence and nondeceptive nature to get evidence that deductively entails, with metaphysical certainty, that he has a body [*Meditations*; AT VII, 78–81; HR I, 190–192].

3. Some think that whenever Descartes clearly and distinctly perceives a proposition, even a first-person report of the content of his mental state or a simple necessary truth, his evidence for the proposition is the first-person report that he clearly and distinctly perceives it. Consider H. A. Prichard, *Knowledge and Perception* (Oxford: Clarendon Press, 1950), pp. 80–104. We lose an important part of the difference between clear and distinct perception and sensation if we interpret Descartes in this way; we end up saying that every clearly and distinctly perceived proposition is ultimately evidenced by the internal sensation report that it is clearly and distinctly perceived. We also fail to capture Descartes's position that propositions clearly and distinctly perceived directly, like his *de se* report that he thinks, are known *per se* rather than on the basis of evidence [*Rules*, III; AT X, 368; HR I, 7].

Descartes does not argue for P3 in and of itself. He tries to show that whole classes of sensory-evidenced propositions, some of which include his belief in his body, are metaphysically uncertain for him. He gives four arguments in Meditation One. The argument from sensory illusion [AT VII, 18; HR I, 145] concerns propositions evidenced under poor perceptual conditions, which does not include his belief in his body. The argument from madness [AT VII, 18–19; HR I, 145] is more a passing fancy than a series of premises leading to a conclusion. The Dream Argument and the Deceiver Argument are Descartes's defense of P3; it is time to look at them.

The Dream Argument: Interpretation

The Dream Argument comes in two parts. First, Descartes argues that it is a metaphysical possibility that he is dreaming. Second, he argues that the hypothesis that he is dreaming indicates how a host of his sensory-evidenced beliefs, including his belief in his body, might be false. Put the two together and the conclusion follows by the definition of a reason for doubt (D3) and the criterion for metaphysical certainty (EP1): those sensory-evidenced beliefs are metaphysically uncertain.

Take a close look at the first part of this argument:

> At this moment it does indeed seem to me that it is with eyes awake that I am looking at this paper; that this head which I move is not asleep, that it is deliberately and of set purpose that I extend my hand and perceive it; what happens in sleep does not appear so distinct as does all this. But in thinking over this I remind myself that on many occasions I have in sleep been deceived by similar illusions, and in dwelling carefully on this reflection I see so manifestly that there are no certain indications by which we may distinguish wakefulness from sleep that I am lost in astonishment. And my astonishment is such that it is almost capable of persuading me that I sleep. [*Meditations*; AT VII, 19; HR I, 146*]

Descartes reasons from

i. I recall having dreams similar to my present sense experience.

to

    ii. There are no certain indications by which I can distinguish wakefulness from sleep.

to the unstated but implied conclusion:

    iii. It is a metaphysical possibility for me that I am dreaming.

He leaves the details as an exercise for the reader, and we can begin by wrestling with the first premise.

Descartes's point is not that he recalls having dreams with all the qualities of his present experience. One of those qualities is, in fact, being a waking experience, and he surely does not recall having a dream with that quality. He just wants to say that he recalls having dreams with *some* of the qualities of his present experience. Which ones? The ones, like distinctness, to which he might appeal to show that his experience is not a dream. This is a slippery point. We might try to capture it as follows:

    1′. If Q is a property such that (1) it is reasonable for me to believe the proposition that my present experience has Q, and (2) it is reasonable for me to believe the proposition that dreams generally do not have Q, then I recall the proposition that I have had dreams with Q.[4]

This comes close. It is reasonable for Descartes to believe that his present experience is distinct and that dreams generally are not, and he recalls having distinct dreams. Yet it is also reasonable for Descartes to believe that his present experience is a waking experience and that

    4. I write here of *the* unique proposition that Descartes's experience has the property Q when no such proposition exists. Descartes can express different propositions to the effect that his experience has Q by using different, nonsynonymous expressions to designate his experience and to designate Q. I do not want to employ the complex moves necessary to reformulate Descartes's premise to avoid this problem. I merely assume that we are concerned only with the proposition Descartes would express by using 'this' to refer to his experience and the canonical designation of the property involved to refer to it. The canonical designation for distinctness, for example, is 'distinctness,' not 'the property Descartes now contemplates.' We are concerned with propositions like the one Descartes would express in English by "this, my present experience, has distinctness." My talk of *the* proposition that dreams generally lack Q and of *the* proposition that Descartes has had dreams with Q should be understood in a similar way.

dreams generally are not.[5] Does he recall having a dream that was a waking experience? It does not help to make his premise

> 1″. If Q is a property such that (1) I am *metaphysically* certain of the proposition that my present experience has Q, and (2) it is reasonable for me to believe the proposition that dreams generally lack Q, then I recall the proposition that I have had dreams with Q.

This puts Descartes on the edge of begging the question. Should a critic argue that the property of being a waking experience falsifies the premise, Descartes's only defense would be to say he is metaphysically uncertain whether he is awake; he would have to use what he is supposed to derive from his premise to defend it.

The best way to characterize Descartes's first premise is to distinguish between the intrinsic and extrinsic qualities of an experience. Intrinsic qualities are, roughly, those that do not require the existence of anything other than the subject and the subject's experience and do not entail that the experience is or is not caused by a particular source. Being distinct, being vivid, being internally coherent, and involving a representation of heat are all intrinsic qualities. Extrinsic qualities are qualities that are not intrinsic. Being veridical, being caused by a deceptive god, and being caused by a fire are extrinsic qualities. Descartes's first premise concerns the intrinsic qualities of his experience:

> 1‴. If Q is an intrinsic property such that (1) it is reasonable for me to believe the proposition that my present experience has Q, and (2) it is reasonable for me to believe the proposition that dreams generally lack Q, then I recall the proposition that I have had dreams with Q.

The premise seems true of intrinsic qualities. It is reasonable for Descartes to believe that his experience has them and that dreams generally do not, but he recalls having dreams with them. It is not falsified by the quality of being a waking experience. That quality is extrinsic, since it entails that Descartes's experience is not produced by his imagination in sleep.

---

5. That Descartes's belief that he is awake is metaphysically uncertain does not prevent it from being reasonable from the standard epistemic perspective. Recall my discussion of moral and metaphysical certainty in Chapter 2.

Suppose though that Q is the conjunction of all the intrinsic qualities of Descartes's experience. My version of his premise has Descartes recalling a dream with Q, a dream like his present experience down to the finest intrinsic detail, a dream in which he is seated by a fire, dressed in a blue robe, wiggling his toes, and so on. Descartes does not have anything this strong in mind when he says, "I have in sleep been deceived by similar illusions." We must restrict his premise to intrinsic qualities of a suitable level of generality. How do we define that level of generality? I wish I knew. Being distinct is general enough, involving a representation of toe-wiggling is not, but I cannot capture the difference between them in a definition. So I simply use 'general intrinsic quality' to describe intrinsic qualities that are appropriately general—whatever that may be—and begin my statement of the first stage of the Dream Argument as follows:

1. If Q is a general intrinsic quality such that (1) it is reasonable for me to believe the proposition that my present experience has Q, and (2) it is reasonable for me to believe the proposition that dreams generally lack Q, then I recall the proposition that I have had dreams with Q.[6]

Let us see what we can do with this premise. We can make some important inferences if we combine it with the claim that Descartes's memories are a source of reasonable belief, though not of metaphysical certainty:

2. If I recall the proposition that I have had dreams with Q, then, since I lack sufficient counterevidence against my recollection, it is reasonable for me to believe that some dreams have Q.

Descartes's first premise combines with this plausible conditional to imply:

3. If Q is a general intrinsic quality such that (1) it is reasonable for me to believe the proposition that my present experience has Q, and (2) it is reasonable for me to believe the proposition that dreams generally

6. Edwin Curley uses a distinction between intrinsic and extrinsic features of an experience in his interpretation of the Dream Argument, but he does not explain his distinction or its motivation, so I am unsure how close his position is to mine. See his *Descartes against the Skeptics* (Cambridge: Harvard University Press, 1978), Chapter 3.

lack Q, then it is reasonable for me to believe the proposition that some dreams have Q.   [from 1 and 2]

Every general intrinsic quality Descartes finds in his present experience as a reasonable sign that he is not dreaming is such that it is reasonable for him to believe it has exceptions. This in turn implies:

> 4. No general intrinsic quality Q is such that I am metaphysically certain of the proposition that my experience has Q and metaphysically certain of the proposition that no dream has Q.   [from 3 and D2]

The easiest way to see this implication is by way of a *reductio ad absurdum*. Suppose Descartes is metaphysically certain that his experience has (the general intrinsic quality) Q and that no dream has Q. Whatever is metaphysically certain is reasonable (D2); what all dreams lack, they generally lack. It is reasonable, then, for Descartes to believe his experience has Q and that dreams generally lack it. According to what we have already seen, then, it is reasonable for Descartes to believe some dreams have Q. He is not metaphysically certain no dreams have Q after all.

We are ready to consider Descartes's next major step in stage one of the Dream Argument: that there are no "certain indications" by which he can distinguish wakefulness from sleep. "Certain indications" would be qualities in Descartes's experience that enabled him to reason with metaphysical certainty in this way:

> i. This, my present experience, has Q.
> ii. No dream has Q.
> iii. Therefore, I am not dreaming.

Descartes needs only one more premise to show that there are no such "certain indications":

> 5. A property Q is such that I am metaphysically certain of the proposition that my present experience has Q and metaphysically certain of the proposition that no dream has Q, only if a general intrinsic quality is such that I am metaphysically certain of the proposition that my present experience has it and metaphysically certain of the proposition that no dream has it.

According to premise (5), Descartes has a criterion by which to become metaphysically certain that he is not dreaming only if he has one limited to general intrinsic qualities. It is backed by two considerations. First, the only way Descartes can be metaphysically certain that his experience has a particular extrinsic quality is to deduce the quality's presence from that of some intrinsic quality; intrinsic qualities must, therefore, be the basis of any criterion for separating waking experiences from dreams. Second, any criterion must concern general intrinsic qualities to have a sufficiently wide range of application. Premise (5) enables Descartes to infer his denial of "certain indications":

6. No property Q is such that I am metaphysically certain of the proposition that my experience has Q and metaphysically certain of the proposition that no dream has Q.   [from 4 and 5]

One more premise takes Descartes to his conclusion that it is a metaphysical possibility that he is dreaming:

7. I am metaphysically certain that I am not dreaming, only if there is a property Q such that I am metaphysically certain of the proposition that my present experience has Q and metaphysically certain that no dream has Q.

The only way he can gain metaphysical certainty that he is not dreaming is the route closed by the preceding steps in the argument. He may then conclude:

8. Therefore, it is a metaphysical possibility for me that I am dreaming.   [from 6 and 7]

That is stage one of the Dream Argument. Premises (1), (2), (5), and (7) do the work: according to (1), Descartes recalls dreams like his present experience in their general intrinsic qualities; (2) says his recollection has enough epistemic weight to make it reasonable for him to believe there are such dreams; according to (5), any criterion Descartes can use to gain metaphysical certainty he is not dreaming must ultimately rely on general intrinsic qualities; and (7) says a criterion is the only way he can gain metaphysical certainty he is not dreaming.

The second stage of the Dream Argument concerns what beliefs are made metaphysically uncertain by the Dream Hypothesis. Descartes again makes general comments and leaves the details to us. It is best to begin with some elementary points.

Recall that Descartes assumes, for the sake of argument, that all his beliefs are ultimately evidenced, if at all, by sensation reports. He adopts the principle that metaphysical certainties are those moral certainties he has no reason to doubt (EP1), and he defines a reason to doubt (D3) as a metaphysical possibility that indicates how his belief, or an essential part of his evidence for it, might be false. The question to be answered by the second stage of the Dream Argument, then, is this: What propositions are such that, no matter what evidence sensation provides to make them moral certainties, they are metaphysical uncertainties because the Dream Hypothesis indicates how they or an essential part of the evidence for them might be false? Note that the Dream Hypothesis suggests more than that Descartes is asleep and having ideas. It is about his being "deceived" [*Meditations*; AT VII, 19; HR I, 146] and so making false judgments. The judgments concern the external cause of his ideas, for he tells us the standard "error . . . in our dreams consists in their representing to us various objects in the same way as do our external senses" [*Discourse*; AT VI, 39; HR I, 105]. The Dream Hypothesis is that Descartes is asleep, forming complex ideas in his imagination, and incorrectly taking them to be produced in him by external things.

Some beliefs based on present external sensation are clearly vulnerable to this hypothesis. Suppose Descartes reasons this way:

  i. I seem to see light, hear noise, feel heat.
  ii. Therefore, there is a fire here.

The Dream Hypothesis indicates how his conclusion might be false despite his evidence. He may be asleep, forming a complex idea of light, noise, and heat in his imagination, and incorrectly taking it to be caused by a fire outside him. Some beliefs based on recollections of past external sensations are also vulnerable:

  i. I recall seeming to see light, hear noise, and feel heat.
  ii. Hence, I saw light, heard noise, and felt heat.
  iii. Therefore, there was a fire.

The Dream Hypothesis indicates how the second and third steps might be false despite the first. Perhaps there was no fire; Descartes never saw light, heard noise, and felt heat. The recollection he now takes to be produced in him by a fire through past external sensation and memory is really just a complex idea he produces as part of a dream.

Only three types of belief can resist the Dream Hypothesis, according to Descartes.

Sensation reports are immune:

> I see light, I hear noise, I feel heat. But it will be said that these phenomena are false and that I am dreaming. Let it be so; still it is at least quite certain that it seems to me that I see light, that I hear noise and that I feel heat. [*Meditations*; AT VII, 29; HR I, 153]

The hypothesis that Descartes is asleep, forming complex ideas in his imagination, and incorrectly taking them to be caused by external things does not indicate how his *de se* beliefs about the content of his mental state might be false. Those beliefs only concern the content of his ideas; not what causes them. (There is a bonus here: since sensation reports are immune, so is whatever Descartes immediately and correctly deduces from them, e.g., that he himself exists, that something seems to see light.)

Descartes introduces a second group of exceptions right after the first stage of the Dream Argument.

> Although these general things, to wit, eyes, a head, hands, and such like, may be imaginary, we are bound at the same time to confess that there are at least some other objects yet more simple and more universal, which are real and true; . . . To such a class of things pertains corporeal nature in general, and its extension, the figure of extended things, their quantity or magnitude and number, as also the place in which they are, the time which measures their duration and so on. [*Meditations*; AT VII, 20; HR I, 146]

These simple, universal "objects" are the unanalyzable properties Descartes styles "material and common simple natures" in the *Rules* [XII; AT X, 419; HR I, 41]. The Dream Hypothesis does not work against propositions to the effect that one of these "objects" is exemplified by some unspecified thing, for example, that something is extended.

Suppose Descartes decides that the best explanation of how he obtained a simple idea of extension is that some extended thing caused it in him:

    i. I have an idea of extension.
    ii. My idea of extension is simple (unanalyzable).
    iii. Therefore, there was, perhaps is, an extended thing.

The Dream Hypothesis does not indicate how his premises, which are sensation reports, might be false. It does not indicate how his conclusion might be false despite his premises: the chance that he is asleep, forming *complex* ideas, and making mistakes about what caused them does not indicate how he might be wrong about what caused his *simple* idea of extension.[7]

"Eternal truths," such as those of mathematics, are the third exception to the Dream Hypothesis:

> Whether I am awake or asleep, two and three together always form five, and the square can never have more than four sides, and it does not seem possible that such perspicuous truths can be suspected of any falsity. [*Meditations*; AT VII, 20; HR I, 147*]

Descartes's point is best understood through his examples. His evidence for believing two and three equals five and squares have four sides must, by assumption, be sensory, and he goes on to say that he "adds two and three" and "counts the sides of a square" [*Meditations*; AT VII, 21; HR I, 147]. He is most likely concerned, then, with these inferences:

    i. I mentally add two and three and get five.
    ii. Therefore, two and three is five.

    i. I conceive of a square, count its sides, and get four.
    ii. Therefore, squares have four sides.

---

7. Do not overlook the difference between the preceding example and another one. Suppose Descartes reasons: (i.) I seem to see light, hear noise, feel heat; (ii.) Hence, there is a fire; (iii.) Hence, something is extended. The Dream Hypothesis casts doubt on his final conclusion by indicating how his intermediate conclusion might be false despite his evidence for it. The moral: Whether a proposition resists the Dream Hypothesis or any other reason for doubt depends in part on its evidence.

The Dream Hypothesis is irrelevant to his premises, for they do not assert the existence of an external cause of his ideas. That Descartes may be asleep, forming complex ideas in his imagination, and making the mistake of believing they are caused by something outside him has nothing to do with whether he is adding two and three to get five or counting the sides of an imagined square to get four. Descartes thinks that his conclusions resist the Dream Hypothesis for the same reason. They, like external truths in general, do not assume the existence of external objects. The eternal truth *ex nihilo nihil fit*, for example, "is not to be considered as an existing thing, or the mode of a thing, but as a certain eternal truth which has its seat in our mind, and is a common notion or axiom" [*Principles*, I, xlix; AT VIII, 23; HR I, 239; consider too: *Meditations*; AT VII, 64; HR I, 179–180; *Discourse*; AT VI, 36; HR I, 103].[8]

If we put what we have just seen in the form of premises and a conclusion, we get the second stage of the Dream Argument.

The Dream Argument: Stage Two

1. Suppose *p* is not a first-person sensation report or immediately and correctly deduced by me from one, but *p* is ultimately evidenced for me solely by such reports in a way that makes it a moral certainty for me.
2. Suppose an essential part of my evidence for *p* is either a first-person

---

8. Some commentators have had difficulty appreciating why the Dream Hypothesis does not cast doubt on mathematical propositions evidenced by first-person reports of mental operations like addition, even though they have been willing to assume mathematical propositions do not make assertions of external existence. Consider Anthony Kenny, *Descartes: A Study of His Philosophy* (New York: Random House, 1968), pp. 33–34, and Margaret Wilson, *Descartes*, p. 226. After all, does the Dream Hypothesis not give Descartes a reason to doubt his internal sensation reports; could he not just dream that he adds two and three and gets five? The question is based on a misunderstanding of the Dream Hypothesis. It is the hypothesis that Descartes is asleep, forming complex ideas in his imagination, and incorrectly taking them to be caused by things outside him, and, as such, it is irrelevant to propositions like his sensation report that he adds two and three and gets five. There is, of course, another hypothesis that does cast doubt on Descartes's mathematical beliefs: He is asleep, performing mathematical operations, and getting incorrect results. Yet this is not the hypothesis that interests Descartes in the Dream Argument, and one way to see that it is not is to note that he is interested in a hypothesis that does not cast doubt on his mathematical beliefs, while this one does.

report of a complex external sensation or a first-person report of my
recollection of a complex external sensation.

3. The hypothesis that I am dreaming indicates how p, or an essential
part of my evidence for p, might be false, despite my evidence for
it. [from 1 and 2]

4. I have a reason to doubt p.   [from 3, the conclusion of stage one,
and D3]

5. Therefore p is a metaphysical uncertainty for me.   [from 1, 2, 4, and
EP1]

The first premise partially defines a target set of propositions: those that
are not sensation reports or correctly deduced immediately from them
but are strongly enough evidenced by sensation reports to be moral
certainties and so have a shot at metaphysical certainty. The second
premise zeros in on members of the set for which complex external
sensations, past or present, play a crucial evidentiary role. According
to (3) the Dream Hypothesis indicates how such propositions or an
essential part of the evidence for them might be false. Premise (4) uses
this result, the earlier conclusion of stage one that the Dream Hypothesis is a metaphysical possibility, and the definition of rational doubt to
conclude that Descartes has a reason to doubt the propositions. His
metaphysical uncertainty of them (5) follows by the metaphysical certainty criterion (EP1).

I have designed the first two premises to reflect Descartes's exceptions to the Dream Hypothesis. The first premise excludes sensation
reports and what Descartes immediately and correctly deduces from
them. The second excludes indefinite propositions about simple
natures, when they are evidenced by reports of simple ideas, and
eternal truths, when they are evidenced by reports of mental operations
like addition. The argument's conclusion is devastating: sensation is
not an independent source of metaphysical certainty about complex
objects in the external world. If we try to gain metaphysical certainty
about such objects by sensation, we will be forced to rely on reports of
complex external sensations, and the Dream Hypothesis will block our
way. We can remove it only by becoming metaphysically certain we
are not dreaming, and that, according to Descartes, requires the use of
clear and distinct perception.

Descartes can now argue for P3 in particular.

The Dream Argument Defense of P3

1. Suppose all my evidence for the proposition that I have a body ultimately consists solely of sensation reports.
2. That I have a body is either a moral uncertainty or a moral certainty for me.
3. If it is a moral uncertainty for me, then it is a metaphysical uncertainty for me. [from D1 and D2]
4. If it is a moral certainty for me, then it falls into the category of moral certainties made metaphysically uncertain by the Dream Hypothesis (it is not a sensation report or correctly deduced immediately from one, it is ultimately evidenced by sensation reports, and an essential part of the evidence is either a first-person report of a complex external sensation or a first-person report of my recollection of one).
5. Therefore, if my evidence for the proposition that I have a body ultimately consists solely of sensation reports, I am metaphysically uncertain that I have a body.

This is the Dream Argument for P3. Now I want to look at some criticisms, first of my interpretation of the Dream Argument and then of the argument itself.

Objections to the Interpretation

Other commentators interpret the Dream Argument in several different ways, and my interpretation contradicts all of them in one way or another. Consider first my reading of the Dream Hypothesis. I read the hypothesis as the proposition that Descartes is *now* dreaming. W. H. Walsh says it is that Descartes is *always* dreaming, and Margaret Wilson says the Dream Hypothesis must concern the past as well as the present to question the existence of all ordinary physical objects.[9]

Descartes formulates the hypothesis in terms of both the past and present in *The Search after Truth* [AT X, 511; HR I, 314] and *Discourse* [AT VI, 32; HR I, 101], but those works contain unsophisticated versions of the argument that are hard to take seriously. The "argument" in the first is all of three sentences; that in the second, all

9. W. H. Walsh, *Metaphysics* (London: Hutchinson University Library, 1963), p. 91; Wilson, *Descartes*, p. 18.

of two. Neither mentions such fine points as that propositions about simple natures can resist the Dream Hypothesis. The *Meditations* contains Descartes's most detailed and subtle statement of the Dream Argument, and he there restricts his attention to his present experience. Consider once again his presentation of the Dream Hypothesis:

> At *this moment* [*Atqui nunc*] it does indeed seem to me that it is with eyes awake that I am looking at this paper; that this head which I move is not asleep, that it is deliberately and of set purpose that I extend my hand and perceive it; what happens in sleep does not appear so distinct as does all this. But in thinking over this I remind myself that on many occasions I have in sleep been deceived by similar illusions, and in dwelling carefully on this reflection I see so manifestly that there are no certain indications by which we may clearly distinguish wakefulness from sleep that I am lost in astonishment. And my astonishment is such that it is almost capable of persuading me that I sleep [*fere hic ipse stupor mihi opinionem somni confirmet*]. [AT VII, 19; HR I, 146*; my emphasis][10]

Must the Dream Hypothesis concern the past to question the existence of all ordinary physical objects? Margaret Wilson thinks so:

> The major objection to this interpretation of the argument [that which restricts the Dream Hypothesis to the present] is that it simply does not lead to the conclusion that, I would hold, Descartes clearly desires. As I hope to have shown above, Descartes takes the Dreaming Argument to establish that there is reason to doubt the world is *anything like* what the senses seem to reveal. In other words, the argument calls into question the existence of *all* 'composites' or ordinary physical objects—not just

10. Haldane and Ross translate the end of the passage "it is almost capable of persuading me that I *now* dream" [HR I, 146; my emphasis]. Although other aspects of the text make Descartes's concern with the present clear, neither the Latin nor French text justifies their use of the indexical 'now.' I have given the relevant part of the Latin; the French is "Il me semble bien à présent que ce n'est point avec des yeux endormis que je regarde ce papier; que cette tête que je remue n'est point assoupie; que c'est avec dessien et de propos délibéré que j'étends cette main, et que je la sens: ce qui arrive dans le sommeil ne semble point si clair ni si distinct que tout ceci. Mais, en y pensant soigneusement, je me ressouviens d'avoir été souvent trompé, lorsque je dormais, par de semblables illusions. Et m'arrêtant sur cette pensée, je vois si manifestement qu'il n'y a point d'indices concluants, ni de marques assez certaines par où l'on puisse distinguer nettement la veille d'avec le sommeil, que j'en suis tout étonné; et mon étonnement est tel, qu'il est presque capable de me persuader que je dors" [AT IX, 14–15].

any particular one that I happen to be 'viewing' at a given time. The question Descartes wishes to raise is not whether I can now know that this or that sense experience is veridical, but whether I can know with certainty that the senses ever afford us truth at all (apart from the reality of simples).[11]

Wilson finds it clear that if we restrict the Dream Hypothesis to the present, it will not cast doubt on some assertions that there are composite physical objects, even though Descartes wants it to do so. The troublesome assertions are, I suppose, those evidenced by recollections of past external sensation rather than reports of present external sensation. Suppose, then, that Descartes reasons like this:

   i. I recall seeming to see light, hear noise, feel heat.
  ii. Hence, I saw light, heard noise, felt heat.
 iii. Therefore, there was a fire.

The Dream Hypothesis, restricted to the present, casts doubt on his final conclusion by indicating how it and the intermediate conclusion might be false despite his present recollection. Perhaps he is *now* asleep and creating in his imagination the recollection he takes to be caused in him by a fire through past external sensation and present memory.

Wilson seems to have missed the fact that whenever Descartes bases his belief in the existence of a composite physical object on external sensation, he bases it on his *present* external sensations or his *present* recollection of past external sensations. He considers an external sensation and takes it to be caused in him by an external thing through present perception, or he considers a recollection and takes it to be caused in him by an external thing through past perception and present memory. The Dream Hypothesis, restricted to the present, casts doubt in each case. It indicates to Descartes how he, not some external thing, might be the source of what he finds in his mind (a present external sensation; a present recollection of a past external sensation).[12]

11. Wilson, *Descartes*, p. 18.
12. Frankfurt, *Demons, Dreamers and Madmen*, pp. 51–52, also argues against extending the Dream Hypothesis to Descartes's past experiences. His argument is based on his particular interpretation of Meditation One as a whole, however, and that interpretation is well criticized by Wilson, *Descartes*, pp. 38–42.

My interpretation of the Dream Hypothesis is controversial in another way. I take it to be the hypothesis that Descartes is *dreaming*. Wilson takes it to be that Descartes's waking experiences are non-veridical, just as dreams are. She thinks interpretations like mine make Descartes's attempt in Meditation Six to rule out the Dream Hypothesis implausible. Here is her first of two arguments:

> According to all the interpretations considered so far, the problem Descartes sets himself in the First Meditation is to find 'certain marks to distinguish dreaming from waking,' where this is understood to mean 'marks by which one may certainly *tell* on a given occasion *whether* one is, on that occasion, dreaming or waking.' It is because he doesn't 'see' any such marks in the First Meditation that he is said to conclude that he can't know for certain that he isn't dreaming. Now suppose (as seems obvious) that to seek marks by which one may certainly *tell whether* one is dreaming or waking is to seek criteria, satisfied by waking experience but not by dreams, which one may *apply* to one's current experience to determine whether or not one is dreaming. Unfortunately, this seems to describe a nonsensical quest. For first, the description of the objective implies that it is possible to apply a criterion to dreaming experience while one is dreaming. But in fact (one common objection runs) under such circumstances one can only *dream* one applies a criterion.[13]

Wilson misses an important distinction. It is one thing for Descartes to develop a criterion for dreaming that he can apply to his experience *when he dreams* to gain metaphysical certainty that he dreams; it is another for him to develop a criterion for being awake that he can apply to his experience *when awake* to gain metaphysical certainty that he is awake. The first requires an argument of the form

   i. This, my present experience, has Q.
   ii. Everything with Q is a dream.
   iii. Therefore, I am dreaming.

Descartes must be able to gain metaphysical certainty of these premises when they are true. The second task requires

   i. This, my present experience, has Q.
   ii. No dream has Q.
   iii. Therefore, I am not dreaming.

13. Wilson, *Descartes*, p. 19.

Descartes again must be able to gain metaphysical certainty of the premises when they are true. Descartes may run into Wilson's objection if he tries the first task: when he is dreaming, he can only dream his experience satisfies the criterion for being a dream. He does not have to worry about her objection if he tries the second. It calls for him to apply a criterion for being awake to his experience when he is awake, not when he is dreaming. Descartes needs only to accomplish the second task to rule out my version of the Dream Hypothesis; that is, to become metaphysically certain he is not dreaming, when he is not.[14]

Wilson's second reason for not taking the Dream Hypothesis to be about dreaming *per se* is that Descartes cannot show that he is not dreaming without begging the question. If he argues

  i.   This, my present experience, has Q.
  ii. No dream has Q.
  iii. Therefore, I am not dreaming.

he begs the question as soon as he claims metaphysical certainty of the first premise; the hypothesis that he is dreaming gives him a reason to doubt that his experience has Q: "We can adapt Descartes's own reasoning and argue: How many times in the past have I concluded my experience satisfied the criterion of waking experience, only to decide subsequently that I was only dreaming that it did."[15] Descartes sets the stage for this objection, according to Wilson, when he admits to Hobbes that someone might mistakenly apply the criterion for being awake to a dream:

> Someone who sleeps and dreams, cannot join and assemble, perfectly and with truth, his dreams with the ideas of past things, even if he can

14. Wilson, *Descartes*, pp. 21–22, assumes that the two tasks I outline are connected, so that Descartes accomplishes the second only if he accomplishes the first: "But suppose for a moment we take seriously Descartes's implication [*Reply to the Third Objections*; AT VII, 196; HR II, 78] that the conclusion of Meditation VI is not meant to be that (as a result of the discovered 'mark') we can now infallibly 'tell' we are dreaming when we are dreaming. If this is so, it seems that the conclusion can neither be that, as a result of the discovered mark, we can now infallibly *ascertain* we are awake when we are awake." Yet would we say that, since Descartes cannot develop a test for telling whether he is dead drunk when he is dead drunk, he cannot develop one for telling whether he is sober when he is sober? Consider Bernard Williams, *Descartes: The Project of Pure Inquiry* (New York: Penguin Books, 1978), pp. 309–313.

15. Wilson, *Descartes*, p. 19.

dream that he assembles them. For who denies that one who sleeps can deceive himself? But after, when awake, he will easily know his error. [*Third Objections and Replies*; AT VII, 196; HR II, 78*][16]

Wilson does not seem to appreciate the details of Descartes's argument against the Dream Hypothesis in Meditation Six. He opens with the premise that his reports of external sensation, memory, and other mental operations all "cohere" with each other, which he knows by clear and distinct perception; he adds the premise that, if the parts of his experience "cohere," he is not dreaming, which he deduces clearly and distinctly from the metaphysical certainty that God is not a deceiver; and he concludes that he is not dreaming. He sums up the argument this way:

> I ought in no wise to doubt the truth of such matters [external sensation], if, after having called up all my senses, my memory and my understanding, to examine them, nothing is brought to evidence by any one of them which is repugnant to what is set forth by the others. For because God is in no wise a deceiver, it follows that I am not deceived in this. [AT VII, 90; HR I, 199]

If Wilson offers the Dream Hypothesis as a reason for Descartes to doubt his first premise, he will say, as he often does [*Discourse*; AT VI, 39; HR I, 105; *Principles*, I, xxx; AT VIII, 16–17; HR I, 231–232], that that hypothesis does not cast doubt on what he clearly and distinctly perceives. He does not retract this position in his remark to Hobbes. He admits to Hobbes that he might falsely believe his experiences "cohere" when he is actually asleep, but that is not to say that he can be asleep and incorrectly clearly and distinctly perceive that his experiences "cohere." Indeed that cannot happen, since all his clear and distinct perceptions are true.

Descartes is also right, and Wilson wrong, about whether the Dream Hypothesis casts doubt on his premise that all the parts of his experience "cohere." Since the premise does not say that his complex ideas are caused by things outside him, the hypothesis that he is asleep, forming complex ideas in his imagination, and incorrectly taking them to be caused by external things is irrelevant to it.

Some may agree with all I have said and still feel the tug of Wilson's basic point: it is implausible to believe that Descartes can develop a

16. I follow Wilson's translation of the passage; *Descartes*, p. 20.

criterion for being awake and apply it to his experience to gain meta-physical certainty that he is awake. Even if he does not beg the question when he says the criterion is satisfied, the criterion itself is problematic. Surely Descartes could have a dream in which all the parts of his experience "cohere." The only basis he can find for the criterion is the quicksand claim that God exists and is not a deceiver.

Wilson's move ultimately does not save Descartes from these difficulties. Let the Dream Hypothesis be that his waking experiences are nonveridical. His position in Meditation Six is then that he can be metaphysically certain that the parts of his experience cohere and that, when they do, his experience is veridical. Could not Descartes have a coherent, nonveridical experience? What basis, other than the claim that God exists and is not a deceiver, can he give for his criterion for a veridical experience? We do not make Descartes's problems disappear by talking about nonveridical waking experiences instead of dreams.[17]

My interpretation of the Dream Argument is likely to offend sensibilities in another way. I say the Dream Hypothesis is irrelevant to eternal truths because neither they nor Descartes's evidence for them in Meditation One entails the existence of external objects. Other commentators see things differently. Harry Frankfurt believes that

> in the First Meditation, Descartes does in fact regard the truth of mathematical judgments as depending upon the existence of things that exhibit the simple characteristics with which he presumes mathematics to deal. He does not suppose that the superior certainty he ascribes to mathematics derives from the indifference of mathematics to all questions of existence, but rather from the ease with which the existential requirements of mathematics may be satisfied. Since *whatever* exists must possess the simple characteristics, mathematics does not depend as other sciences do upon the existence of any specific objects or types of object. What it needs so far as existence goes is provided by the existence of *any* material thing.[18]

According to Frankfurt, Descartes thinks that mathematical truths entail the claim that some unspecified thing has the material and

16. I follow Wilson's translation of the passage; *Descartes*, p. 20.

17. I ignore the question of whether the text supports my interpretation of the Dream Hypothesis over Wilson's. She admits that Descartes often states the hypothesis so that it clearly concerns whether he is dreaming; she claims that other statements of it may be read as presenting the chance that his waking experiences are nonveridical; see *Descartes*, pp. 23–24. She is right on both counts.

18. Frankfurt, *Demons, Dreamers and Madmen*, p. 75.

common simple natures, though they do not entail more specific existential claims; the Dream Hypothesis does not cast doubt on mathematical truths, Frankfurt suggests, because it does not call into question the existence of some unspecified thing with the simple natures.

Frankfurt appeals to a point we have already accepted:

> The First Meditation is devoted to beliefs that are thought to be derived "from or through the senses." Since it discusses mathematical propositions, Descartes must be regarding these propositions as somehow based on sensory testimony; he cannot be construing their truth, accordingly, as independent of all questions of existence.[19]

Frankfurt misses the point that some sensory reports are not reports of external sensation. When Descartes says, "I've added two and three and obtained five; therefore, two and three is five," he bases his mathematical belief on a sensation report, and that sensation report does not concern the existence of an external thing, any more than the sensation report "I think" does. Frankfurt continues:

> Descartes says, for instance, that the mathematical sciences deal with very simple and general things and "scarcely care whether those things are in nature or not." But if no questions of existence are relevant to mathematics, why should mathematics care about existence even scarcely?[20]

The answer is that when Descartes says mathematics scarcely cares whether corporeal objects exist [*Meditations*; AT VII, 20; HR I, 147], and when he later says "corporeal nature . . . is the object of pure mathematics" [*Meditations*; AT VII, 71; HR I, 185; AT VII, 74; HR I, 187], his point is that mathematical truths describe how corporeal objects must be, *if they exist*. That all squares have four sides does not entail that there are corporeal objects. It just entails that if there are corporeal objects, they are squares only if they have four sides.[21]

19. Frankfurt, *Demons, Dreamers and Madmen*, p. 73.

20. Frankfurt, *Demons, Dreamers and Madmen*, p. 75.

21. Consider Alan Gewirth, "The Cartesian Circle Reconsidered," *Journal of Philosophy*, 67 (October 8, 1970), pp. 668–684, and "Descartes: Two Disputed Questions," *Journal of Philosophy*, 68 (May 6, 1971), pp. 288–298, as well as Anthony Kenny, "The Cartesian Circle and the Eternal Truths," *Journal of Philosophy*, 67 (October 8, 1970), pp. 685–696.

Frankfurt's last piece of evidence is this:

Descartes's assertion that mathematical truths seem immune to doubt is followed almost immediately by the question: "how do I know he [a deceptive god] has not brought it about that there is no earth at all, no sky, no extended thing, no shape, no size, no place, and that all these things should nevertheless seem to me to exist just as they do now?" It is apparent that Descartes conceives the possibility he describes in his question as providing a basis for doubting the truth of mathematics.[22]

It is not apparent to me. Descartes offers the Deceiver Hypothesis as a reason to doubt indefinite propositions about corporeal objects and as a reason to doubt mathematical propositions, but he never says it casts doubt on the latter by casting doubt on the former.

Frankfurt cannot explain several passages. I have already presented one in which Descartes affirms the independence of eternal truths from corporeal existence and cited others in which he makes the point with regard to mathematics in particular. Note too that Descartes claims metaphysical certainty of mathematics in Meditation Five [AT VII, 71; HR I, 185] but does not claim metaphysical certainty about the existence of corporeal objects until Meditation Six [AT VII, 80; HR I, 191].

Why would Descartes, or anyone, adopt the position Frankfurt describes? Consider the proposition that all squares have four sides. It is plausible to read it as having no existential presuppositions: if there are squares, then they have four sides. It is also plausible to read it as having existential presuppositions: there are squares all of which have four sides. But Frankfurt strands Descartes in the implausible middle ground with a proposition that does not go so far as to say there are squares but does presuppose the existence of extended objects. Why should we think that the proposition does not assert the existence of squares but does assert the existence of extended objects? It is as much about squares as it is about extended objects.

Anthony Kenny and, perhaps, Margaret Wilson disagree with another aspect of my interpretation of Descartes's views on mathematics. I say Descartes assumes that his mathematical beliefs are evidenced solely by sensation, and he thinks his beliefs, so evidenced, resist the Dream Hypothesis because neither they nor his evidence assert the existence of

22. Frankfurt, *Demons, Dreamers and Madmen*, p. 76.

external things. Kenny claims that several passages "explicitly contradict" the claim that Descartes takes sensation to be his sole source of evidence; Kenny thinks Descartes regards mathematical propositions as clearly and distinctly perceived.[23] Wilson writes: "Descartes holds explicitly in the *Discourse*, the *Principles* (I, 30), and the *VII Replies* that a clear and distinct perception cannot fail to be true, even in a dream. It is for this reason that the Dreaming Argument is not supposed to be sufficient to call in doubt mathematical knowledge."[24] Descartes believes he can clearly and distinctly perceive mathematical truths, and he believes that clear and distinct perceptions resist the Dream Hypothesis. The question is this: Does Descartes, in Meditation One, assume for the sake of argument that sensation is his sole source of evidence and then claim relative to that assumption that mathematical truths resist the Dream Hypothesis, or does he believe he clearly and distinctly perceives mathematical propositions at that point and offer that as the reason they resist the Dream Hypothesis? I choose the former; Kenny and, perhaps, Wilson, choose the latter.

I have already given the evidence for my view. Descartes opens Meditation One with the explicit assumption that sensation is his sole source of evidence. There is nothing to indicate that he gives up this assumption for the case of mathematics. He cites mental operations, such as addition, which can be described by sensation reports, and does not even mention clear and distinct perception.[25] Wilson does not present any evidence that Descartes is concerned with clear and distinct perception; Kenny cites two passages from outside Meditation One:

23. Kenny, "The Cartesian Circle and the Eternal Truths," p. 691.

24. Wilson, *Descartes*, pp. 28–29. I am not sure Wilson adopts the same position as Kenny. She seems to do so in the passage I quote, but she later says that Descartes does not offer the Deceiver Hypothesis as a reason to doubt clear and distinct perceptions in Meditation One (*Descartes*, p. 40) even though it is evident that he offers that hypothesis as a reason to doubt mathematical truths at that point.

25. Haldane and Ross translate one of Descartes's remarks so that he does seem to appeal to clear and distinct perception to explain why his mathematical beliefs resist the Dream Hypothesis. They have him say: "For whether I am awake or asleep, two and three together always form five, and the square can never have more than four sides, and it does not seem possible that truths *so clear and apparent* can be suspected of any falsity" [HR I, 147; my emphasis]. Descartes does not describe his mathematical beliefs as "clear and apparent." The Latin text is "Nam sive vigilem, sive dormiam, duo & tria simul juncta sunt quinque, quadratumque non plura habet latera quàm quatuor; nec fieri posse videtur ut tam perspicuæ veritates in suspicionem falsitatis incurrant" [AT VII, 20]. In the French text, he describes his beliefs as "vérités si apparentes."

The nature of my mind is such that I could not help holding [geometrical truths] to be true so long as I perceive them clearly; and I remember that even at the time when I was most strongly immersed in the objects of sense, I counted as most certain those truths which I clearly recognized concerning shapes, numbers and other arithmetical and geometric matters, concerning pure and abstract mathematics. [*Meditations*; AT VII, 65; HR I, 180]

Before I had liberated myself from the prejudices of the senses, I rightly perceived that two and three make five. . . . Children no sooner learn to count two and three than they are capable of judging that they make five. [*Reply to the Sixth Objections*; AT VII, 445; HR I, 257][26]

In each passage, Descartes admits having clear and distinct perceptions in mathematics during the time he was immersed in his senses, but this does not, in itself, tell us anything about his strategy in Meditation One and what he does or does not assume there for the sake of argument. Kenny might say Meditation One "represents" the period of Descartes's immersion in the senses. Even if it does, it is one thing for Descartes to perceive a mathematical truth clearly and distinctly and another for him to take his clear and distinct perception as the source of his justification for believing it; if Descartes really is immersed in his senses, he does not realize he has clear and distinct perceptions but instead takes sensation to be his only source of evidence after all. If Descartes wants Meditation One to represent his period of sensory slavery, he will assume for the sake of argument in that meditation the same understanding of his intellectual abilities he unwittingly adopted during his slavery: all his evidence comes from sensation. This is just what I say he does.

Standard Objections to the Dream Argument[27]

Anyone who gives the Dream Argument contradicts himself, according to G. E. Moore. Moore interprets the argument as containing an inference from:

26. I follow Kenny's translation of the passages.
27. Two recent discussions of objections to the Dream Argument are David Blumenfeld and Jean Beer Blumenfeld's "Can I Know That I Am Not Dreaming?" and George Nakhnikian's "Descartes's Dream Argument," both in *Descartes: Critical and Interpretive Essays*, ed. Michael Hooker (Baltimore: Johns Hopkins University Press, 1978).

M1: Some of the sensory experiences I am now having are similar in important respects to dream images that have actually occurred in dreams.

to:

M2: I do not know that I am not now dreaming.

to:

M3: I do not know propositions evidenced by my sense experience.

Moore argues as follows:

There is a very serious objection to the procedure of using [M1] as a premise in favor of the derived conclusion [M2]. For a philosopher who does use [M1] as a premise, is, I think, in fact *implying*, though he does not expressly say, that he himself knows it to be true. He is *implying* therefore that he himself knows that dreams have occurred. And, of course, I think he would be right. All the philosophers I have ever met or heard of certainly did know that dreams have occurred: we all know that dreams *have* occurred. But can he consistently combine this proposition that he knows that dreams have occurred, with his conclusion that he does not know that he is not dreaming? Can anybody possibly know that dreams have occurred, if, at the time, he does not himself know that he is not dreaming? If he *is* dreaming, it may be that he is only dreaming that dreams have occurred; and if he does not know that he is not dreaming, can he possibly know that he is *not* only dreaming that dreams have occurred? Can he possibly know therefore that dreams *have* occurred? I do not think he can; and therefore I think that anyone who uses this premise and also asserts the conclusion that nobody ever knows that he is not dreaming, is guilty of an inconsistency.[28]

Moore thinks anyone who uses M1 as a premise is committed to the claim that he knows it:

M4: I know that M1, that is, that some of my present sensory experiences are similar in important respects to dream images that have actually occurred in dreams.

28. George Edward Moore, "Certainty," in *Philosophical Papers* (New York: Macmillan, 1959), pp. 248–249. The references to M1 and M2 are mine.

M4 is inconsistent with M2. Just as M2 implies M3, that the person giving the argument does not know propositions evidenced by his senses, it implies that the person does not know there have been dreams qualitatively indistinguishable from his present experience.[29]

We can tailor Moore's objection to fit my interpretation of the Dream Argument. When Descartes gives the first stage of the argument, he commits himself to

> i. I am metaphysically certain of the premises of stage one of the Dream Argument.

The conclusion of stage one is

> ii. That I am dreaming is a metaphysical possibility for me.

When he gives stage two, he implies that

> iii. The hypothesis that I am dreaming indicates how some premises of stage one might be false despite my evidence for them.

The last two commitments jointly contradict the first, by the metaphysical certainty criterion (EP1) and the definition of rational doubt (D3).

The problem with Moore's objection is that Descartes is not committed to premise (i) above—M4 in Moore's own statement of the objection—and to think he is is to misunderstand the context and purpose of the Dream Argument. Descartes is engaged in an inquiry into truth. He guides his attitudes by the standard epistemic imperative (Believe all and only what is true on the matter at hand) and the Cartesian imperative (Accept under the heading of 'Science' only what is true and metaphysically certain) (see Chapter 2). He believes the premises in stage one of the Dream Argument, so he must say they are true and reasonable for him to believe from the standard perspective, but because he does not place those premises under the heading of 'Science'—no proposition gains a place under that heading until Med-

---

29. Other commentators agree with Moore; consider David and Jean Beer Blumenfeld, "Can I Know That I Am Not Dreaming?," p. 240, and W. H. Walsh, *Metaphysics*, p. 91.

itation Two—he does not have to say they are metaphysically certain. The Dream Argument's purpose is not to make Descartes metaphysically certain some propositions evidenced by sensation are metaphysically uncertain; its purpose is to make it reasonable for him to believe that those propositions are metaphysically uncertain. That reasonable belief combines with his commitment to the Cartesian imperative to make it reasonable for him to exclude those propositions from his science. The Dream Argument needs only reasonable premises to accomplish its purpose.[30]

J. L. Austin gives the best statement of another objection:

> [An] erroneous principle which the argument here seems to rely on is this: that it *must* be the case that 'delusive and veridical experiences' are not (as such) 'qualitatively' or 'intrinsically' distinguishable—for if they were distinguishable, we should never be 'deluded'. But of course, this is not so. From the fact that I am sometimes 'deluded', mistaken, taken in through failing to distinguish A from B, it does not follow at all that A and B must be *indistinguishable*.[31]

Austin is aiming at a version of the Dream Argument given by Ayer and Price, but Edwin Curley thinks he hits Descartes's argument as well.[32]

Yet Descartes does not reason, "I have failed to distinguish dreams from waking experiences in the past; therefore, I cannot do so in the present and am metaphysically uncertain whether I am dreaming." He is not, after all, the village idiot. He starts with the information that he recalls an exception to every general intrinsic criterion by which he might distinguish his present experience from a dream. He infers (1) that it is reasonable to believe that every such criterion has an exception, (2) that he is not metaphysically certain of an exceptionless criterion, and (3) that he is, therefore, metaphysically uncertain whether

---

30. My reply to Moore's objection is also contained in my "Dreams and Deceivers in Meditation One," *Philosophical Review*, 90 (April 1981), pp. 185–209; that article contains a survey of the unsuccessful replies to Moore's objection that have been given. Edwin Curley, *Descartes against the Skeptics*, pp. 50–51, gives a similar reply to Moore, but Curley does not relate his point to the different degrees of certainty and different imperatives guiding Descartes's epistemic attitudes.

31. J. L. Austin, *Sense and Sensibilia* (New York: Oxford University Press, 1964), pp. 51–52.

32. Curley, *Descartes against the Skeptics*, p. 57.

he is dreaming. He is innocent of the blunder described by Austin and attributed to him by Curley.

Anthony Kenny objects to Descartes's assumption (premise 7, stage one of the Dream Argument) that we can only be metaphysically certain we are not dreaming if we deduce that fact in an argument of this form:

    i. This, my present experience, has Q.
   ii. No dream has Q.
  iii. Therefore, I am not dreaming.

According to Kenny,

> The question, "Am I awake or am I dreaming?" is not senseless, if that means that it has no possible answer. For there is a true answer to the question—namely, "I am awake." Moreover, I know this answer. If I am asked *how* I know it, however, I can give no answer. I can give no grounds for the assertion. There is no fact better known to me than the fact that I am awake, that I can offer as a reason for saying that I am awake. When I say "I am awake," I do so without grounds, but not without justification. [33]

Kenny's point is not that we are always metaphysically certain we are awake or even that whenever we are awake we are metaphysically certain we are. He realizes as well as anyone that we can be awake, fail to consider that fact, and so be metaphysically uncertain of it. His point is that we need only be awake and consider whether we are to be metaphysically certain that we are; our *de se* belief that we are awake has roughly the same "self-evident" status Descartes awards to other *de se* beliefs about our mental state, such as that we seem to see light. [34]

What leads Kenny to this view? "I can give no grounds for my assertion that I am awake, for whatever grounds I give will be at least as much open to doubt as the assertion that I am awake. Let the reason I give be p. Then the sceptic can always ask, 'How do you know that you are not merely dreaming that p?' " [35] We have already seen Descartes's reply, weak as it may be: his best grounds for saying he is awake are a

33. Kenny, *Descartes*, p. 30.
34. Kenny, *Descartes*, p. 31.
35. Kenny, *Descartes*, p. 30.

clearly and distinctly perceived criterion for being awake and the clearly and distinctly perceived fact that his experience satisfies the criterion; the Dream Hypothesis does not apply to clear and distinct perceptions. We can give a stronger reply of our own: there is a tremendous
gap between Kenny's premises and intended conclusion. Suppose we
always have a reason to doubt whether a criterion for being awake is
true and satisfied. It does not follow that we can gain metaphysical
certainty we are awake without a criterion. Perhaps we can never be
metaphysically certain we are awake.

Kenny may have another argument:

> The judgment "I am awake" cannot be mistaken. "But can't I dream
> that I am awake?" Descartes objects. Yes, but to dream I am awake is
> not to judge that I am awake. It is impossible falsely to believe that one
> is awake, because one cannot entertain beliefs in sleep. In contrast to "I
> am dreaming," the judgment "I am awake" can only be made truly,
> never falsely. The question "Am I awake?" is not senseless; it is pointless
> only to the extent that if a man is in a position to ask the question, he is
> also in a position to answer it. [36]

Perhaps Kenny is thinking this: We cannot have beliefs when asleep,
so we cannot believe falsely that we are awake (our *de se* belief that we
are awake is incorrigible); hence, our belief that we are awake is self-
evident (we need only consider it when it is true to be metaphysically
certain it is true). Descartes will reject Kenny's undefended claim that
we cannot have beliefs when we are asleep. [37]

We have good reason to be sceptical of Kenny's basic position. All
the standard candidates for self-evident metaphysical certainties about
our mental state—that we think, that we seem to see light—concern
the content, rather than the cause, of our mental state. Indeed, that is
what makes them plausible candidates for self-evident status. It is

36. Kenny, *Descartes*, p. 31.

37. Kenny cites Norman Malcolm's arguments for the claim that we cannot have
beliefs when asleep, but he does not say he accepts those arguments. Malcolm's
arguments are in *Dreaming* (London: Routledge and Kegan Paul, 1959) and "Dreaming and Scepticism," in *Descartes*, ed. Willis Doney (New York: Anchor Doubleday,
1967), pp. 54–79. They have been widely discussed and criticized; see, for example,
A. J. Ayer, "Professor Malcolm on Dreams," *Journal of Philosophy*, 57 (1960), pp.
517–535, John V. Canfield, "Judgments in Sleep," *Philosophical Review*, 70 (1961),
pp. 224–230, and Edwin M. Curley, "Dreaming and Conceptual Revision," *Aus-
tralasian Journal of Philosophy*, 53 (1975), pp. 119–141.

reasonable to think we need only "look" to see what our mind contains. The proposition that we are awake concerns the cause of our mental state; it entails that we are not producing the contents of our mind, whatever they are, as part of a dream. It is not reasonable to think we need only "look" to see the cause. We must infer the cause of our mental state from the content, and Descartes's point is that the inference must use a metaphysically certain criterion to yield a metaphysically certain conclusion.

Dreaming and the Body

Descartes believes that, as long as he relies solely on sensation, the Dream Hypothesis (1) is a metaphysical possibility for him and (2) indicates how his *de se* belief in his body might be false. Critics generally concentrate on the first point. What about the second? Does the Dream Hypothesis really indicate to Descartes how his sensation based belief in his body might be false?

We do not give someone a reason to doubt a belief by citing a hypothesis that supports his belief. We do not give Descartes a reason to doubt Arnauld's existence by telling him Arnauld deceives him; we do not give Descartes a reason to doubt his own existence by telling him some god deceives him.

> But there is some deceiver or other, very powerful and very cunning, who ever employs his ingenuity in deceiving me. Then without doubt I exist also if he deceives me. [*Meditations*; AT VII, 25; HR I, 150]

This part of Descartes's concept of a reason for doubt is captured by

EP13: q indicates to S how S's morally certain belief p might be false despite S's evidence for p only if either (1) it is logically necessary that p, or (2) it is logically possible that q is true and p is false.

A hypothesis indicates to Descartes how one of his contingent moral certainties might be false despite his evidence only if the hypothesis does not entail the belief.[38]

38. I add the disjunct that p is logically necessary to the consequent of EP13 to keep the principle from implying that no hypothesis indicates how a logically necessary truth might be false.

Is it logically possible for the Dream Hypothesis to be true and the content of Descartes's *de se* belief in his body false? It depends on what propositions they are. We can now reap some benefit from our examination of Descartes's position on the content of his *de se* attitudes. Descartes would express the Dream Hypothesis in English by "I am dreaming" and his *de se* belief in his body by "I have a body." We have seen that in each case he would assign 'I' the same individual concept that differentiates him from all things without relating him to any; the most likely candidate is his property of being identical to himself. The Dream Hypothesis is true just when something satisfies that individual concept and also dreams. Descartes's *de se* belief in his body is true just when something satisfies that concept and also has a body. The question, then, is whether dreaming entails having a body. If it does, the Dream Hypothesis entails Descartes's *de se* belief in his body and does not cast doubt on it.

Descartes does not say much about dreaming, except for this:

> It is, however, easily proved that the soul feels those things that affect the body, not insofar as it is in each member of the body, but only insofar as it is in the brain, where the nerves by their movements convey to it the diverse actions of the external objects which touch the parts of the body. For, in the first place, there are many natural maladies which, though they affect the brain alone, yet either disorder or altogether take away from us the use of our senses; just like sleep itself which is only in the brain [*qui est in solo cerebro*], and yet every day takes from us during a great part of our time the faculty of perception, which is afterwards restored to us on awakening. [*Principles*, IV, cxcvi; AT VIII, 319; HR I, 293*]

Sleep is a brain state and so a property of the body. Since every property "that may be attributed to body presupposes extension" [*Principles*, I, liii; AT VIII, 25; HR I, 240], nothing can sleep unless it is extended. Nothing can dream unless it or its body sleeps, so Descartes is committed to the view that nothing dreams without being or having a body. He must say the Dream Hypothesis does not cast doubt on his *de se* belief in his body after all.

Descartes can slide out of this difficulty by surrendering either EP13 or his belief that sleep is a brain state. It would be foolish to give up EP13; it contains a compelling insight, and it is crucial to his defense of his claim to be metaphysically certain he thinks and exists (P1 and P2). Descartes is also right that sleep is a bodily state. A being without a body might think, conceive, imagine, even cease mental operations for a while, but how could it properly be said to do what we mean by 'sleep'? Descartes's best move is to admit that the Dream Hypothesis does not cast doubt on his *de se* belief in his body. He can revise the second part of the Dream Argument to take this new exception into account, and the argument will still show that many of his sensory-evidenced beliefs about the external world are metaphysically uncertain. He can give a new defense of P3 by appealing to the Deceiver Argument.

The Deceiver Argument: Interpretation

The Deceiver Argument will always represent the state of the art in attacks on sensation. It pushes the limits of Descartes's metaphysical uncertainty past the point where the Dream Argument stalls, all the way to indefinite propositions about simple natures, eternal truths, and the proposition that he has a body. Descartes opens with an observation and a question:

> Nevertheless I have long had fixed in my mind the belief that God who is all powerful has created me such as I am. But how do I know that He has not brought it to pass that there is no earth, no heaven, no extended body, no magnitude, no place and that nevertheless they seem to me to exist just exactly as I now see them? And, besides, as I sometimes imagine that others deceive themselves in the things which they think they know best, how do I know that I am not deceived every time that I add two and three, or count the sides of a square, or judge of things yet simpler, if anything simpler can be imagined? [*Meditations*; AT VII, 21; HR I, 147*]

Some may say deception is contrary to God's goodness:

> If, however, it is contrary to His goodness to have made me such that I constantly deceive myself, it would also appear to be contrary to His goodness to permit me to be sometimes deceived, and nevertheless I cannot doubt that He does permit this. [*Meditations*; AT VII, 21; HR I, 147]

Others may say God does not exist:

> Nevertheless in whatever way they suppose that I have arrived at the
> state of being that I have reached, . . . since to err and deceive oneself
> is a defect, it is clear that the greater will be the probability of my being
> so imperfect as to deceive myself ever, as is the Author to whom they
> assign my origin the less powerful. [*Meditations*; AT VII, 21; HR I,
> 147]

It follows that

> there is nothing in all that I formerly believed to be true, of which I
> cannot in some measure doubt, and that not merely through want of
> thought or through levity, but for reasons which are very powerful and
> maturely considered. [*Meditations*; AT VII, 21; HR I, 147–148]

Descartes's definitions and epistemic principles enable us to state his
argument in a more precise, but still provisional, way.

The Deceiver Argument: Preliminary Version

1. It is metaphysically possible for me that God always deceives me
   (makes all my judgments at all times false).
2. If p is one of my beliefs, p is a moral certainty or a moral uncertainty
   for me.
3. If p is a moral uncertainty for me, p is a metaphysical uncertainty for
   me.   [from D1 and D2]
4. If p is a moral certainty for me, the hypothesis that God always
   deceives me indicates how p, or an essential part of my evidence for
   p, might be false despite my evidence for it.
5. If p is a moral certainty for me, I have a reason to doubt p, so that it is
   a metaphysical uncertainty for me.   [from 1, 4, D3 and EP1]
6. Therefore, none of my beliefs is a metaphysical certainty for
   me.   [from 2, 3, and 5]

This is close to what Descartes has in mind, but a few adjustments are
necessary.

The conclusion is that Descartes is metaphysically uncertain of all
his beliefs. He says that in the last passage quoted, and he says it again
when he reconsiders the Deceiver Hypothesis in Meditation Three:

> I must inquire whether there is a God as soon as the occasion presents
> itself; and if I find that there is a God, I must also inquire whether He

may be a deceiver; for without a knowledge of these two truths I do not see that I can ever be certain of anything. [AT VII, 36; HR I, 159]

Descartes has no right to such a strong conclusion. He begins Meditation One by assuming sensation is his only source of evidence, so the most he may conclude in the Deceiver Argument of that meditation is that all his beliefs are metaphysically uncertain *as long as sensation is his only source of evidence.* Even that conclusion goes too far. He claims in Meditation Two that his *de se* belief in his existence resists the Deceiver Hypothesis, and we shall soon see he immediately deduces that belief from his sensation report that he thinks. Descartes must limit the conclusion of the Deceiver Argument of Meditation One to "I am metaphysically uncertain of any proposition that (1) is not the content of one of my first-person sensation reports or immediately and correctly deduced by me directly from such reports but (2) is ultimately evidenced for me solely by them." The set of metaphysical uncertainties defined by this conclusion does not include Descartes's *de se* beliefs that he thinks, seems to see light, or exists. It does include propositions inductively evidenced by reports of external sensation, by reports of what simple ideas he has, and by reports of what mental operations, such as addition, he performs. It includes all the Dream Argument shows to be doubtful and more.

The Deceiver Hypothesis also needs attention; Descartes has in mind something both less broad and less restrictive than that God always deceives him. He does not intend to raise the possibility that he is deceived in all his beliefs, and he does not intend to specify God, in particular, as the one and only source of his deception. Recall his description of how he might be deceived:

> But how do I know that He has not brought it to pass that there is no earth, no heaven, no extended body, no magnitude, no place *and that nevertheless they seem to me to exist just exactly as I now see them?* And, besides, as I sometimes imagine that others deceive themselves in the things which they think they know best, how do I know that I am not deceived *every time that I add two and three, or count the sides of a square?* [AT VII, 21; HR I, 147; my emphasis]

Descartes raises the possibility that God gives him sensations when the things represented by those sensations do not exist. If that is so, some of his beliefs—sensation reports like "I seem to see light"—will still be true; it is the conclusions he inductively draws from them that will be false.[39] Descartes initially cites God as the source of this possible defect and ends with a more general description: one way or another, he has been created so that all the beliefs he inductively draws from his sensation reports are false:

> There may indeed be those who would prefer to deny the existence of a God so powerful, rather than believe that all other things are uncertain. But let us not oppose them for the present, and grant that all that is here said of a God is a fable; nevertheless in whatever way they suppose that I have arrived at the state of being that I have reached, . . . since to err and deceive oneself is a defect, it is clear that the greater will be the probability of my being so imperfect as to deceive myself ever, as is the Author to whom they assign my origin the less powerful. [*Meditations*; AT VII, 21; HR I, 147; consider too: *Principles*, I, v; AT VIII, 6; HR I, 220; *Reply to the Sixth Objections*; AT VII, 428; HR II, 245]

Descartes uses different instances of the general hypothesis as he moves through the *Meditations*. First, it is God who deceives him:

> Nevertheless I have long had fixed in my mind the belief that God who is all powerful has created me such as I am. But how do I know that He has not brought it to pass that there is no earth, no heaven, no extended body, no magnitude, no place and that nevertheless they seem to me to exist just exactly as I now see them? [AT VII, 21; HR I, 147*]

Then it is an evil spirit:

> I will suppose, then, not that there is a supremely good God, the source of truth; but that there is an evil spirit [*genium aliquem malignum*] who is supremely powerful and cunning, and does his utmost to deceive me. [AT VII, 22; HR I, 148*]

---

39. Consider too the French text: "Or qui me peut avoir assuré que ce Dieu n'ait point fait qu'il n'y ait aucune terre, aucun ciel, aucun corps étendu, aucune figure, aucune grandeur, aucun lieu (et que néanmoins j'aie les sentiments de toutes ces choses), et que tout cela ne me semble point exister autrement que je le vois? Et même, comme je juge quelquefois que les autres se méprennent, même dans les choses qu'ils pensent savoir avec le plus de certitude, il se peut faire qu'il ait voulu que je me trompe toutes les fois que je fais l'addition de deux et de trois, ou que je nombre les côtés d'un carré" [AT IX, 16]. The phrase in parentheses is added in the French text and properly amplifies Descartes's position.

Then it is just some deceiver or other:

> But there is some deceiver or other, very powerful and very cunning,
> who ever employs his ingenuity in deceiving me [*Sed est deceptor nescio
> quis, summe potens, summe callidus, qui de industriâ me semper fallit*].
> [AT VII, 25; HR I, 150]

These are all nearly equivalent variations on a theme: one way or
another—God, an evil spirit, an experiment in genetic engineering—
Descartes has been created in such a way that all his inductive conclusions from sensation are false.[40]
    Let us restate the Deceiver Argument of Meditation One in light of
these observations.

The Deceiver Argument: Revised Version

1. Let p be a proposition that (1) is not one of my first-person sensation
   reports or immediately and correctly deduced by me from them but
   (2) is ultimately evidenced for me solely by them.
2. p is either a moral certainty or a moral uncertainty for me.
3. If p is a moral uncertainty for me, p is a metaphysical uncertainty for
   me.　[from D1 and D2]
4. It is a metaphysical possibility for me that I have been created so that,
   while all my first-person sensation reports and what I immediately
   and correctly deduce from them are true, the rest of what I believe on
   the basis of them is false.
5. If p is a moral certainty for me, the hypothesis that I have been
   created in the way just described indicates how p, or an essential part
   of my evidence for p, might be false despite my evidence for it.
6. If p is moral certainty for me, I have a reason to doubt p so that it is a
   metaphysical uncertainty for me.　[from 4, 5, D3, and EP1]
7. Therefore, p is a metaphysical uncertainty for me.

This argument establishes the metaphysical uncertainty of propositions
about material and common simple natures evidenced by reports of
simple ideas. Suppose Descartes reasons as follows:

---

40. The specific hypotheses do not have exactly the same force as reasons for doubt
in light of EP13. The hypothesis that God deceives him does not indicate to Descartes
how his belief in God might be false; that an evil spirit deceives him does indicate how
his belief in God might be false.

    i. I have an idea of extension.
   ii. My idea of extension is simple (unanalyzable).
  iii. Therefore, something was, perhaps is, extended.

The Deceiver Hypothesis indicates how his conclusion might be false despite his evidence. Perhaps Descartes was created with the simple idea of extension in a world in which there are no extended things. The argument also applies to eternal truths evidenced by sensation. Descartes may have been created in a way that allows, even requires, him to make mistakes when he adds two numbers and obtains a third, recalls proving something in the past, and so on.

Descartes can now establish P3.

The Deceiver Argument Defense of P3

1. Suppose all my evidence for the proposition that I have a body ultimately consists solely of sensation reports.
2. The proposition that I have a body is not one of my first-person sensation reports or immediately and correctly deduced by me from them.
3. If p is a proposition that (1) is not one of my first-person sensation reports or immediately and correctly deduced by me from them but (2) is ultimately evidenced for me solely by them, then p is a metaphysical uncertainty for me.
4. Therefore, that I have a body is a metaphysical uncertainty for me.

My objection to the Dream Argument defense of P3 does not apply here. Descartes is not committed to the view that inductively drawing false beliefs from first-person sensation reports entails having a body.

Objections to the Interpretation

I have contradicted some popular opinions in my interpretation of the Deceiver Argument. Let me try to meet the main objections likely to come my way.

I have left clear and distinct perception out of the Deceiver Argument. Those who think Descartes is interested in clear and distinct perception in Meditation One will object: Descartes thinks the Dream Hypothesis does not threaten truths of mathematics because they are clearly and distinctly perceived, he thinks the Deceiver Hypothesis does apply to them, so that hypothesis must concern and cast doubt on clear and distinct perceptions. Those who think Descartes is interested in clear and distinct perception in Meditation Three may object: Descartes says in Meditation Three that the Deceiver Hypothesis gives him a reason to doubt clear and distinct perceptions [AT VII, 36; HR I, 158]; we will not capture his view if we restrict the Deceiver Hypothesis to sensations from the start in Meditation One.

I have answered the first complaint already. Descartes does not appeal to clear and distinct perception in Meditation One to explain how mathematical beliefs resist the Dream Hypothesis. He never mentions clear and distinct perception at that point, he explicitly says sensation is his only source of evidence, and we can understand his position without bringing clear and distinct perception into play. The second objection is also easy to meet. The Deceiver Hypothesis of Meditation One is similar, but not identical, to the hypothesis Descartes offers as a reason to doubt clear and distinct perception in Meditation Three. The Meditation One hypothesis concerns his being deceived with regard to his sensations:

> But how do I know that He has not brought it to pass that there is no earth, no heaven, no extended body, no magnitude, no place and that nevertheless they seem to me to exist just exactly as I now see them? [*Meditations*; AT VII, 21; HR I, 147]

The Third Meditation hypothesis concerns his being deceived with regard to his clear and distinct perceptions:

> But every time that this preconceived opinion of the sovereign power of a God presents itself to my thought, I am constrained to confess that it is easy to Him, if He wishes it, to cause me to err, even about the things which I think I intuit as evidently as possible by the eye of the mind [*etiam in iis quæ me puto mentis oculis quàm evidentissime intueri*]. [*Meditations*; AT VII, 36; HR I, 158*][41]

---

41. This time the French text obscures Descartes's position by changing the end of his Meditation Three remark from a reference to mental vision to a more obscure reference to beliefs for which he has the greatest evidence: "je suis contraint d'avouer qu'il lui est facile, s'il le veut, de faire en sorte que je m'abuse, même dans les choses que je crois connaître avec une évidence très grande" [AT IX, 28].

Descartes shifts from questioning his eyesight to questioning his mental vision.

Some commentators think Descartes assigns different jobs to the hypothesis that God deceives him and the hypothesis that an evil spirit does so; they may find my broad reading of the Deceiver Hypothesis (that one way or another, Descartes has been created to have deceptive sensations) misguided. Margaret Wilson argues that Descartes uses the evil spirit hypothesis to cast doubt on propositions about external existence and the God hypothesis to cast doubt on eternal truths:

> It seems likely, then, that Descartes wishes to divide the doubts engendered in the First Meditation into two classes: doubts about external existence, and doubts about mathematics and other questions of essence (the so-called 'eternal truths'). The idea of a 'certain malign spirit, maximally powerful and clever' is used to undermine my initial certainties about real existence. This idea is confronted, and in some sense banished, by the *Cogito* argument at the beginning of Meditation II. The question whether *optimus Deus* himself may be supposed a deceiver is not, then, really addressed till the Third Meditation, when it is reintroduced in connection with the problem of the certainty of (apparent) eternal truths.[42]

Wilson has two pieces of circumstantial evidence for her view: Descartes does not include any eternal truths in the list of metaphysical uncertainties that accompanies the evil spirit hypothesis at the end of Meditation One; Descartes appeals to the God hypothesis when he considers the metaphysical uncertainty of eternal truths in Meditation Three. But Wilson's interpretation does not fit Descartes's own account of his situation. When he is concerned with sensation in Meditation One, he says the hypothesis that God deceives him gives him a reason to doubt both eternal truths (two and three is five) and propositions about external existence (something is extended), and he can't escape this doubt by denying God's existence, since the same doubt is cast by hypotheses that assign his creation to less impressive sources [AT VII, 21; HR I, 147]; the evil spirit hypothesis is such an alternative. Descartes takes the same line when he later concentrates on

---

42. Wilson, *Descartes*, p. 33. Kenny contemplates a similar view, *Descartes*, p. 36. Consider also in this regard Henri Gouhier, *Essais sur Descartes* (Paris: Vrin, 1937), p. 143fn.

clear and distinct perception. That God deceives him gives an atheist a reason to doubt mathematical propositions he perceives clearly and distinctly [*Reply to the Second Objections*; AT VII, 141; HR II, 39], and the atheist will get nowhere by denying God's existence, since hypotheses that assign his creation to other sources work just as well:

> As to the Atheist's knowledge, it is easy to prove that it is not immutable and certain. For, as I have already in a former place said, in proportion to the impotence assigned to the author of his being, the greater will be his reason for doubting whether he may not be of such an imperfect nature as to be deceived in matters which appear most evident to him. [*Reply to the Sixth Objections*; AT VII, 428; HR II, 245]

Let the belief be an assertion of external existence or an eternal truth; let the source of evidence be sensation or clear and distinct perception. The evil spirit and God hypotheses cast doubt equally well.[43]

Objections to the Deceiver Argument

Critics frequently charge that the Deceiver Argument or Deceiver Hypothesis is incoherent.[44] It is not always clear what kind of incoherence they have in mind, so let us look at some options.

43. Descartes can say that the evil spirit and God hypotheses both cast doubt on eternal truths without contradicting his view that God and God alone can change the eternal truths [*Correspondence*; Letter to Mersenne, May 6, 1630; AT I, 150]. An evil spirit can deceive us about what the eternal truths are even if he cannot change what they are. Wilson agrees with this point, *Descartes*, pp. 31–37, 120–131. A great deal has been written, mainly by French commentators, concerning Descartes's doctrine about the creation of eternal truths and its connection to the Deceiver Hypothesis: F. Aliqué, *La découverte métaphysique de l'homme chez Descartes* (Presses Universitaires de France, 1950), p. 171fn; E. M. Curley, "Descartes on the Creation of the Eternal Truths," *Philosophical Review*, 93 (October 1984), pp. 569–597; H. Frankfurt, "Descartes on the Creation of Eternal Truths," *Philosophical Review*, 86 (January 1977), pp. 36–57; M. Gouhier, *La pensée metaphysique de Descartes* (Paris: Vrin, 1967), p. 114fn; H. Gueroult, *Descartes selon l'ordre des raisons* (Paris: Aubier, 1968), p. 42fn; A. Kenny, "The Cartesian Circle and the Eternal Truths," *Journal of Philosophy*, 67 (October 8, 1970), pp. 685–699.

44. O. K. Bouwsma, "Descartes's Evil Genius," *Philosophical Review*, 58 (January 1949), p. 150, was one of the first to raise the issue. Discussion of Bouwsma's position can be found in James Cornman and Keith Lehrer, *Philosophical Problems and Arguments: An Introduction* (New York: Macmillan, 1974), pp. 87–92; Kenny, *Descartes*, pp. 36–37, and Michael Slote, *Reason and Scepticism* (London: George Allen and Unwin, 1970), pp. 141–151.

If the Deceiver Hypothesis is incoherent in the sense of being logically impossible, Descartes can be hoisted with his own epistemic petard:

> EP13: q indicates to S how S's morally certain belief p might be false despite S's evidence for p only if either (1) it is logically necessary that p, or (2) it is logically possible that q be true and p be false.

If the Deceiver Hypothesis is logically impossible, it does not satisfy EP13 with regard to any contingent moral certainty and the fifth premise of the Deceiver Argument is false. Is it logically impossible? We might argue that Descartes cannot be deceived in all his beliefs, since if he is deceived, he thinks and has the true belief that he does; but the Deceiver Hypothesis is not that Descartes is deceived in all his beliefs, only that he is continually deceived in what he inductively draws from his true first-person sensation reports. Kenny alludes to unidentified critics who "have argued that sense deception is only possible against a background of veridical perception. There cannot be errors, it is reasoned, where there is no possibility of correction, for if it makes no sense to talk of something's being corrected, then it makes no sense to talk of its being wrong."[45] He may be thinking of Austin's remark: "It is important to remember that talk of deception only *makes sense* against a background of general non-deception. (You can't fool all of the people all of the time.) It must be possible to *recognize* a case of deception by checking the odd cases against the more normal ones."[46] Other commentators have already done a fine job of defending Descartes against this objection.[47] I have nothing to add beyond an observation: Even if we agreed with Austin that Descartes cannot be continually deceived in the conclusions he inductively draws from his sensations, we could revise the Deceiver Argument to avoid the problem. Just restrict the Deceiver Hypothesis to the present: Descartes is *now* such that his sensation reports and what they entail are true, but

---

45. Kenny, *Descartes*, p. 25.
46. J. L. Austin, *Sense and Sensibilia*, p. 11.
47. One of the best and most recent defenses is that given by David Blumenfeld and Jean Beer Blumenfeld in "Can I Know That I Am Not Dreaming?" pp. 245–248.

all the rest of what he now believes on the basis of them is false. This hypothesis allows for the possibility that Descartes's sense perceptions have been veridical in the past and will be so in the future. It just says that at this very moment all he inductively concludes from his sensations is false. It contains no contradiction, and even though Descartes writes of his being continually deceived [*Meditations*; AT VII, 21; HR I, 147; *Principles*, I, v; AT VIII, 6; HR I, 220; *The Search after Truth*; AT X, 511–512; HR I, 314], the Deceiver Argument only requires the hypothesis that he is deceived in the present, just as the Dream Argument only requires that he dream in the present.

The idea that Descartes's position is incoherent can take another form. Might not his claims about the Deceiver Hypothesis be contradictory? EP13 forces him to say that the hypothesis is logically possible, whereas his understanding of God's nature seems to entail that it is logically impossible:

1. It is logically necessary that God exists and is not a deceiver.
2. It is logically necessary that if God exists and is not a deceiver, then I am not created such that all my first-person sensation reports and what I immediately and correctly deduce from them are true while the rest of what I believe on the basis of those reports is false.
3. Therefore, it is logically impossible that I have been created such that all my first-person sensation reports and what I immediately and correctly deduce from them are true but the rest of what I believe on the basis of them is false.

Descartes himself says:

> That it is self-contradictory that men should be deceived by God is clearly demonstrated from the fact that the form of deception is non-existence, towards which the supreme existent cannot incline. [*Reply to the Sixth Objections*; AT VII, 428; HR II, 245]

Descartes's views about God are not as simple as this objection assumes. He is not committed to the second premise in the line of reasoning above; he would say God's existence and nondeceptive nature are consistent with his being created such that his sensation reports and their entailments are true while the inductive conclusions he draws from them are false. Take a close look at the implications of

God's goodness for Descartes's intellectual faculties. That God exists and is not a deceiver entails that none of Descartes's *clear and distinct perceptions* is false:

> Every clear and distinct perception is without doubt something, and hence cannot derive its origin from what is nought, but must of necessity have God as its author—God, I say, who being supremely perfect, cannot be the cause of any error; and consequently we must conclude that it is true. [*Meditations*; AT VII, 62; HR I, 178*]

God's existence and nondeceptive nature are consistent with the fact that *some* of Descartes's inductive conclusions from sensation are false. Those conclusions are not clearly and distinctly perceived, and Descartes has no one but himself to blame when he assents to them:

> If I determine to deny or affirm, I no longer make use as I should of my free will, and if I affirm what is not true, it is evident that I deceive myself. . . . And it is in the misuse of the free will that the privation which constitutes the characteristic nature of error is met with. Privation, I say, is found in the act, in so far as it proceeds from me, but it is not found in the faculty which I have received from God, nor even in the act in so far as it depends on Him. [*Meditations*; AT VII, 59–60; HR I, 176–177]

I believe Descartes would say that, for similar reasons, God's existence and nondeceptive nature are consistent with his being such that *all* his inductive conclusions from sensation are false. He, not God, would be to blame, as long as he drew each false conclusion of his own free will.

Could God create Descartes in a way that guaranteed that all his inductive conclusions from sensation would be false yet allowed him to draw each conclusion freely? Descartes seems to think so. He finds no problem with the opposite case: "God could easily have created me so that I never should err, although I still remained free" [*Meditations*; AT VII, 61; HR I, 177]. If God can do one, He can do the other.

Descartes may, of course, be wrong in his conception of what God can and cannot do. That is not the issue. What is important is that his views about God, correct or incorrect, well defended or ill defended, do not commit him to the claim that the Deceiver Hypothesis (of Meditation One) is logically impossible and so do not contradict what he is required to say by EP13 when he offers that hypothesis as a reason for doubt.[48]

There is one other way to charge Descartes with incoherence. Margaret Wilson notes that his attempt in Meditation Three to remove the Deceiver Hypothesis is problematic:

> He [Descartes] will ultimately attempt to [prove] . . . that he is in the hands of an omnipotent, benevolent being, who would not permit him to be deceived in what seems to him most certain. But according to the most common form of the circularity objection, one cannot know the premises of a proof are true, unless one already knows one is not subject to systematic deception.

> This line of reasoning leads to an interesting conclusion. Since the Deceiver Argument itself involves premises, it is in a certain sense self-annihilating.[49]

---

48. Does this version of the incoherence objection work against the Meditation Three version of the Deceiver Hypothesis, which asserts that Descartes is mistaken in his clear and distinct perceptions? Here is how the objection runs: EP13 commits Descartes to the view that the hypothesis is logically possible. Descartes's views on God force him to say that it is logically impossible. Since he deduces the principle that all his clear and distinct perceptions are true from (what he takes to be) necessary truths about God's existence and nature, he must say that it is logically impossible for some of his clear and distinct perceptions to be false.

Descartes can meet this objection in two ways. First, EP13 forces him to say the clear and distinct perception version of the Deceiver Hypothesis is logically possible only if he uses the hypothesis to indicate how a contingent moral certainty might be false. He does not use it in that way; he uses it to indicate how necessary truths, such as that two and three is five, might be false. Second, we can interpret the clear and distinct perception version of the Deceiver Hypothesis so that it is consistent with the principle that all Descartes's clear and distinct perceptions are true. Let the hypothesis be: I (Descartes) have been created so all my clear and distinct perceptions are false, except those which concern the content of my mental state (e.g., that I think) or involve my immediately deducing a conclusion from a clear and distinct perception of my mental content (e.g., I think, therefore I am). This hypothesis is consistent with the principle that all Descartes's clear and distinct perceptions are true; the hypothesis and the principle can both be true when Descartes's clear and distinct perceptions are limited to his sensation reports and what he immediately deduces from them.

Descartes can slide around this version of the charge of incoherence in these two ways. Keep in mind, too, that this charge of incoherence does not threaten the Deceiver Argument of Meditation One or Descartes's defense of P3, since they use another version of the Deceiver Hypothesis.

49. Wilson, *Descartes*, p. 35.

In other words, the Deceiver Hypothesis casts doubt on the premises of the Deceiver Argument itself.

We can make Wilson's point in terms of my interpretation of the argument. Descartes assumes that all his beliefs are evidenced solely by sensation, including the premises of the Deceiver Argument. Each morally certain premise is open to the Deceiver Hypothesis. None is a metaphysical certainty.

What is the problem for Descartes here? Wilson describes her point as an objection. Yet we do not have the makings of one unless Descartes is committed to the metaphysical certainty of the premises of the Deceiver Argument, and he is not. Recall what we learned from the failure of Moore's objection to the Dream Argument. Descartes's premises must be reasonable to believe from the standard epistemic perspective: since his premises are reasonable, his conclusion is reasonable, and as long as his conclusion is reasonable, given his allegiance to the Cartesian imperative, it is reasonable for him to exclude beliefs inductively evidenced by sense preception from his science. That is how Descartes's argument works. He does not, and need not, claim to be metaphysically certain of his premises.[50]

50. I have examined Wilson's objection in "Dreams and Deceivers in Meditation One," *Philosophical Review*, 90 (April 1981), pp. 185–209.

Chapter 5

THE MIND, CLEAR
AND DISTINCT PERCEPTION,
AND CERTAINTY

After demonstrating his metaphysical uncertainty that he has a body (P3), Descartes moves to establish P1 and P2, that he is metaphysically certain he thinks and metaphysically certain he exists. His argument generates the infamous *cogito* puzzle: How do Descartes's several individually insightful but apparently mutually inconsistent remarks about P1 and P2 form a single cogent defense? We see the answer once we place his remarks within the context of his views on the nature and content of certainty.

The Main Pieces of the Puzzle

Descartes must explain why he is metaphysically certain he thinks and exists even though he is metaphysically uncertain he has a body. He may not say the first two beliefs concern himself, while the third does not, and that he has a special access to himself that he has to no other thing. All three are *de se* beliefs. Descartes believes, in each, that he himself has a property, and he directs his attention to himself by considering a concept that individuates him from all things without relating him to any. The only difference of content between these beliefs is in the properties Descartes attributes to himself: on the one hand, thought and existence; on the other, having a body (being either extended or having an extended thing as one's body). The question is this: Why are Descartes's self-attributions of thought and existence metaphysically certain for him, whereas his self-attribution of having a body is not?

We have seen part of Descartes's answer. Sensation is his only source of evidence for believing he has a body, the relation between his *de se* belief in his body and his sensation reports is inductive, and reasons for doubt operate in the inductive gap. His belief that he thinks is not evidenced by sensation reports; it is a sensation report. His *de se* belief that he exists might be evidenced by such sensation reports as that he thinks, but, if it is, the evidential relation is deductive rather than inductive. In short, Descartes's beliefs in his thought and existence are not inductively evidenced by sensation in the way his belief in his body is assumed to be.

How, then, are Descartes's beliefs that he thinks and exists evidenced? Why does this source of evidence make them metaphysically certain? Descartes's earliest answer is contained in the *Rules*. He there takes intuition to be his source of metaphysical certainty:

> By *intuition* I understand, not the fluctuating testimony of the senses, nor the misleading judgment that proceeds from the blundering constructions of the imagination, but the conception which an unclouded and attentive mind gives us so readily and distinctly that we are wholly freed from doubt about that which we understand. [III; AT X, 368; HR I, 7]

Intuition takes two forms. We intuit some propositions directly (without deducing them from others). These are "primary and self-evident principles" [*Rules*, VII; AT X, 387; HR I, 19], which we behold as "existing *per se*" [*Rules*, VI; AT X, 383; HR I, 16]. We intuit other propositions by deducing them from intuited premises. In this process, we keep our "imagination moving continuously in such a way that while it is intuitively perceiving each fact it simultaneously passes on to the next"; the result is that we have "the whole [deduction] in intuition before [us] at the same time" [*Rules*, VII; AT X, 388; HR I 19]. Descartes's first explanation of how he gains metaphysical certainty that he thinks and that he exists is that he directly intuits each proposition. In his discussion of direct intuition in the *Rules*, three paragraphs before he even introduces deductive intuition, he writes:

> Each individual can mentally have intuition of the fact that he exists, and that he thinks; that the triangle is bounded by three lines only, the sphere by a single superficies, and so on. Facts of such a kind are far more numerous than many people think, disdaining as they do to direct their attention upon such simple matters. [III; AT X, 368; HR I, 7]

Descartes's talk of intuition in the *Rules* gives way to that of clear and distinct perception in the *Discourse, Meditations*, and *Principles*. He never announces that the faculties are the same, but their equivalence is strongly suggested by the fact that he designates them by similar descriptions: 'the light of reason' and 'the light of nature.' We are told in the *Rules* that

> intuition is the undoubting conception of an unclouded and attentive mind, and springs from the light of reason [*rationis luce*] alone. [III; AT X, 368; HR I, 7]

and in the *Principles* that

> the light of nature [*lumen naturæ*], or the faculty of knowledge which God has given us, can never disclose to us any object which is not true, inasmuch as it comprehends it, that is, inasmuch as it apprehends it clearly and distinctly. [I, xxx; AT VIII, 16; HR I, 231; consider too: *Meditations*; AT VII, 38–39; HR I, 160–161][1]

In the language of his later works, then, Descartes's first explanation is that direct clear and distinct perception makes him metaphysically certain he thinks and he exists. We get a hint of this explanation in the *Meditations*:

> I am certain that I am a thing which thinks; but do I not then likewise know what is requisite to render me certain of a truth? Certainly in this

---

1. Descartes uses 'natural reason' (*ratio naturalis*) and 'the light of nature' (*lumen naturale*) interchangably in *Notes against a Programme* [AT VIII-2, 353; HR I, 438–439]. In "Clear and Distinct Perception and Metaphysical Certainty," *Mind*, 88 (January 1979), pp. 101–102, I claim that intuition is a necessary but not a sufficient condition for clear and distinct perception; I now think that is incorrect.

first knowledge there is nothing that assures me of its truth, excepting the clear and distinct perception of that which I state. [AT VII, 35; HR I, 158]

Yet in works after the *Rules*, Descartes frequently suggests that he has only a deductive clear and distinct perception of his existence:

> Substance cannot first be discovered merely from the fact that it is a thing that exists, for that fact alone is not observed by us. [*Principles*, I, lii; AT VIII, 25; HR I, 240]

> But immediately afterwards I noticed that whilst I thus wished to think all things false, it was absolutely essential that the 'I' who thought this should be somewhat, and remarking that this truth '*I think, therefore I am*' was so certain and so assured that all the most extravagant suppositions brought forward by the sceptics were incapable of shaking it, I came to the conclusion that I could receive it without scruple as the first principle of the Philosophy for which I was seeking. [*Discourse*; AT VI, 32; HR I, 101]

> There is a contradiction in conceiving that what thinks does not at the same time as it thinks, exist. And hence this cognition *I think, therefore I am*, is the first and most certain of all that occurs to one who philosophises in an orderly way. [*Principles*, I, vii; AT VIII, 6–7; HR I, 221*]

Descartes seems to be deducing the proposition that he exists from the proposition that he thinks.

The puzzle has a third piece. Descartes appears to ignore both direct and deductive clear and distinct perception when he claims metaphysical certainty of his existence in Meditation Two. He emphasizes that he has no reason to doubt his existence, since potential reasons for doubt entail that he exists (they violate EP13):

> But there is some deceiver or other, very powerful and very cunning, who ever employs his ingenuity in deceiving me. Then without doubt I exist also if he deceives me, and let him deceive me as much as he will, he can never cause me to be nothing so long as I think that I am something. [*Meditations*; AT VII, 25; HR I, 150]

Descartes can make the same point about his belief that he thinks. These are the main pieces of the *cogito* puzzle. I now want to consider two unsuccessful, but instructive, attempts to fit them together.

Unsuccessful Interpretations

According to what might be called the 'Naive Inference Interpretation,' Descartes never changes his mind about why he is metaphysically certain he thinks. He believes that when he apprehends the proposition that he thinks, he clearly and distinctly perceives it directly, and any proposition he clearly and distinctly perceives is a metaphysical certainty for him. He does change his mind between the *Rules* and his later works, however, about how he gains metaphysical certainty that he exists. The idea that he can directly perceive clearly and distinctly that he exists gives way to the insight that existence does not have the sort of content that allows him to recognize its presence in a particular thing noninferentially; he decides he deduces his existence from the metaphysically certain fact that he thinks.

We can generate different versions of this interpretation by giving different accounts of Descartes's inference from thought to existence: (1) it is immediate, (2) it uses the premise that whatever thinks, exists, or (3) it uses a premise to the effect that if Descartes, in particular, thinks, then he exists. I want to concentrate on the immediate inference version. This interpretation has several attractive features. It captures Descartes's dictum, "*Cogito, ergo sum,*" and his remark that we do not observe *per se* the fact of a thing's existence. It helps us appreciate the role of clear and distinct perception in his metaphysical certainty: direct clear and distinct perception makes him metaphysically certain he thinks; deductive clear and distinct perception makes him metaphysically certain he exists. We can even make sense of two difficult passages.

Descartes tells the Marquis of Newcastle:

> You will surely admit that you are less assured of the presence of the objects you see than of the truth of the proposition: I experience, therefore I am? Now this knowledge is no product of your reasoning, no lesson that your masters have taught you; it is something that your mind sees, feels, handles; and although your imagination, which insistently

mixes itself up with your thoughts, reduces the clearness of this knowledge, it is, nevertheless, a proof of our soul's capacity for receiving from God an intuitive kind of knowledge. [*Correspondence*; AT V, 137; AG, 301][2]

Descartes presents the inference that he thinks and therefore exists, yet he also says his knowledge of his existence is intuitive and does not involve reasoning. How can his knowledge involve the inference but be intuitive and not involve reasoning? The Naive Immediate Inference Interpretation has an answer: Descartes's knowledge does not involve reasoning in that it does not involve a syllogism or a series of inferences; it is intuitive in that he intuits (clearly and distinctly perceives directly) that he thinks and immediately infers that he exists. I have already noted that Descartes extends the title 'intuitive' to knowledge gained by an inference from simultaneously intuited premises [*Rules*, III; AT X, 369–370; HR I, 8; *Rules*, VIII; AT X, 389; HR I, 20; *Rules*, XI; AT X, 407–408; HR I, 33].

Descartes tells Mersenne:

> When we become aware that we are thinking beings, this is a primitive act of knowledge derived from no syllogistic reasoning. He who says, '*I think, hence I am, or exist,*' does not deduce existence from thought by a syllogism, but, by a simple act of mental vision, recognises it as if it were a thing that is known *per se*. [*Reply to the Second Objections*; AT VII, 140; HR II, 38]

Descartes again presents the inference that he thinks and therefore exists. He again suggests his knowledge of his existence is intuitive; this time he claims to gain his knowledge in a simple act of mental vision in which he recognizes something as if it were known *per se*. It is not clear what this "something" is. It may be that he exists, or it may be the inference that he thinks and therefore exists. Whatever it is, how can his knowledge both involve that inference and be gained in a simple act of mental vision? The Naive Immediate Inference Interpretation contains an answer: Descartes infers that he exists immediately from the premise that he thinks, and he apprehends his inference in a simple act of mental vision in that he clearly and distinctly per-

---

2. I follow Anscombe and Geach's translation.

ceives the premise directly and infers the conclusion simultaneously. In the *Rules*, Descartes describes as "simple and clear" inferences "grasped as a whole at the same time by the mind" and "presented to us by intuition" [XI; AT X, 407–408; HR I, 33].

So what is wrong with the Naive Immediate Inference Interpretation? Two things trip it up. First, it does not use all of the pieces of the *cogito* puzzle. It ignores Descartes's observation that he has no reason to doubt his existence because all potential reasons for doubt entail that he exists. Margaret Wilson is one of the few commentators to see this difficulty:

> [The interpretation] does not bring out the peculiar relation of the *cogito* to the enterprise of Cartesian doubt. Since 'I doubt,' or 'I am deceived,' or 'I entertain the possibility I am deceived,' are themselves *examples* of *cogito* judgments, they themselves entail the truth of 'I exist,' according to the connection between *cogito* and *sum* alleged in the *cogito* reasoning. In other words, it surely is an important feature of the cogito reasoning that doubt and/or the supposition of deception *itself* is supposed to *lead to*, rather than undermine, the certainty of 'I exist.'[3]

Second, the Naive Immediate Inference Interpretation uses something it is not allowed to use—the principle that clear and distinct perceptions are always metaphysically certain. Some commentators think Descartes accepts this principle.[4] He actually tosses it aside, thinking that versions of the Deceiver Hypothesis cast doubt on his direct clear and distinct perceptions of simple necessary truths and on any deduc-

---

3. Margaret Wilson, *Descartes* (London: Routledge and Kegan Paul, 1978), pp. 60–61.

4. Commentators who have attributed this principle to Descartes include Willis Doney, "The Cartesian Circle," *Journal of the History of Ideas*, 16 (1955), p. 325; Anthony Kenny, *Descartes: A Study of His Philosophy* (New York: Random House, 1968), p. 192; Harry Frankfurt, *Demons, Dreamers and Madmen: The Defense of Reason in Descartes's 'Meditations'* (New York: Bobbs-Merrill, 1970), p. 164; and James Van Cleve, "Foundationalism, Epistemic Principles and the Cartesian Circle," *Philosophical Review*, 88 (January 1979), p. 69. Doney has since decided that Descartes does not accept the principle; "Descartes's Conception of Perfect Knowledge," *Journal of the History of Philosophy*, 8 (1970), pp. 387–403. Those who think that Descartes regards at least some clear and distinct perceptions as metaphysically uncertain include Alan Gewirth, "The Cartesian Circle," *Philosophical Review*, 50 (1941), pp. 368–395, and Fred Feldman, "Epistemic Appraisal and the Cartesian Circle," *Philosophical Studies*, 27 (1975), pp. 37–55.

tive clear and distinct perception based on them. Let us look at the text.[5]

Does Descartes ever say clear and distinct perceptions are always metaphysically certain? He indicates that intuitions are always metaphysically certain in the *Rules* [III; AT X, 368; HR I, 7], and if we identify intuition with clear and distinct perception, we may take him to be saying all clear and distinct perceptions are metaphysically certain. Yet Descartes does not really test his beliefs against potential reasons for doubt in the *Rules*, and what he takes to be metaphysically certain there, he may well take to be metaphysically uncertain when he examines his beliefs more critically in the *Meditations*. We need to consider what he says in that later work.

Two passages in the *Meditations* are often taken to affirm the metaphysical certainty of all clear and distinct perceptions. Descartes writes in Meditation Three:

> When I say that I am so instructed by nature, I merely mean a certain spontaneous inclination which impels me to believe in this connection, and not a natural light which makes me recognise that it is true. But these two things are very different; for I cannot doubt that which the natural light causes me to believe to be true, as, for example, it has shown me that I am from the fact that I doubt, or other facts of the same kind. And I possess no other faculty whereby to distinguish truth from falsehood, which can teach me that what this light shows me to be true is not really true, and no other faculty that is equally trustworthy. [AT VII, 38; HR I, 160]

We know that Descartes identifies perception by the natural light with clear and distinct perception [*Principles*, I, xxx; AT VIII, 16; HR I, 231], and he here says he cannot doubt what the natural light causes him to believe. Anthony Kenny thinks that Descartes is here affirming the metaphysical certainty of clear and distinct perceptions.[6] I think he is only affirming their psychological certainty. He does not say he has no reason to doubt the revelations of the natural light, only that he cannot doubt them. The contrast between the instructions of nature, which he receives in sensation, and the revelations of the natural light

---

5. Some of what follows appeared in my "Clear and Distinct Perceptions and Metaphysical Certainty."
6. Kenny, *Descartes*, p. 178.

is that he has a resistible inclination to believe the former and an irresistible compulsion to believe the latter. The second passage also comes from Meditation Three:

> Always when I direct my attention to things which I believe myself to perceive very clearly, I am so persuaded of their truth that I let myself break out into words such as these: Let who will deceive me, He can never cause me to be nothing while I think that I am, or some day cause it to be true to say that I have never been, it being true now to say that I am, or that two or three make more or less than five, or any such thing in which I see a manifest contradiction. [AT VII, 36; HR I, 158–159]

Kenny and James Van Cleve both take Descartes to be affirming the metaphysical certainty of all clear and distinct perceptions. Yet, once again, he only explicitly affirms their persuasive power or psychological certainty.[7]

Two passages from works after the *Rules* indicate that Descartes thinks clear and distinct perceptions can be metaphysically uncertain. Mersenne observes that

> an Atheist knows clearly and distinctly that the three angles of a triangle are equal to two right, yet he is far from believing in the existence of God. [*Second Objections*; AT VII, 125; HR II, 26]

Descartes replies:

> That *an atheist can know clearly that the three angles of a triangle are equal to two right angles,* I do not deny, I merely affirm that, on the other hand, such knowledge on his part cannot constitute true science, because no knowledge that can be rendered doubtful should be called science. Since he is, as supposed, an Atheist, he cannot be sure that he is not deceived in the things that seem most evident to him. [*Reply to the Second Objections*; AT VII, 141; HR II, 39]

Descartes denies that the atheist's clear and distinct perception will yield "true science," because, in his ignorance of God, the atheist

---

7. Kenny, *Descartes*, pp. 182–183; Van Cleve, "Foundationalism, Epistemic Principles and the Cartesian Circle," pp. 66–69. For more discussion of this passage, see the exchange between Alan Gewirth, "The Cartesian Circle Reconsidered," *Journal of Philosophy*, 67 (1970), pp. 668–685 and "Descartes: Two Disputed Questions," *Journal of Philosophy*, 68 (1971), pp. 288–296, and Anthony Kenny, "The Cartesian Circle and the Eternal Truths," *Journal of Philosophy*, 67 (1970), pp. 685–700.

cannot be sure that all his clear and distinct perceptions are true.[8]
Descartes's requirements for science are truth and metaphysical certainty (see Chapter 2). The theorem is true, so metaphysical certainty
must be what the atheist lacks.

Commentators who think that clear and distinct perceptions are
always metaphysically certain have tried to slide around this passage.
Kenny says Descartes demands "Cartesian certainty," not metaphysical certainty, for science.[9] As I understand Kenny, a proposition
is a Cartesian certainty for someone just when it is a metaphysical
certainty for him and there is no later time at which it is a metaphysical
uncertainty for him; the atheist's problem is that his clear and distinct
perception does not give him Cartesian certainty. I have already argued (Chapter 2) that Descartes does not set such an impossibly high
standard for scientific knowledge. Not even knowledge of God can
place Descartes in such a position that his clear and distinct perception
of a proposition at one moment insures that he will not lose his clear
and distinct perception and end up metaphysically uncertain at the
next.

According to Willis Doney, Descartes wants to admit that the atheist's clear and distinct perception generates metaphysical certainty but
also to deny that the atheist's recollection of having a clear and distinct
perception does so. Only those with a knowledge of God can be metaphysically certain of a proposition on the evidence that they have
clearly and distinctly perceived it in the past.[10] There is textual support
for Doney's view:

> First, we are sure that God exists because we have attended to the proofs
> that established this fact, but afterwards it is enough for us to remember
> that we have perceived something clearly, in order to be sure that it is
> true; but this would not suffice, unless we knew that God existed and
> that he did not deceive us. [*Reply to the Fourth Objections*; AT VII,

8. Descartes explicitly refers only to the clarity of the atheist's perception, but it is
unlikely that his quarrel with Mersenne is over whether an atheist can have a perception that is both clear and distinct. He does not deny Mersenne's claim that an atheist
can have both a clear and a distinct perception; he instead denies that an atheist can
have scientific knowledge.

9. Kenny, *Descartes*, p. 192.

10. Doney, "The Cartesian Circle," p. 326. A more extensive critique of Doney's
proposal is given by Frankfurt, *Demons, Dreamers and Madmen*, pp. 156–169.

246; HR II, 115; consider too: *Reply to the Second Objections*; AT VII, 146; HR II, 42–43]

There is also strong evidence against Doney's proposal. We can be metaphysically certain of a proposition on the evidence that we have clearly and distinctly perceived it in the past only if we can be metaphysically certain of our evidence. Even after he proves God's existence, Descartes admits that his memories of past clear and distinct perceptions are fallible and so metaphysically uncertain:

> We frequently err when we presume we have known certain things as being stored up in our memory, to which on recollection we give our assent, and of which we have never possessed any knowledge at all. [*Principles*, I, xliv; AT VIII, 21; HR I, 236]

Descartes cannot consistently combine this view with the one described by Doney, and since this is the more plausible of the two, it is the one we should take seriously.

Another occasion on which Descartes says that clear and distinct perceptions are metaphysically uncertain is early in Meditation Three:

> When I took anything very simple and easy in the sphere of arithmetic or geometry into consideration, e.g. that two and three together made five, and other things of the sort, did I not at least intuit these things perspicuously enough that I might affirm them to be true? Certainly if I since judged that such matters could be doubted, this would not have been so for any other reason than that it came to my mind that perhaps some God might have endowed me with such a nature that I may have been deceived even concerning things which seemed to me most manifest. But every time that this preconceived opinion of the sovereign power of a God presents itself to my thought, I am constrained to confess it is easy to Him, if He wishes it, to cause me to err, even in what I think I intuit as evidently as possible by the eye of the mind [*etiam in iis quæ me puto mentis oculis quàm evidentissime intueri*]. [AT VII, 36; HR I, 158*]

Descartes presents a version of the Deceiver Hypothesis and claims that it gives him a reason to doubt simple necessary truths he intuits; intuition and clear and distinct perception are one and the same.

Those who embrace the principle that clear and distinct perceptions are always metaphysically certain interpret this passage in a different way. Kenny and Van Cleve say Descartes is not giving a reason to doubt particular clear and distinct perceptions; he is giving a reason to doubt the general principle that all clear and distinct perceptions are true.[11] Yet look at the passage. Descartes focuses on particular simple propositions in arithmetic and geometry, asks whether he has a reason to doubt them when he intuits them, and offers a version of the Deceiver Hypothesis. He does not even present the general principle that all clear and distinct perceptions are true. Moreover, how could he consistently claim that all his clear and distinct perceptions are metaphysically certain while admitting that it is a metaphysical possibility for him that some of them are false? The metaphysical possibility that some god gives him false clear and distinct perceptions should give him a reason to doubt some of his direct clear and distinct perceptions.[12]

In all, the Naive Immediate Inference Interpretation has serious problems. It ignores Descartes's insight that potential reasons for doubt entail that he thinks and exists; it makes use of the principle that clear and distinct perceptions are always metaphysically certain, which Descartes rejects. The two flaws are related. It is only when we interpret

11. Kenny, *Descartes*, pp. 183–184 and "The Cartesian Circle and the Eternal Truths," p. 689; Van Cleve, "Foundationalism, Epistemic Principles and the Cartesian Circle," pp. 66–69.

12. In the French edition, the reference to intuition at the end of the passage is replaced by one to propositions for which there is the greatest evidence: "les choses que je crois connaître avec une évidence très grande" [AT IX, 28]. Some may argue that direct clear and distinct perceptions do not fit this description, since they do not involve evidence, and hence that the change in wording shows that Descartes came to regard direct clear and distinct perceptions as capable of resisting the versions of the Deceiver Hypothesis. Consider John Morris, "A Plea for the French Descartes," *Dialogue*, 6 (September 1967), pp. 236–239. The argument ignores the fact that Descartes does not change the examples with which the passage begins. They are candidates for direct clear and distinct perception.

Some may object that my position on the metaphysical uncertainty of clear and distinct perception leaves Descartes twisting in the Cartesian Circle: he cannot rule out the Deceiver Hypothesis (those versions of it that cast doubt on clear and distinct perception) unless he becomes metaphysically certain that God exists. He cannot become metaphysically certain of that unless he becomes metaphysically certain of the premises in his proof of God's existence. He cannot become metaphysically certain of those premises unless he becomes metaphysically certain of some simple necessary truths by direct clear and distinct perception. He cannot do that unless he rules out the Deceiver Hypothesis (those versions of it that cast doubt on clear and distinct perception). I think Descartes's philosophy contains this problem; it represents his inability to gain metaphysical certainty of matters beyond his thought and existence and is one of the most important things we can learn from him.

Descartes as thinking that some clear and distinct perceptions are metaphysically uncertain that we face the question: Why does he think his clear and distinct perceptions that he thinks and that he exists are metaphysically certain when others are not? It is only when we raise this question that we are in a position to appreciate Descartes's insight that hypotheses that cast doubt on some of his clear and distinct perceptions do not cast doubt on his clear and distinct perception of his thought and existence because they entail that he thinks and exists.

Edwin Curley's response to the *cogito* puzzle emphasizes Descartes's insight that reasons for doubt entail that he thinks and exists. Curley's interpretation illustrates the problems we face when we try to combine this piece of the puzzle with the others, even if we decide some clear and distinct perceptions are metaphysically uncertain. According to Curley,

> [A] reasonable ground for doubting a proposition must offer some expla-
> nation of how it is that we might erroneously believe the proposition
> even if the explanation is only conjectural.
>
> That is why "I exist" survives the systematic doubt. Set up any skep-
> tical hypothesis you like—that I am deceived by my senses, that I am
> dreaming, that I am deceived by an omnipotent demon or any other
> you can imagine. Each of these hypotheses involves, in one way or
> another, the supposition that I am thinking. And it must involve that
> supposition if it is to explain how my thinking might be erroneous, and
> so satisfy the conditions for being a reasonable ground of doubt. But that
> supposition entails my existence.[13]

Curley gives a similar interpretation to Descartes's claim to be meta-physically certain he thinks: "For it seems to me that the claim of 'I think' to be a first principle can be defended in the same way that the claim of 'I exist' can, that is, a proposition entailing 'I think' is a common element in any reasonable skeptical hypothesis which might be invoked as a ground for doubting that I think."[14] In short, Descartes is metaphysically certain that he thinks and that he exists because every potential reason for doubt entails those propositions.

What about the rest of the puzzle: Descartes's references to clear and

13. Edwin Curley, *Descartes against the Skeptics* (Cambridge: Harvard University Press, 1978), p. 86.
14. Curley, *Descartes against the Skeptics*, p. 88.

distinct perception and to an inference from thought to existence? Curley ignores the role of clear and distinct perception. Indeed, there is no room for it in his interpretation, since the entailment relation between potential reasons for doubt and Descartes's belief that he thinks and exists is independent of any act of clear and distinct perception Descartes performs. Curley tries to make room for Descartes's talk of an inference. The dictum "I think, therefore, I am" is Descartes's way of saying that every potential reason for doubt entails that he exists by entailing that he thinks: "So 'I exist' is inferred from 'I think.' But 'I think' is not a premise of a proof. It is, rather, an essential element in any hypothesis which might cast reasonable doubt on my existence."[15] This does not work. Descartes claims that the insight contained in "I think, therefore I am" is contained in any conditional in which he infers his existence from a true description of his thought, for example, "I seem to see light, therefore I am" [*Principles*, I, ix; AT VIII, 7–8; HR I, 222]. The proposition that Descartes seems to see light is not an essential element of any hypothesis that gives him a reason for doubt.

Here, then, is our problem. If we concentrate on Descartes's talk of clear and distinct perception and an inference, we risk ignoring his discovery that some clear and distinct perceptions are metaphysically uncertain and his insight that potential reasons for doubt entail that he thinks and exists. If we concentrate on Descartes's view that some clear and distinct perceptions are metaphysically uncertain and his insight about the implications of potential reasons for doubt, we risk leaving out his references to clear and distinct perception and an inference. It may be tempting to solve this puzzle with a knife: Descartes has two explanations of why he is metaphysically certain that he thinks and exists; one affirms the metaphysical certainty of all clear and distinct perceptions and uses an inference from thought to existence, while the other denies the metaphysical certainty of some clear and distinct perceptions and uses the insight that potential reasons for doubt entail that he thinks and exists.[16] There is no need for such drastic measures.

---

15. Curley, *Descartes against the Skeptics*, p. 86.

16. Curley may split Descartes's position in something like this way. When he presents the interpretation I have just sketched, he also says Descartes "sometimes is tempted" to think he gains metaphysical certainty he exists by an inference from metaphysically certain premises about his mental state; *Descartes against the Skeptics*, p. 88.

We can assemble all the pieces of the puzzle if we look at them in the context of Descartes's views about certainty.

A Solution to the *Cogito* Puzzle

I argue in Chapter 2 that Descartes's claim (P1) to be metaphysically certain he thinks has two parts: He is morally certain he thinks, and he has no reason to doubt his morally certain belief that he thinks.[17] His claim (P2) to be metaphysically certain he exists is similarly complex: He is morally certain he exists, and he has no reason to doubt his morally certain belief that he exists.

Since Descartes's claims are complex, his defense of them must be so, too. He must explain what makes him morally certain he thinks and exists and why no hypothesis casts doubt on those morally certain beliefs. Descartes's references to clear and distinct perception and an inference from thought to existence contain the makings of the first part of his defense. His insight that potential reasons for doubt entail that he thinks and exists contains the makings of the second part. Descartes does not give different explanations of why he is metaphysically certain he thinks and exists. He emphasizes different parts of his explanation in different places. The way to solve the *cogito* puzzle is to bring all the parts to the fore and see how they work together.

The Defense of P1 and P2 (Part One)

1. All my clear and distinct perceptions are morally certain.
2. I clearly and distinctly perceive directly that I think.
3. I clearly and distinctly perceive deductively that I exist, by inferring immediately that I exist from the premise that I think.
4. Therefore, I am morally certain that I think and that I exist.

I have recast the Naive Immediate Inference Interpretation as an account of Descartes's *moral* certainty of his thought and existence. All the advantages of that interpretation remain. I can explain Descartes's references in the *Meditations* to clear and distinct perception as a

17. Some of the material in this section appeared in my "The *Cogito* Puzzle," *Philosophy and Phenomenological Research*, 43 (September 1982), pp. 59–81.

source of his metaphysical certainty: to be metaphysically certain that he thinks and exists, he must be morally certain of those facts; direct clear and distinct perception makes him morally certain of the former and deductive clear and distinct perception of the latter. I can explain his frequent references to an inference from thought to existence: he clearly and distinctly perceives that he exists by immediately deducing that fact from his direct clear and distinct perception that he thinks. I can make sense of Descartes's remarks to the Marquis of Newcastle and to Mersenne on the inferential yet intuitive nature of his knowledge: he gains moral certainty that he exists in a deductive clear and distinct perception in which he grasps the entire inference, "I think, therefore I am," in one mental act.

I interpret Descartes as adopting

EP14: If S clearly and distinctly perceives that p, then S is morally certain that p.

Descartes never explicitly states this principle, but it gives us a way to understand the relation between clear and distinct perception and his moral certainty that he thinks and exists. It is consistent with his view that some clear and distinct perceptions are metaphysically uncertain.

Descartes still has to show that he has no reason to doubt his morally certain beliefs that he thinks and exists; why do they resist all reasons for doubt, when other clear and distinct perceptions succumb? This is where his insight into the implications of potential reasons for doubt comes into play. He presents it most clearly in the *Meditations*, where he concentrates on the topic of reasons for doubt.

At the start of Meditation Two, Descartes reflects on the results he has obtained so far:

But I was persuaded that there was nothing in all the world, that there was no heaven, no earth, that there were no minds, nor any bodies: was I not then likewise persuaded that I did not exist? Not at all; of a surety I myself did exist since I persuaded myself of something. [AT VII, 25; HR I, 150]

In pointing out that his being persuaded of something entails his existence, he calls attention to the sort of inference by which he gains moral certainty he exists. (His intention is clearer in the French text

[AT IX, 19], where he says his thinking of something entails his existing.) He next explains why his belief that he exists resists the major reason for doubt of Meditation One:

> But there is some deceiver or other, very powerful and very cunning, who ever employs his ingenuity in deceiving me. Then without doubt I exist also if he deceives me, and let him deceive me as much as he will, he can never cause me to be nothing so long as I think that I am something. [AT VII, 25; HR I, 150]

The hypothesis that some god deceives him just entails that he exists. Descartes concludes:

> So that after having reflected well and carefully examined all things, we must come to the definite conclusion that this proposition: I am, I exist, is necessarily true each time that I pronounce it, or that I mentally conceive it. [AT VII, 25; HR I, 150]

Descartes sometimes says that a proposition is necessarily true when he obviously intends to say that it is a metaphysical certainty for him [*Meditations*; AT VII, 27; HR I, 152]; I think this is what he is doing here. His point is that there is no way his assertion or belief that he exists can be mistaken, or more precisely, it is a metaphysical certainty. Indeed, in the next paragraph, in the French text [AT IX, 19; HR I, 150], he describes himself as "I who am certain that I am."

Descartes repeats his position at the end of Meditation Two:

> What then, I who seem to perceive this piece of wax so distinctly, do I not know myself . . . with much more truth and certainty? . . . If I judge that the wax exists from the fact that I touch it, the same thing will follow, to wit, that I am; and if I judge that my imagination, or some other cause, whatever it is, persuades me that the wax exists, I shall still conclude the same. And what I have here remarked of wax may be applied to all other things which are external to me. [AT VII, 33; HR I, 156]

Descartes offers two points in defense of the claim that he is more certain of his own existence than that of the wax. First, his evidence for the wax's existence is evidence for his own. Both beliefs, we may say, are made morally certain by sensation reports of what he seems to experience. Second, hypotheses about his imagination or some other cause deceiving him give him reason to doubt his morally certain belief in the wax's existence, but not his morally certain belief in his own; they just entail that he exists.

Descartes's argument needs tightening. At the beginning and end of Meditation Two, he indicates the inference that makes him morally certain he exists, claims that some hypotheses about his being deceived do not cast doubt on his existence because they entail he exists, and decides he has no reason to doubt his existence. He needs to show that *no* metaphysically possible hypothesis indicates how his belief that he exists might be false despite the evidence that he thinks. He needs to show that *no* metaphysically possible hypothesis indicates how his belief that he thinks might be false despite his direct clear and distinct perception that he thinks.

We have seen one principle he can use:

> EP13: q indicates to S how S's morally certain belief p might be false despite S's evidence for p only if (1) it is logically necessary that p, or (2) it is logically possible that q is true and p is false.

EP13, based on the idea that we do not give someone a reason to doubt a contingent moral certainty by citing a hypothesis that entails it, explains why some hypotheses do not cast doubt on Descartes's *de se* beliefs that he thinks and exists. Consider the hypothesis he would express by "Some god deceives me" if he assigned 'me' the same individual concept he assigns 'I' in "I exist" and "I think" (say, the individual concept of being him). That hypothesis cannot be true unless something satisfies that individual concept and thinks; that is, unless the propositions he would express by "I exist" and "I think" are true.

What about the hypotheses Descartes would express by "Some god deceives the greatest seventeenth-century philosopher" and "Some god deceives everyone?" These do not entail that Descartes himself exists and thinks. I believe he can best rule them out by

> EP15: q indicates to S how S's morally certain belief p might be false despite S's evidence for p only if (1) q entails that proposition that is the content of S's *de se* belief that S exists, and (2) q entails that proposition that is the content of S's *de se* belief that S thinks.

No hypothesis gives Descartes a reason to doubt his beliefs unless the information it contains includes the content of his *de se* belief that he exists and the content of his *de se* belief that he thinks. The first condition in EP15 is based on the idea that each person must relate a metaphysical possibility to himself before it gives him a reason to doubt. A person relates a metaphysical possibility to himself by making his existence part of the metaphysical possibility. He does this by formulating the metaphysically possible hypothesis so that it includes the content of his *de se* belief that he exists. The hypotheses Descartes would express by "Some god deceives the greatest seventeenth-century philosopher" and "Some god deceives everyone" do not give him a reason to doubt his beliefs, but the ones he would express by "Some god deceives the greatest seventeenth-century philosopher *and I am that philosopher*" and "Some god deceives everyone *and I am some-one*" do. The second requirement in EP15 is based on the idea that all our reasons for doubt must include the information that our intellectual abilities are leading us astray, either due to their own intrinsic limitations or to someone's manipulation of them, and any hypothesis to that effect will include the information that we think. I believe Descartes would accept EP15. He sticks to hypotheses that satisfy it throughout the *Meditations* and, in particular, in the Meditation Two passages we have just examined and the Meditation Five list of reasons for doubt [AT VII, 70–71; HR I, 184–185].

The Defense of P1 and P2 (Part Two)

1. I have reason to doubt my morally certain beliefs that I think or that I exist only if a metaphysically possible hypothesis indicates how my belief that I think might be false despite my direct clear and distinct perception of it or how my belief that I exist might be false despite my evidence that I think.   [from D3]
2. A hypothesis indicates how my morally certain belief that I think might be false only if it does not entail the content of my belief and does entail the content of my belief.   [from EP13 and EP15]
3. A hypothesis indicates how my morally certain belief that I exist might be false only if it does not entail the content of my belief and does entail the content of my belief.   [from EP13 and EP15]
4. I have no reason to doubt my morally certain belief that I think or my morally certain belief that I exist.   [from 1, 2, and 3]

5. Therefore, I am metaphysically certain that I think and that I exist. [from 4 and EP1]

It is important to note two points here. First, see how the second part of Descartes's defense of P1 and P2 is based on his position about the content of his *de se* attitudes. Some hypotheses, for example, the one Descartes would express by "Some god deceives everyone," do not give him a reason to doubt his thought and existence, because they are not about him *in the appropriate way*. They do not entail his *de se* beliefs that he thinks and exists. They do not entail those beliefs because they do not contain the individual concept by which he individuates himself in his *de se* attitudes. Other hypotheses, for example, the one Descartes would express by "Some god deceives me," are about him in the appropriate way. Yet they do not cast doubt on his *de se* beliefs that he thinks and exists because they entail those beliefs. They entail those beliefs in part because they contain the individual concept by which Descartes individuates himself in his *de se* attitudes. Second, this formulation of Descartes's defense of P1 and P2 does justice to his insight that potential reasons for doubt entail that he thinks and exists, and it does so without diminishing the significance of clear and distinct perception and the inference from thought to existence.

This is my solution to the *cogito* puzzle. I want to develop it by considering Descartes's claim to be metaphysically certain of specific propositions about the content of his mental state, such as that he seems to see light. I also want to take a closer look at clear and distinct perception and its central role in Descartes's Gambit. Before I do these things, though, I need to consider some objections to what I have said so far. There is no point in going further if I am on the wrong track.

Objections to the Interpretation

What are we to make of Descartes's statement in the *Principles:*

When I stated that this proposition *I think, therefore I am* is the first and most certain which presents itself to those who philosophise in orderly fashion, I did not for all that deny that we must first of all know *what is knowledge, what is existence, and what is certainty,* and that *in order to think we must be,* and such like. [I, x; AT VIII, 8; HR I, 222]

Is Descartes not saying he must be metaphysically certain that whatever thinks exists before he can be metaphysically certain that he exists, and does this not show that he uses the general proposition as a premise in his inference from thought to existence? Perhaps he does not *immediately* deduce his existence from his thought after all.

Descartes says he must know what knowledge, existence, and certainty are and that whatever thinks exists, before he can do something else. What he means by "know" and what he takes the something else to be are unclear. We will make a hash of his remark if we take him to be saying that, in order to be metaphysically certain he exists, he must first be metaphysically certain what knowledge, existence, and certainty are and that whatever thinks exists. He surely does not need to be metaphysically certain what knowledge and certainty are to be metaphysically certain he exists.[18]

I believe that Descartes's point is that he must know with moral certainty what knowledge, existence, and certainty are and that whatever thinks exists in order to know with moral certainty his account of why he is metaphysically certain he exists. He is not offering the principle that whatever thinks exists as part of his evidence for his belief that he exists. He is offering it as part of his account of why his evidence—that he thinks—makes him metaphysically certain he exists. Part of his account is that he infers his existence from his thinking; part is that hypotheses about his being deceived entail that he thinks and thereby that he exists. Note that it is enough for Descartes to be *morally* certain of his account of why he is metaphysically certain he thinks and exists; the premises and conclusions in his two-part defense of P1 and P2 do not have to be metaphysical certainties, any more than the premises and conclusions of the Dream and Deceiver Arguments for P3 must be. All he requires is that his premises and conclusions be reasonable from the standard epistemic perspective. Once it is reason-

18. Commentators who nonetheless read Descartes in this way include Frankfurt, *Demons, Dreamers and Madmen,* p. 96; Curley, *Descartes against the Skeptics,* p. 90; Bernard Williams, *Descartes: The Project of Pure Inquiry* (New York: Penguin Books, 1978), pp. 90–91; and Wilson, *Descartes,* p. 57.

able for him to believe he is metaphysically certain he thinks and exists, it is reasonable, given his adoption of the Cartesian imperative, for him to list that he thinks and that he exists under the heading of 'science.'

We should also keep in mind Descartes's reply to Mersenne, which is worth quoting again:

> He who says, '*I think, hence I am, or exist*' does not deduce existence from thought by a syllogism, but, by a simple act of mental vision, recognises it as if it were a thing that is known *per se*. This is evident from the fact that if it were syllogistically deduced, the major premise, *that everything that thinks is, or exists*, would have to be known previously; but yet that has rather been learned from the experience of the individual—that unless he exists he cannot think. For our mind is so constituted by nature that general propositions are formed out of the knowledge of particular ones. [*Reply to the Second Objections*; AT VII, 140–141; HR II, 38*]

There is no way to reconcile Descartes's position here with his remark in the *Principles* if we take the message of the latter to be that the general principle that whatever thinks exists is an essential part of his evidence for his existence.[19]

Descartes could use some other proposition to join his premise that he thinks to his conclusion that he exists, for example, that it is logically necessary that whatever thinks exists; that if he thinks, then he exists.[20] These additional premises, like the general principle that whatever thinks exists, are all objects of clear and distinct perception, however, and we have seen that in Meditation Three Descartes admits

---

19. Burman (*Conversation*, AT V, 147) reports that Descartes explains the relation between his reply to Mersenne and his remark in the *Principles* by drawing a distinction between explicit knowledge and implicit knowledge. When he explicitly knows that he thinks and therefore exists, he only implicitly knows that whatever thinks exists. The difference between explicit and implicit knowledge escapes me; it may or may not be related to the points I have made. One thing is clear: if Burman is to be trusted, Descartes does not believe he must know that whatever thinks exists, in the same way he must know that he thinks, in order to be metaphysically certain that he exists. That whatever thinks exists is not an equally essential part of his inference from thought to existence.

20. Consider, for instance, F. Aliqué, *La découverte métaphysique de l'homme chez Descartes* (Paris: Presses Universitaires de France, 1950), p. 152; Williams, *Descartes*, p. 91.

that he has a reason to doubt such propositions. No metaphysically uncertain premise is an essential part of the evidence that makes him metaphysically certain he exists.

I may seem to be digging Descartes's grave. Commentators have been quick to criticize any even apparent attempt on his part to infer his existence immediately from the premise that he thinks. Let us take a look at their objections.

Margaret Wilson asserts that the immediate inference lacks "formal validity."[21] Her point is not that the premise fails to entail the conclusion or that the immediate inference is not an instance of a valid argument form in any formal system. The premise entails the conclusion. The immediate inference is valid in first-order quantification theories with existential presuppositions (those in which all constants refer to actually existing entities). Wilson's point is that the immediate inference is not valid in first-order quantification theories without existential presuppositions (those in which some constants do not refer to actually existing entities). Wilson is right, but why must Descartes use an inference valid in formal systems without existential presuppositions to gain metaphysical certainty that he exists? She does not say, except to note that some of Descartes's mathematical claims and his argument in Meditation Five for God's existence can only be correctly translated into such systems. That some of Descartes's arguments and claims can only be correctly translated into a particular type of system does not commit him to only giving arguments valid in that type of system.

Jaakko Hintikka thinks the immediate inference is question begging because it is only valid in formal systems with existential presuppositions: Descartes must interpret his premise that he thinks so it entails that he exists, but then the premise presupposes his existence, and he can only know it if he already knows he exists.[22] The flaw in Hintikka's criticism has already been exposed.[23] He relies on the principle that if *p* entails *q*, we cannot know *p* without first knowing *q*, which falsely implies that we never get knowledge by valid deductive reasoning.

Edwin Curley advises caution at this point: "Still, I am not sure that

21. Wilson, *Descartes*, p. 55; consider too Kenny, *Descartes*, pp. 169–170.

22. Jaakko Hintikka, "*Cogito, Ergo Sum*: Inference or Performance," *Philosophical Review*, 71 (January 1962), pp. 7–8.

23. Consider, for example, Wilson, *Descartes*, p. 63.

Descartes would feel that he could take it for granted that some deductive reasoning is probative. As we have seen above, criticisms of the syllogism like Mill's had been raised by the skeptics as early as Sextus Empiricus, repeated by the Renaissance skeptics, and apparently accepted by Descartes himself in the *Regulae*. If Descartes would have taken Hintikka's objection seriously, that is reason enough for us to do so.[24] Do Descartes's criticisms of syllogistic reasoning commit him to Hintikka's position, with its implication that we do not gain knowledge by deductive reasoning? Descartes does not think so. Just before he criticizes syllogistic reasoning, he says:

> Hence we must give ourselves practice first in those easier disciplines, but methodically, so that by open and familiar ways we may ceaselessly accustom ourselves to penetrate as easily as though we were at play into the very heart of these subjects. For by this means *we shall afterwards gradually feel (and in a space of time shorter than we could at all hope for) that we are in a position with equal facility to deduce from evident first principles many propositions which at first sight are highly intricate and difficult.* [*Rules*, X; AT X, 405; HR I, 32; my emphasis]

After he presents his criticisms of syllogistic reasoning, he says:

> Mankind has no road towards certain knowledge open to it, save those of self-evident intuition and *necessary deduction.* [*Rules*, XII; AT X, 425; HR I, 45; my emphasis]

Descartes thus treats deductive reasoning as a source of knowledge both before and after his attack on syllogisms. He aims his attack at dialecticians who

> prescribe certain formulae of argument, which lead to a conclusion with such necessity that, if the reason commits itself to their trust, even though it slackens its interest and no longer pays a heedful and close attention to the very proposition inferred, it can nevertheless at the same time come to a sure conclusion by virtue of the form of the argument alone. [*Rules*, X; AT X, 405–406; HR I, 32]

24. Curley, *Descartes against the Skeptics*, p. 81. Wilson raises the issue in a footnote, *Descartes*, p. 229.

These dialecticians miss the fact that

> this style of argument contributes nothing at all to the discovery of
> truth, [for] the Dialecticians are unable to devise any syllogism which
> has a true conclusion, unless they have first secured the material out of
> which to construct it, i.e. unless they have already ascertained the very
> truth which is deduced in that syllogism. [*Rules*, X; AT X, 406; HR I,
> 32]

Descartes's remark is vague, and, if we read it out of context, it is
tempting to take him to be saying that no deductive argument is a
source of knowledge because, if p entails q, we cannot know p unless
we first know q. Yet that is clearly not what he intends to say; we have
just seen his belief that deductions provide knowledge. It seems likely
that Descartes is concerned with syllogisms in which a general and a
particular premise yield a particular conclusion, ones like

   i. All men are mortal.
   ii. Socrates is a man.
   iii. Therefore, Socrates is mortal.

Descartes is not objecting to the view that we can know that Socrates is
mortal by this argument, but to the view that, for every man there is,
we can know that he is mortal by this sort of inference. We know the
first premise only if there are some men we already know to be moral,
so where those men are concerned, we do not gain knowledge of their
mortality by this sort of inference. More generally, we cannot obtain
knowledge from scratch by using valid syllogistic forms like

   i. All M are P.
   ii. Some S is M.
   iii. Therefore, some S is P.

To know the universal premise we first must know some of its instances, and if we try to deduce those instances in an argument of this
form, we fall into circular reasoning.

Descartes makes this point elsewhere. Recall his reply to Mersenne
that he cannot gain knowledge that he exists by a syllogism because the
"mind is so constituted by nature that general propositions are formed

out of the knowledge of particular ones" [*Reply to the Second Objections*; AT VII, 140–141; HR I, 38]. When Gassendi objects that the inference "I think, therefore I am" contains the assumption that whatever thinks, exists, Descartes writes:

> The greater error here is our critic's assumption that the knowledge of particular truths is always deduced from universal propositions in consonance with the order of the sequence observed in the syllogism of dialectic. This shows that he is but little acquainted with the method by which truth should be investigated. For it is certain that in order to discover the truth we should always start with particular notions, in order to arrive at general conceptions subsequently, though we may also in the reverse way, after having discovered the universals, deduce other particulars from them. [*Letter to Clerselier*; AT IX, 205–206; HR II, 127]

Most important of all, if we read Descartes's objection to syllogistic reasoning as I suggest, he does not endorse the principle that, if p entails q, we cannot know p unless we already know q. He just affirms the weaker principle that, if p is a general proposition, we cannot know it unless we first know some of its instances.[25]

Two final criticisms might be directed against Descartes's immediate inference: (1) he cannot be morally certain that he exists solely on the evidence that he thinks without such additional evidence as that whatever thinks exists; (2) even if his immediate inference gives him moral certainty of his existence, the mere evidence that he thinks does not place his belief in his existence beyond rational doubt. Yet Descartes's sensation reports give him moral certainty about the external world, so his sensation report that he thinks should be able to make him morally certain he exists, and I have explained why Descartes has no reason to doubt his existence without once extending his evidence beyond the single premise that he thinks.

25. Curley, *Descartes against the Skeptics*, pp. 27–28, seems to think that Descartes may not adopt this weaker principle unless he also adopts the stronger one. I fail to see why, and Curley does not explain his claim. I do not endorse Descartes's objection to syllogistic reasoning, as I interpret it, or even claim that it is consistent with the rest of his philosophy. (How can he combine it with his view that we can know general mathematical truths, e.g., all squares have four sides, without knowing any of their instances, e.g., some squares have four sides.) My only claim is that Descartes does not commit himself to the principle that if p entails q, we cannot know p unless we already know q.

Cogitatio Propositions

Thought takes many forms: affirmation, denial, hope, and more. Descartes believes he can be metaphysically certain what form his thoughts take just as he can be metaphysically certain that he thinks:

> I am the same who feels, that is to say, who perceives certain things, as by the organs of sense, since in truth I see light, I hear noise, I feel heat. But it will be said that these phenomena are false and that I am dreaming. Let it be so; still it is at least quite certain that it seems to me that I see light, that I hear noise and that I feel heat. That cannot be false; properly speaking it is what is in me called feeling; and used in this precise sense that is no other thing than thinking. [*Meditations*; AT VII, 29; HR I, 153]

Propositions about the form of his thought can replace the one that he thinks as his evidence for believing he exists.

> For if I say I see, or I walk, I therefore am, and if by seeing and walking I mean the action of my eyes or my legs, which is the work of my body, my conclusion is not absolutely certain; because it may be that, as often happens in sleep, I think I see or I walk, although I never open my eyes or move from my place, and the same thing perhaps might occur if I had not a body at all. But if I mean only to talk of my sensation, or my consciously seeming to see or to walk, it becomes quite true because my assertion now refers only to my mind, which alone is concerned with my feeling or thinking that I see and I walk. [*Principles*, I, ix; AT VIII, 7–8; HR I, 222]

Descartes's position is limited in several ways. He is not saying that any proposition about his mental state—even the one he would express by "The greatest seventeenth-century philosopher seems to see light"—is a metaphysical certainty for him when he believes it. He is only concerned with those that can be the content of a *de se* belief. Even within that group he is selective. The propositions he would express by "I doubt" and "I seem to see light" qualify; those he would express by "I am awake" and "I am not deceived by a god" do not. I shall call the ones that interest Descartes '*cogitatio* propositions.' His claim is that all his *cogitatio* beliefs are metaphysically certain for him. Whenever he believes he seems to see light, his belief is maximally reasonable.

Descartes never explains exactly which propositions are *cogitatio* propositions or why they are metaphysically certain whenever he believes them. He seems to think these points are as self-evident as the propositions themselves, and his contemporary critics did not push the issue. Recent sceptics have been less polite. Keith Lehrer offers a space-age version of the Deceiver Hypothesis as a reason to doubt *cogitatio* beliefs:

> The kind *K* of basic beliefs may be specified differently by philosophers of different epistemic biases, which already offers succor to the sceptic, but the dogmatists have generally agreed that at least some kinds of perceptual beliefs, memory beliefs and beliefs concerning our conscious states are among them.
>
> Now it is not at all difficult to conceive of some hypothesis that would yield the conclusion that beliefs of the kind in question are not justified, indeed, which if true would justify us in concluding that the beliefs in question were more often false than true. The sceptical hypothesis might run as follows. There are a group of creatures in another galaxy, call them Googols, whose intellectual capacity is 10^{100} that of men, and who amuse themselves by sending out a peculiar kind of wave that affects our brain in such a way that our beliefs about the world are mostly incorrect. This form of error infects beliefs of every kind, but most of our beliefs, though erroneous, are nevertheless very nearly correct. This allows us to survive and manipulate our environment.[26]

Descartes cannot meet Lehrer's objection by the same moves he used to establish his metaphysical certainty that he thinks and exists. Direct clear and distinct perception may make each of his true *cogitatio* beliefs a moral certainty, but not every potential reason for doubt entails every *cogitatio* belief. That some god, or Googol, deceives Descartes entails that he thinks, but not that he seems to see light.

Descartes needs to supplement EP13 and EP15 with a principle that handles the case of *cogitatio* beliefs:

> EP16: *q* indicates to *S* how *S*'s morally certain belief *p* might be false
> despite *S*'s evidence for *p* only if either (1) it is logically necessary

26. Keith Lehrer, "Why Not Scepticism?" in *Essays on Knowledge and Justification*, ed. George Pappas and Marshall Swain (Ithaca: Cornell University Press, 1978), p. 356. Lehrer's paper originally appeared in *Philosophical Forum*, 2:3 (1971), pp. 283–298.

that p, or (2) it is logically possible that q is true, S believes p, and p is false.

The idea is simple. To indicate to someone how one of his contingent moral certainties might be false, we must cite a hypothesis that indicates how he could have been misled, how he could have come to believe the proposition when it was false. We do not do this by citing a hypothesis that combines with the supposition that he has his belief to entail that his belief is true; all this does is indicate another way his belief might be true.

Descartes can use EP16 to defend the metaphysical certainty of *cogitatio* beliefs:

A *Defense of* Cogitatio *Propositions*

1. Suppose I believe that I seem to see light.
2. My belief that I seem to see light is incorrigible (it is logically impossible that I believe that I seem to see light but do not seem to see light).
3. I correctly believe that I seem to see light.   [from 1 and 2]
4. I clearly and distinctly perceive directly that I seem to see light.   [from 3]
5. I am morally certain that I seem to see light.   [from 4 and EP14]
6. I have a reason to doubt that I seem to see light only if some hypothesis q is such that it is logically possible that (1) q is true, (2) I believe that I seem to see light, and (3) I do not seem to see light.   [from D3 and EP16]
7. I have no reason to doubt that I seem to see light.   [from 2 and 6]
8. Therefore, whenever I believe that I seem to see light, I am metaphysically certain that I seem to see light.   [from 1, 5, 7, and EP1]

The argument starts with the assumption that Descartes believes he seems to see light. According to the second premise, he cannot be mistaken in his belief. The third premise follows from the first two, and the fourth follows from the third by the assumption that whenever Descartes seems to see light and considers whether he does, he has a direct clear and distinct perception that he does. This assumption is, I think, part of what Descartes has in mind when he tells Mersenne, "Thought is a word that covers everything that exists in us in such a way that we are immediately conscious of it" [*Reply to The Second Objections*; AT VII, 160; HR II, 52]. Premise (5) follows from the principle (EP14) that all clear and distinct perceptions are morally certain. Premise (6) follows from the definition of a reason for doubt (D3) and the epistemic principle just introduced to help govern reasons for doubt (EP16). Descartes can combine premise (6) with his claim that he cannot be mistaken in his belief, premise (2), to conclude, in lines (7) and (8), that he has no reason to doubt, and so is metaphysically certain of, his belief. He can repeat the argument for any other proposition he takes to be a *cogitatio* proposition.

Let me emphasize that Descartes never gives this argument; it is my best attempt to plug another hole in his boat. His critics are bound to say it leaks. They will, of course, deny that his belief is incorrigible. Lehrer writes:

> The best candidates for such incorrigible beliefs are ones concerning one's present sensations or thoughts. But it is logically possible for such beliefs to be mistaken. Consider sensations first. Suppose it is affirmed that if a person believes that he is having sensation S, a pain for example, then it is logically impossible that such a belief should be mistaken. This is not so. One might believe one is having a sensation S, a pain for example, because one is having a different sensation, S*, an itch for example, and one has mistaken S* for S, that is, one has mistaken an itch for a pain. How could this happen? It might happen either because of some general belief, to wit, that itches are pains, which one has been led to believe by some authority, or one may simply be misled on this occasion because one has been told by some authority that one will experience a pain. In short, one might have some false belief which together with the sensation of an itch produces the belief that one is in pain. Beliefs about sensations can be inferential, and one can infer that one is in a conscious state that one is not in by inferring from some false belief that this is so.[27]

Descartes might try to tough it out in reply: Lehrer's case cannot happen. If the person is not in pain, then he does not believe he is; he may have a belief he expresses by the words "I am in pain," but the content of his belief is not that he is in pain, since he clearly does not understand what a pain is. Descartes might also weaken his position: if we believe a *cogitatio* proposition and our belief is true and noninferential, then it is a metaphysical certainty for us. He can defend this position by a new principle about rational doubt:

---

27. Lehrer, "Why Not Scepticism?" pp. 351–352; consider too Kathryn Parsons, "Mistaking Sensations," *Philosophical Review*, 79 (1970), pp. 201–213.

EP16(a): q indicates to S how S's morally certain noninferential belief that p might be false despite S's evidence for p only if either (1) it is logically necessary that p, or (2) it is logically possible that q is true, S believes p noninferentially, and p is false.

He can use a weakened incorrigibility thesis that if we noninferentially believe a *cogitatio* proposition, then the proposition must be true. Lehrer's counterexample will not apply to this thesis.

It is important to note that even if we reject Descartes's position on *cogitatio* judgments—and perhaps we should—it does not follow that we should reject his defense of P1, that he is metaphysically certain he thinks. His defense of P1 rests on two claims: (1) in the particular case at hand, he is noninferentially morally certain that he thinks, and (2) no hypothesis indicates to him how his belief that he thinks might be false. To accept the first is not to say we are always right about the content of our mental state; to accept the second is unavoidable.

Clear and Distinct Perception: A Problem

Clear and distinct perception comes to the fore in Descartes's defense of P1 and P2. He presents his clear and distinct perception that he thinks and that he exists as the source of his justification for believing those propositions. The more we know about clear and distinct perception, the more we can understand his overall position.

We have been working with a partial account since Chapter 2. Truths about the content of our mental state and simple necessary truths are such that we need only apprehend them to "see" they are true; they are the objects of direct clear and distinct perception. Other propositions—that we exist, that God exists, complex necessary truths, and more—can be deduced from direct clear and distinct perceptions; this is deductive clear and distinct perception. Clear and distinct perception has miraculous results. Whatever we clearly and distinctly perceive is true, psychologically certain, and morally certain for us. It is our only source of metaphysical certainty. Clear and distinct perceptions that only concern the content of our mental state and the fact of our existence are always metaphysically certain; those that contain more information are metaphysically uncertain until we rule out such reasons for doubt as the Deceiver Hypothesis of Meditation Three.

Yet what is it to perceive a proposition clearly and distinctly? When we perceive a proposition in this way, we consider it; but that is not all, since not every proposition we consider is true, psychologically certain, and morally certain for us. So what plus consideration equals clear and distinct perception?[28]

Descartes indicates in the *Principles* [I, xlv; AT VIII, 21–22; HR I, 237] that the concept of a clear and distinct perception can be analyzed into that of a clear perception and that of a distinct perception, and that distinctness can itself be defined by clarity. He also writes of degrees of clarity and distinctness. All this suggests that we proceed as follows. Define what it is to perceive a proposition with a particular degree of clarity, use that concept to define what it is to perceive a proposition with a particular degree of distinctness, use both concepts to define what it is to perceive a proposition with a particular degree of clarity and distinctness, and, finally, decide what degrees of clarity and distinctness are sufficient for truth, psychological certainty, and moral certainty and what degree is necessary for metaphysical certainty. No commentator has even come close to defining clear and distinct perception in this way. Descartes's remarks simply do not give us enough to go on.[29]

I want to try something else. Let us assume that a particular degree of clarity and distinctness is sufficient for truth, psychological certainty, and moral certainty and necessary for metaphysical certainty. Descartes's remarks permit this assumption. Can we give necessary and sufficient conditions for perceptions of that degree of clarity and dis-

---

28. This question is really only one of a family of questions, since, besides writing of his clear and distinct perception of propositions (e.g., *Discourse*; AT VI, 33; HR I, 102), Descartes also writes, without adequate explanation, of his clear and distinct perception of ideas (e.g., *Principles*, I, xlv–xlvi; AT VIII, 21–22; HR I, 237), of clear and distinct propositions (e.g., *Principles*, I, xxx; AT VIII, 17; HR I, 231), and of clear and distinct ideas (e.g., *Meditations*; AT VII, 46; HR I, 166). I concentrate on the question of what it is to perceive a proposition clearly and distinctly because it is the one directly relevant to Descartes's defense of P1 and P2. Harry Frankfurt, *Demons, Dreamers and Madmen*, p. 131, thinks the clear and distinct perception of ideas "reduces" to that of propositions.

29. Two discussions of Descartes's suggestions about how to understand clear and distinct perception are Anthony Kenny's in *Descartes*, pp. 121–125, and Alan Gewirth's "Clearness and Distinctness in Descartes," in *Descartes: A Collection of Critical Essays*, ed. Willis Doney (New York: Doubleday, 1967). Gewirth's paper first appeared in *Philosophy*, 18 (April 1943), pp. 17–36. Gewirth offers a positive interpretation of Descartes's position after criticizing it, but I must confess that his interpretation eludes my comprehension.

tinctness using concepts we understand better than clear and distinct perception itself? If we can, we can at least explicate the sort of clear and distinct perception crucial to Descartes's defense of P1 and P2. Let us start with some explications that do not work to see what is required of one that does.

We might locate what is special about clear and distinct perception in the proposition perceived; that is, to have a clear and distinct perception is to consider a proposition with special intrinsic characteristics. What special intrinsic characteristics? The main options are these:

a. S clearly and distinctly perceives that p if and only if S considers that p and p is necessarily true.
b. S clearly and distinctly perceives that p if and only if S considers that p and p is logically possible.
c. S clearly and distinctly perceives that p if and only if S considers that p and p is true.

We can distinguish between direct and deductive clear and distinct perception in each case on the ground that some propositions can be considered without an act of inference while others cannot.

Each explication has a serious flaw. The first conflicts with Descartes's claim to perceive contingent propositions, for example, that he thinks, clearly and distinctly. The second makes absurd his association of clear and distinct perception with the truth. The third lets a lucky guess or "mere prejudice" be a clear and distinct perception. What is special about clear and distinct perception does not lie in the intrinsic characteristics of what is perceived. Descartes would, I think, admit that a person might consider a proposition without clearly and distinctly perceiving it and then later perceive it clearly and distinctly, even though it does not change any of its intrinsic traits. An atheist might consider and deny the proposition that God exists without perceiving it clearly and distinctly, only to later "see the light" and affirm it in an act of clear and distinct perception. The atheist's psychological and epistemic state will change, but the proposition will remain the same.[30]

---

30. Harry Frankfurt, *Demons, Dreamers and Madmen*, p. 124, tries to make the same point by a different example: I clearly and distinctly perceive that I am in pain while you apprehend that I am in pain but not clearly and distinctly; hence one and the same proposition is clearly and distinctly perceived by one of us but not by the other. Frankfurt overlooks the fact that in this case you and I apprehend different propositions; at least we do according to the position I attribute to Descartes in Chapter 3.

The special nature of clear and distinct perception lies in our relation to the perceived content, perhaps in our apprehension of its intrinsic traits. Commentators have flirted with

>   d. S clearly and distinctly perceives that p if and only if S apprehends that not-p is contradictory.[31]

Here the difference between direct and deductive clear and distinct perception presumably resides in whether we use an inference to apprehend that a proposition's denial is contradictory. But how are we to understand the concept of apprehension used in the explicans? If it amounts to mere consideration or even consideration plus belief, the explication makes it highly implausible that all clear and distinct perceptions are true. I might apprehend, in the sense of considering and believing, that a proposition's denial is contradictory, when, all the while, it is the proposition itself that is contradictory and false. If we are dealing with a form of apprehension that amounts to consideration plus *true* belief, the explication prohibits the clear and distinct perception of contingent propositions.

Similar problems are likely to infect any other attempt to explicate clear and distinct perception as the apprehension of a proposition's intrinsic traits. Suppose we try this:

>   e. S clearly and distinctly perceives that p if and only if S apprehends that p is true.

If the form of apprehension cited in the explicans is mere consideration or consideration plus belief, the explication makes it implausible that all clear and distinct perceptions are true. If it is consideration plus true belief, the explication fails to distinguish a lucky guess from a clear and distinct perception.

Harry Frankfurt thinks that clear and distinct perception involves our apprehension of our epistemic relation to a proposition: "When a person perceives something clearly and distinctly, his basis for believing it is so complete that no additional evidence could strengthen it. Since there is nothing further that he must consider, there is no reasonable basis for him to withhold assent or to doubt. His clear and

---

31. Margaret Wilson, *Descartes*, pp. 142–143.

distinct perception consists in the recognition that this is the case."[32]
When we perceive a proposition clearly and distinctly, we believe it,
consider our basis for believing it, and recognize (believe correctly)
that our basis for belief is enough to yield metaphysical certainty. All
this is the element of "clarity" in our perception. The element of
distinctness involves more: "A proposition is clearly perceived when
the perceiver recognizes that his evidential basis for it excludes all
reasonable grounds for doubting it. A perception is distinct, on the
other hand, when the perceiver understands what is and what is not
entailed by the evidential basis that renders his perception clear."[33]
Frankfurt realizes that we never isolate all the propositions entailed by
our evidence for a belief. He decides that our perception is distinct to
the extent that we do so and writes of perceptions being distinct to an
"appropriate degree"; that is, distinct enough to be sufficient for truth,
psychological certainty, and moral certainty and necessary for metaphysical certainty.[34] Frankfurt's proposal is best captured by this:

f. S clearly and distinctly perceives that p if and only if (1) S believes p, S
considers his basis for believing p, and S correctly believes that his
basis for believing p makes him metaphysically certain of p; and (2) if
q is S's basis for believing p, then (a) for an appropriate number of
propositions r entailed by q, S believes r is entailed by q, and (b) for an
appropriate number of propositions t not entailed by q, S believes t is
not entailed by q.

Our basis for believing a proposition can be other propositions, the
proposition itself, or an experience, according to Frankfurt.[35] When
we clearly and distinctly perceive a mathematical theorem by deducing
it from axioms, the axioms are our basis for believing the theorem.
When we clearly and distinctly perceive an axiom directly, the axiom
is our basis for belief. When we clearly and distinctly perceive directly
that we seem to see light, our experience of seeming to see light is our
basis.

Frankfurt's proposal has significant advantages over the others I have
presented. He allows for the clear and distinct perception of contingent

32. Harry Frankfurt, *Demons, Dreamers and Madmen*, p. 124.
33. Harry Frankfurt, *Demons, Dreamers and Madmen*, p. 137.
34. Harry Frankfurt, *Demons, Dreamers and Madmen*, pp. 144–145.
35. Harry Frankfurt, *Demons, Dreamers and Madmen*, p. 134.

propositions. He makes it plausible to think that all clear and distinct perceptions are true. He distinguishes lucky guesses from clear and distinct perceptions. He also runs into two new problems, because he explicates clear and distinct perception by metaphysical certainty. His explication implies that clear and distinct perceptions are always metaphysically certain: we have seen that Descartes thinks they sometimes are not. He undercuts Descartes's attempts to explain the metaphysical certainty of particular propositions by reference to clear and distinct perception. Recall this passage from Meditation Three:

> I am certain that I am a thing which thinks; but do I not then likewise know what is requisite to render me certain of a truth? Certainly in this first knowledge there is nothing that assures me of its truth, excepting the clear and distinct perception of that which I state. [AT VII, 35; HR I, 158]

On Frankfurt's interpretation, Descartes here tells us that he is metaphysically certain that he is a thinking thing because he correctly believes he is metaphysically certain that he is a thinking thing. That is no explanation at all. [36]

Clear and Distinct Perception: A Solution

The special character of clear and distinct perception does not reside in the intrinsic traits of the proposition considered, nor does it

---

36. I have ignored a further wrinkle some commentators add to our problem: how can we define clear and distinct perception so as to make it plausible (1) that all clear and distinct perceptions are true, and (2) that we can be metaphysically certain that we are having a clear and distinct perception whenever we have one? The former requires us to add a normative element to the definition; the latter requires us to delete any such element. Consider Gewirth, "Clearness and Distinctness in Descartes," p. 257. I do not think this dilemma is part of our problem, since I do not think Descartes generally needs to be metaphysically certain that he is having a clear and distinct perception. (There are exceptions noted in Chapters 6 and 7.) He would need such certainty if he wanted to gain metaphysical certainty by inferences of the form (i) I clearly and distinctly perceive that *p*; (ii) All my clear and distinct perceptions are true; (iii) Therefore, *p* is true. I do not think Descartes is very interested in such inferences. He treats clear and distinct perception as an activity that can produce his metaphysical certainty of a proposition. He does not see it as a state he can cite as evidence to make a proposition metaphysically certain for him.

reside in our apprehension of those traits or our recognition of the proposition's metaphysical certainty for us. Where does it reside?

Let us start with direct clear and distinct perception. Descartes limits this to simple necessary truths and true *cogitatio* propositions; what, if anything, do these have in common?

Simple necessary truths are

> so evident and at the same time so simple, that in their case we never doubt about believing them true: e.g. that I, while I think, exist; that what is once done cannot be undone, and other similar truths, about which clearly we can possess this certainty. For we cannot doubt them unless we think of them; but, it is assumed, we cannot think of them without at the same time believing them to be true. Hence we can never doubt them without at the same time believing them to be true; i.e. we can never doubt them. [*Reply to the Second Objections*; AT VII, 145–146; HR II, 42*]

We are naturally compelled to believe the simple necessary truths we consider, according to Descartes.

We are compelled to believe true *cogitatio* propositions in a similar way. Descartes writes in a letter of March 1638:

> When one says, 'I am breathing, therefore I exist,' if he wants to conclude his existence from the consideration that breathing cannot go on without the breather existing, his conclusion is of no value, since he would have to have proved already that it was true that he was breathing, and this is impossible, if he has not already proved that he exists. But if he wants to conclude his existence from the belief or opinion that he has that he is breathing, in the sense that, even if this opinion were not true, all the same one sees that it is impossible that one should have it, unless one existed, then his conclusion is very sound, since this opinion that we are breathing presents itself to our mind before that of our existence, and *we cannot doubt that we have the opinion while we have it*. [*Correspondence*; AT II, 37–38; my emphasis][37]

Descartes's talk of what we cannot doubt is ambiguous in this case. He may mean that when we believe we breathe, we are metaphysically certain we have that belief; this fits the context. He may mean that we

---

37. Bernard Williams's commentary, *Descartes: The Project of Pure Inquiry*, p. 94, brought this passage to my attention. I follow Williams's translation.

are compelled to believe we have that belief; this is what he actually says. I think he wants to make both points: Whenever we believe we breathe, we are metaphysically certain we have that belief; whenever we believe we breathe, we are compelled to believe we have that belief. We have to adjust this interpretation to allow for Descartes's remark in the *Discourse:*

> For since the act of thought by which we believe a thing is different from that by which we know that we believe it, the one often exists without the other. [AT VI, 23; HR I, 95]

We can allow for this remark by taking Descartes's position to be that if we have a belief, and *consider whether we have it*, we are compelled to believe that we have it.[38]

If we interpret Descartes as I suggest, we can explicate direct clear and distinct perception as follows.

> EP17: S clearly and distinctly perceives that *p* directly if and only if either (1) S noninferentially considers *p* and it is naturally necessary that if S noninferentially considers *p*, then S believes *p*, or (2) S noninferentially considers *p*, *p* is true, and it is naturally necessary that if S noninferentially considers *p* and *p* is true, then S believes *p*.

We clearly and distinctly perceive a simple necessary truth directly just when we consider it without deducing it from any other propositions and, as a result, are naturally compelled to believe it. We clearly and distinctly perceive a *cogitatito* proposition directly just when we consider it when it is true without deducing it from other propositions and, as a result, are naturally compelled to believe it.

---

38. Bernard Williams, *Descartes: The Project of Pure Inquiry*, pp. 77–84, 305–308, interprets Descartes as adopting an even stronger principle about *cogitatio* states and belief: It is logically necessary that whenever we are in one of these states, we believe we are in it. The passage I have just presented from the *Discourse* indicates that Descartes does not accept this principle, though he sometimes says things that come close to it. Edwin Curley discusses the relevant passages in detail in *Descartes against the Skeptics*, Chapter 7. Although Descartes's remarks are vague and sometimes seem to conflict, I think it is safe to say that he at least accepts the weak principle I attribute to him here.

Deductive clear and distinct perception can be given a similar explanation recursively:

> EP18: (1) If S considers the deduction of *p* from premises each of which S clearly and distinctly perceives directly, and it is naturally necessary that S believes *p* when S considers that deduction and clearly and distinctly perceives its premises directly, then S clearly and distinctly perceives *p* deductively; and
> (2) If S considers the deduction of *p* from premises each of which S clearly and distinctly perceives directly or deductively, and it is naturally necessary that S believes *p* when S considers that deduction and clearly and distinctly perceives its premises, then S clearly and distinctly perceives *p* deductively; and
> (3) S clearly and distinctly perceives *p* deductively only if S satisfies the conditions in (1) or (2) relative to *p*.

We clearly and distinctly perceive a proposition deductively just when we consider its deduction from premises we clearly and distinctly perceive and, as a result, are compelled to believe it.

EP17 and EP18 are not the sort of analytic definitions of clear and distinct perception Descartes says we can give. They just state necessary and sufficient conditions for clear and distinct perception in terms of other concepts in his philosophy that are easier to grasp. Their value is that they help us appreciate the claims about clear and distinct perception that are most important to Descartes's epistemology in general and to his theory of self-knowledge in particular.

Descartes says all clear and distinct perceptions are psychologically certain:

> I am of such a nature that as long as I understand anything very clearly and distinctly, I am naturally impelled to believe it to be true. [*Meditations*; AT VII, 69; HR I, 183]

> And even although I had not demonstrated this [that all our clear and distinct perceptions are true], the nature of my mind is such that I could not prevent myself from holding them [truths of mathematics] to be true so long as I conceive them clearly. [*Meditations*; AT VII, 65; HR I, 180]

EP17 and EP18 imply that we are naturally compelled to believe each proposition we clearly and distinctly perceive, and as Descartes indi-

cates here, the contingent nature of our mind determines which propositions those are. Descartes cannot help but believe, whenever he
noninferentially considers it, the simple necessary truth that what is
done cannot be undone, but things did not have to be that way. He
might have been created in such a way that this proposition was not in
the range of his clear and distinct perception and thus could be
doubted.[39]

I have not lost sight of Descartes's distinction between clear and
distinct perception and prejudice or his distinction between the understanding and the will, even though I have explicated clear and distinct
perception in terms of compelled belief. We are irresistibly compelled
to believe what we clearly and distinctly perceive, but our prejudices,
which stem from social influences or our own shortsightedness, can be
put aside [*Reply to the Fifth Objections*; AT VII, 361–362; HR II,
214]. When Descartes distinguishes between the activities of the understanding and those of the will, he does not include clear and distinct perception in either list:

> For all the modes of thinking that we observed in ourselves may be
> related to two general modes, the one of which consists in perception,
> or in the operation of the understanding, and the other in volition, or
> the operation of the will. Thus sense-perception, imagining and con-
> ceiving things that are purely intelligible are just different methods of
> perceiving; but desiring, holding in aversion, affirming, denying,
> doubting, all these are different modes of willing. [*Principles*, I, xxxii;
> AT VIII, 17; HR I, 232]

Clear and distinct perception, as I have explicated it, unites the understanding and the will; it amounts to our considering a proposition in a

39. Some may find a reason to object to EP17 and EP18 here. If we treat them as
necessary truths, they imply that there is no logical gap between clearly and distinctly
perceiving a proposition and assenting to it, but Descartes thinks there is such a gap; he
thinks it is a contingent fact that we are compelled to assent to our clear and distinct
perceptions. Consider Margaret Wilson, *Descartes*, p. 142. I think this objection may
be based on a misreading of Descartes's statements. What he finds to be contingent
may be, not that we believe every proposition we clearly and distinctly perceive, but
that particular propositions are within the range of our clear and distinct perception
and, so, our compelled belief. Furthermore, I use EP17 and EP18 to explicate clear
and distinct perception without treating them as necessary truths.

particular way, when our considering that proposition in that way compels us to believe it.

Descartes defends the truth of clear and distinct perceptions in this way:

> Every clear and distinct perception is without doubt something, and hence cannot derive its origin from what is nought, but must of necessity have God as its author—God, I say, who being supremely perfect cannot be the cause of any error; and consequently we must conclude that it is true. [*Meditations*; AT VII, 62; HR I, 178*]

A clear and distinct perception is false only if God is the cause of error; since God cannot be the cause of error, every clear and distinct perception is true. Yet why would a false clear and distinct perception entail that God is the cause of error? Our illusory sense perceptions do not entail that God is the cause of error.

Descartes's argument is easy to appreciate relative to EP17 and EP18. When we clearly and distinctly perceive a proposition, we are compelled by our nature to believe it, and since God has given us the faculty of clear and distinct perception and placed that proposition within its range, He will be the cause of our error if the proposition is false. God has created us with the faculty of sense perception and placed particular propositions within its range, but we are not compelled to believe the propositions evidenced for us by our senses; we have at most a resistible inclination to believe them [*Meditations*; AT VII, 38; HR I, 160]. We are the cause of any errors we make, because we do not refrain from belief when we can and should.

I have avoided the mistake of explaining clear and distinct perception by metaphysical certainty. That I have explained it in nonepistemic terms lets me accommodate the view that Descartes affirms the supervenience of epistemic properties upon nonepistemic ones.[40] He may do so in

> EP14. If S clearly and distinctly perceives that *p*, then S is morally certain that *p*.

---

40. Van Cleve, "Foundationalism, Epistemic Principles and the Cartesian Circle," pp. 74–91.

Now that we have at least a slightly better understanding of clear and distinct perception, lets us take another look at Descartes's defense of P1 and P2.

The Defense of P1 and P2 Reconsidered

Here is a more detailed statement of Descartes's appeal to clear and distinct perception to show that he is morally certain he thinks and exists.

The Defense of P1 and P2: Part One (Expanded Version)

1. All my clear and distinct perceptions are morally certain.   [from EP14]
2. I noninferentially consider that I think, it is true that I think, and it is naturally necessary that if I noninferentially consider that I think when I think, I believe that I think.
3. I clearly and distinctly perceive directly that I think.   [from 2 and EP17]
4. I consider the deduction of the proposition that I exist from the premise that I think, while clearly and distinctly perceiving that premise directly, and it is naturally necessary that if I do so, I believe that I exist.
5. I clearly and distinctly perceive deductively that I exist.   [from 4 and EP18]
6. Therefore, I am morally certain that I think and that I exist.   [from 1, 3, and 5]

Watch out for a potential misunderstanding. The argument may seem circular, since the second premise includes the claim that Descartes thinks. Is not that claim part of the conclusion Descartes wants to establish? No. He wants to show, first, that he is morally certain he thinks and exists, and then, in the second part of his defense, that he is metaphysically certain he thinks and exists. He never tries to *demonstrate* that he thinks. He gets his basis for believing he thinks by an act of direct clear and distinct perception.

How can Descartes establish his first premise, EP14, that the nonepistemic quality of clear and distinct perception implies the epistemic one of moral certainty? He might say EP14 is immediately justified for him by an act of direct clear and distinct perception, except that EP14 does not fall within the range of that faculty. It lacks the "self-present-ing" character of *cogitatio* propositions; even if it is true, we can consider it without being compelled to believe it. It lacks the "self-evident" status of simple necessary truths; we can doubt it. Descartes might argue for the moral certainty of clear and distinct perceptions by an appeal to God, just as he argues for their truth. His argument, in outline form, would run:

i. I have an idea of God.
ii. Therefore, God exists and is supremely perfect.
iii. Therefore, God has made me such that all my clear and distinct perceptions are morally certain.
iv. Therefore, all my clear and distinct perceptions are morally certain.[41]

Descartes will encounter well-known difficulties when he tries to move from (i) to (ii). He will face even more between (ii) and (iii). God allows some clear and distinct perceptions to be metaphysically uncer-tain, so why would God not allow some to be morally uncertain? If God does not violate His perfection by creating Descartes with a natu-ral compulsion to believe propositions that are less than maximally reasonable, it is hard to see how He would do so by creating Descartes with a natural compulsion to believe ones that are less than very reasonable.

Descartes could offer EP14 as the best explanation of some epis-temic data. The best explanation of why he is morally certain that two and three is five is that he perceives that fact clearly and distinctly. The same goes for other moral certainties. (Note that his data only has to make EP14 reasonable for him to believe in order for his defense of P1 and P2 to make it reasonable for him to think he is metaphysically certain he thinks and exists and, thus, reasonable for him to include that he thinks and exists in his science.) Yet where does Descartes get his epistemic data, and how does he show that no other explanation is as good as an appeal to clear and distinct perception? The first problem

41. Van Cleve, "Foundationalism, Epistemic Principles and the Cartesian Cir-cle," p. 72, says Descartes uses a similar argument to show that all clear and distinct perceptions are *metaphysically* certain. Van Cleve fails, however, to provide a passage that contains the argument; I have already argued that Descartes thinks some clear and distinct perceptions are metaphysically uncertain.

is especially tricky. Descartes wants to use EP14 to show his moral certainty that he thinks and exists. He can defend that principle by appealing to epistemic data about the moral certainty of particular propositions, but any data to which he appeals is bound to be no more obvious than the particular epistemic facts he wants to use the principle to establish—that he is morally certain he thinks and exists.

In short, even if we accept that Descartes is morally certain that he thinks and exists, and surely most of us do, it is not evident that Descartes's appeal to clear and distinct perception is the right way to explain his epistemic state. I am not saying that Descartes's explanation is false; I suspect that it—or a similar one from contemporary foundationalists—is true. It is just that Descartes does not show that he is right, and it is hard to see how he might.

Descartes's Gambit Again

The point I just made about EP14 can be made about Descartes's other epistemic principles; he does not defend them and it is often hard to see how he might. Is not this enough to block his Gambit from the start? How can he successfully base his theory of the self on his theory of self-knowledge if he cannot defend the epistemic principles on which the latter rests?

Descartes's Gambit will fail if we demand that he begin with premises we all accept and then reason, first, to his epistemic principles, next, to P1, P2, and P3, and, finally, to his theory of the self. Yet why not just expect Descartes to begin with his epistemic principles and reason correctly from them to P1, P2, and P3 and from there to his theory of the self? He will still accomplish a great deal. He will derive his theory of the self from premises far less controversial and intuitively more reasonable than his theory of the self. Many present-day foundationalists adopt positions on self-knowledge similar to Descartes's but are reluctant to accept his theory of the self. The same is true of many of Descartes's first critics. Hobbes has no reservations about accepting P1, P2, and P3, but he has a host of objections to Descartes's theory of the self [*Third Objections and Replies*; AT VII, 171–174; HR II, 60–62]. Arnauld accepts P1, P2, and P3, but unequivocally rejects Descartes's attempt to move from them to his theory of the self [*Fourth Objections*; AT VII, 197–206; HR II, 80–86].

We should think of Descartes as prepared to address two groups. To those who accept his epistemic principles, he is ready to say: "I have given arguments to show that those principles imply P1, P2, and P3; now I shall give ones that derive my theory of the self from those claims about self-knowledge." To those willing to accept P1, P2, and P3 as the sort of epistemic data with which an epistemology must begin, he is ready to say: "I have given some epistemic principles and shown how they entail and thus explain P1, P2, and P3; now I shall show how those three claims, understood relative to my epistemic principles, imply my theory of the self." To those who reject both his epistemic principles and P1, P2, and P3, Descartes has nothing to say.

Chapter 6

SUBSTANCE AND ESSENCE

Descartes takes a good look at himself and decides:

C1: I am a substance.
C2: I am essentially thinking.
C3: I am not essentially extended.
C4: I am not extended.
C5: I am not numerically identical with my body.
C6: My body and I are such that each can exist without the other.

His first three conclusions concern his nature: he is a substance that is essentially thinking but not essentially extended. The next three concern his relation to his body: he is not extended, so he is not identical with his body; his connection with his body is loose enough that he can exist without it and it can exist without him.

We have already seen the obstacles that now confront Descartes. He cannot justify these claims solely with the data he gathers by external and internal sensation. He cannot deduce them from necessary truths. He can deduce them by combining the premises that he thinks and that his body is extended with some of his general metaphysical principles, but those principles beg the question by dividing substances into the mutually exclusive categories of the thinking and the extended (see Chapter 1).

Some commentators are so impressed by these difficulties that they wonder whether Descartes really argues for his theory of the self. Consider Bernard William's reaction to Stephen Schiffer's interpretation of Descartes's argument:

> The effect of Schiffer's approach is not, then, to produce a longer, more interesting, or less question-begging argument. It is rather to suggest that there is not much of an argument at all, and that the Real Distinction [between minds and bodies] arises almost directly from a primary intuition of the two basic attributes, thought and extension, between which everything is divided and in terms of which everything is to be explained.
>
> There is much to be said for this point of view. The intuition of the dualism is primary, and Descartes does not so much arrive at it by the progress back from the Doubt, as reconstruct the world in terms of it. [1]

I suggest that Descartes has a bolder conception of his procedure; he thinks that he uses his theory of self-knowledge to establish his theory of the self.

I here show that Descartes has strong arguments for each of his six claims. His arguments rely directly or indirectly on his premises about self-knowledge (P_1, P_2, and P_3) in every case but one. He appeals to some of his epistemic principles, and even to some of his metaphysical principles, but he never begs the question by assuming a dualistic picture of the world.

I concentrate in this chapter on Descartes's conception of his nature: He is an essentially thinking, but not essentially extended, substance.

Self and Substance

Descartes has two conceptions of what it is to be a substance and, so, two versions of C_1, his claim to be one. Each version has different implications and different demands for its defense.

Descartes writes in the *Reply to the Second Objections*:

> Everything in which there resides immediately, as in a subject, or by means of which there exists anything that we perceive, i.e. any proper-

---

1. Bernard Williams, *Descartes: The Project of Pure Inquiry* (New York: Penguin Books, 1978), p. 120.

ty, quality or attribute, of which we have a real idea is called a Substance; neither do we have any other idea of substance itself, precisely
taken, than that it is a thing in which this something that we perceive or
which is present objectively in some of our ideas, exists formally or
eminently. For by means of our natural light we know that a real
attribute cannot be an attribute of nothing. [AT VII, 161; HR II, 53]

This suggests

> D6a: x is a substance = $_{df.}$ x has a real attribute.

Descartes seems to rely on this definition in the *Reply to the Fourth
Objections* as well.

For we do not have immediate cognition of substances, as has been
elsewhere noted; rather from the mere fact that we perceive certain
forms or attributes which must inhere in something in order to have
existence, we name the thing in which they exist a *substance*. [AT VII,
222; HR II, 98]

That an entity is a substance is implied by the fact that it has certain
attributes. Which attributes? The answer seems to be those that are
real (see earlier discussion of this passage in Chapter 2).

It is clear what properties Descartes takes to be real attributes, even
though he never defines that category. He reports:

I do not however observe more than two ultimate classes of real
things—the one is intellectual things, or those of the intelligence, that
is, pertaining to the mind or to thinking substance, the other is material
things, or that pertaining to extended substance, i.e. to body. Perception, volition, and every mode of knowing and willing, pertain to thinking substance; while to extended substance pertain magnitude or extension in length, breadth and depth, figure, movement, situation,
divisibility into parts themselves divisible, and such like. [*Principles*, I,
xlviii; AT VIII, 23; HR I, 238]

The set of real attributes consists of thought, extension, and their
modes.

This concept of substance is narrow in some ways and wide in
others. D6a does not let just any entity, any subject of attributes, be a
substance; the attribute of extension has the attribute of being a simple

nature, but it does not have any real attributes. D6a lets complex entities built out of substances be substances; the union of a mind and a body has the real attributes of thought and extension:

> Hence it is clear that that subject in which we understand extension only, with the various modes of extension, is a simple entity. So, too, is a subject in which we comprehend thought only, with the various modes of thought. But that in which we observe extension and thought co-existent is a composite entity, to wit, a Man, who consists of soul and body. [*Notes against a Programme*; AT VIII-2, 351; HR I, 437]

D6a is also neutral with regard to whether a substance can be "reduced" to entities of another sort. Descartes, who denies he is a bundle of experiences, and Hume, who believes he is, may each say he is a substance as defined here. Each admits he somehow or other has the attribute of thought.[2]

Descartes presents a narrower conception of substance in the *Principles*.

> By *substance* we can understand nothing else than a thing which so exists that it needs no other thing in order to exist. And in fact only one single substance can be understood which clearly needs nothing else, namely, God. We perceive that all other things can exist only by the help of the concourse of God. [I, li; AT VIII, 24; HR I, 239]

He loosens this definition just enough to allow for substances other than God:

> Created substances, however, whether corporeal or thinking, may be conceived under this common concept; for they are things which need only the concurrence of God in order to exist. [I, lii; AT VIII, 24–25; HR I, 240]

A substance is an entity that requires only the existence of God in order to exist.

Descartes's new concept is hard to define. We do not want to say:

> x is a substance = $_{df.}$ x is such that it is logically possible that x and nothing other than God exist.

2. Similar points are made by Sidney Shoemaker about a similar conception of substance in *Self-Knowledge and Self-Identity* (Ithaca: Cornell University Press, 1963), pp. 43–44.

Created minds, bodies, and even God fail to satisfy this definition, since none can exist unless its essential properties exist. We need to restrict the description "nothing other than God" in the definiens so its range does not include attributes, and we need to do so without the at least apparent circularity of Descartes's remark that

> really the notion of substance is just this—that which can exist by itself, without the aid of any other substance. [*Reply to the Fourth Objections*; AT VII, 226; HR II, 101]

Our best strategy is to use Descartes's first concept of a substance to define his second.

> D6b: x is a substance $=_{df.}$ (1) x has a real attribute, and (2) there is no y such that y has a real attribute, y is numerically distinct from x, y exists contingently, but it is logically impossible that x exists and y does not.

Created minds, bodies, and God all satisfy this definition, as Descartes understands them. Each has real attributes and exists independently of every other contingent entity with real attributes.

Descartes's second concept of substance is narrower than his first. A complex entity that consists of a mind and a body does not satisfy D6b; it cannot exist without each of the substances (entities with real attributes) that compose it.[3] Because it contains the insight that each substance is simple, D6b takes sides with regard to whether a substance can be "reduced" to a collection of other entities; we are no mere bundle of experiences if we satisfy D6b. If we were, some subset of the bundle would have the real attribute of thought just as we (the whole bundle) do, the subset would be numerically diverse from us (the whole bundle), it would exist contingently, but it would be such that we (the whole bundle) could not exist without it.

Descartes's claim to be a substance thus has two interpretations.

> C1a: I have a real attribute.
> C1b: I have a real attribute, and there is no y such that y has a real attribute, y is numerically distinct from me, y exists contingently, and it is logically impossible that I exist and y does not exist.

---

3. I here assume a form of mereological essentialism: a complex entity consisting of two substances, a body and a mind, will not survive the loss or replacement of one of its two substantial parts.

The first says Descartes is a special sort of entity distinguished by a special sort of attribute. The second says he is a special sort of entity distinguished by both that special sort of attribute and his independence from every other contingent entity with that sort of attribute.

I examine Descartes's argument for C1b in Chapter 7; his argument is a variation on his defense of C6, that he exists independently of his body in particular. I want to concentrate for now on C1a.

Descartes defends C1a in Meditation Two. It is the one part of his theory of the self he thinks is metaphysically certain for him before he establishes the truth of his clear and distinct perceptions and the one part he tries to defend without appealing, directly or indirectly, to his premises about self-knowledge. He just examines himself and decides:

> I do not now admit anything which is not necessarily true: to speak accurately I am not more than a thing which thinks [*res cogitans*], that is to say a mind or a soul, or an understanding, or a reason, which are terms whose significance was formerly unknown to me. I am, however, a true and truly existing thing [*res vera & vere existens*], but what thing [*sed qualis res*]? I have answered: a thing which thinks [*Dixi, cogitans*]. [*Meditations*; AT VII, 27; HR I, 152*]

Descartes regularly uses '*res*' and '*substantia*' interchangably—see, for example, *Principles*, I, xi [AT VIII, 8; HR I, 223]—so it is reasonable to believe he is presenting some version of C1 here when he declares he is a true thing (*res vera*). He is interested in C1a rather than C1b, for he does not dare say he can exist independently of his body, let alone independently of every other contingent thing with real attributes, until Meditation Six.

Descartes has to infer C1a from his direct clear and distinct perceptions of his mental state. Recall his remark in the *Fourth Replies*:

> From the mere fact that we perceive certain forms or attributes which must inhere in something in order to have existence, we name the thing in which they exist a *substance*. [AT VII, 222; HR II, 98]

I think he intends to defend C1a by:

The Cogito Defense of C1a
1. I think.
2. Therefore, I am a substance (have a real attribute).

Direct clear and distinct perception makes him morally certain he thinks; this moral certainty makes him morally certain he has a real attribute. He has no reason to doubt his morally certain conclusion. Every potential reason for doubt simply affirms his premise and conclusion by entailing that he thinks and, so, has a real attribute. He is metaphysically certain of C1a for the same sort of reasons he is metaphysically certain of his existence.[4]

The Concept of Essence

The next parts of Descartes theory are C2, that he is essentially thinking, and C3, that he is not essentially extended. We cannot appreciate his defense of these claims unless we understand his concept of an essential property. Descartes never defines his concept, but we can extract three jointly defining conditions from his remarks. He tells Arnauld:

> Nothing without which a thing can still exist is comprised in its essence. [*Reply to the Fourth Objections*; AT VII, 219; HR II, 97]

A property is essential to a substance only if the substance cannot exist without it.[5]

Descartes does not place every property he cannot exist without in his essence. He cannot exist without the so-called transcendental properties he necessarily shares with every substance, such as having duration, or without such nontranscendental properties as being created, but he says thought is his only essential property [*Meditations*; AT VII, 78; HR I, 190]. Why?

I suggest that Descartes excludes the transcendental properties from his essence because, since he shares them with all substances, they do

---

4. The question of whether the *Cogito* Defense of C1a needs an extra premise, such as that whatever thinks is a substance, is bound to arise here, just as it does with regard to Descartes's inference from "I think" to "I exist." I think the answer to the question is no, for the same reasons it is no with regard to the Descartes's inference from thought to existence; consider my discussion of this point in Chapter 5. Note too that even if we require Descartes to use an extra premise, his argument, with the extra premise, will be sound, even if it does not give him metaphysical certainty.

5. Unless I note otherwise, I use 'substance' relative to D6a.

not help individuate him as a particular kind of substance. He treats the essence of each substance as a way to classify it relative to others.

> There is always one principle property of substance which constitutes its nature and essence, and on which all the others depend. Thus extension in length, breadth and depth constitutes the nature of corporeal substance; and thought constitutes the nature of thinking substance. [*Principles*, I, liii; AT VIII, 25; HR I, 240]

> Of the things we consider as real, the most general are *substance, duration, order, number*, and possibly such other similar matters as range through all the classes of real things. I do not however observe more than two ultimate classes of real things—the one is intellectual things, or those of the intelligence, that is, pertaining to the mind or to thinking substance, the other is material things or that pertaining to extended substance, i.e. to body. [*Principles*, I, xlviii; AT VIII, 22–23; HR I, 238]

A property is essential to a substance, then, only if it is not necessarily possessed by every substance.

Descartes's reason for excluding some nontranscendental properties he cannot exist without, such as being created, is indicated by this remark:

> Thus extension in length, breadth and depth constitutes the nature of corporeal substance; and thought constitutes the nature of thinking substance. *For all else that may be attributed to body presupposes extension, and is but a mode of this extended thing; as everything that we find in mind is but so many diverse forms of thinking.* [*Principles*, I, liii; AT VIII, 25; HR I, 240; my emphasis]

I think Descartes's point is that every nonnecessary, nonrelational property of a substance is a mode or form of its essence. All his nonnecessary, nonrelational properties are modes of thought; all his body's nonnecessary, nonrelational properties are modes of extension.[6] Being created is not essential to Descartes, then, because some of his

---

6. I take Descartes's point to be that every *nonnecessary, nonrelational* property of a substance is a mode of its essence in order to allow for such necessary properties as being a substance and such relational ones as being causally related to a substance. Descartes has each, but neither is a mode of thought.

nonnecessary, nonrelational properties are not modes of being created. Having a free will is not a mode of being created, since God has one.

When we combine these three conditions we get these definitions:

> D7: A property P is essential to a substance $x =_{df}$ (1) it is necessary that if x exists, then x has P, (2) P is a nontranscendental property, and (3) every nonrelational, nonnecessary property of x is a mode of P.
>
> D8: P is a nontranscendental property $=_{df}$ it is possible that some substance lacks P.

What is it for one property to be a mode of another? It is obvious that Q is a mode of P only if it is impossible for a substance to have Q but lack P; to use Descartes's example [*Principles*, I, liii; AT VIII, 25; HR I, 240], imagination is a mode of thought, and it is impossible that something imagines but does not think. This necessary condition is not sufficient. Descartes's beliefs about God imply that it is impossible for a necessarily existent substance to lack thought, but necessary existence is not a mode of thought in the way imagination is. I do not know what suffices to make one property a mode of another, but this bit of vagueness in D7 should not cause us any serious problems.

Descartes's views about God are often seen as an obstacle to understanding his concept of an essence.

> I cannot conceive anything but God himself to whose essence existence pertains. [*Meditations*; AT VII, 68; HR I, 182]

> When mind afterwards considers the diverse conceptions which it has and when it there discovers the idea of a Being who is omniscient, omnipotent and absolutely perfect, which is far the most important of all, in it it recognises not merely a possible and contingent existence, as in all the other ideas it has of things which it clearly perceives, but one which is absolutely necessary and eternal. [*Principles*, I, xiv; AT VIII, 10; HR I, 224]

Existence—more precisely, necessary and eternal existence—is essential to God. Yet, existence does not satisfy D7 relative to God, because it is transcendental, and necessary and eternal existence does not satisfy D7 relative to God, because it does not have all God's nonnecessary, nonrelational properties, such as willing that there be extended objects, among its modes. The other properties Descartes finds in his concept of God, such as being omnipotent, fail to satisfy D7 as well. It looks as though only thought qualifies: thought is necessary to God, it is nontranscendental, and all God's nonnecessary, nonrelational properties are modes of thought.

We must either scrap D7 or find a way to interpret Descartes's remarks about God so they do not conflict with it. Bernard Williams would advise us to scrap D7: "We shall avoid confusion and be nearer Cartesian usage if we take the term 'essence' as basic. We should not, to understand Descartes, define 'essence' as a particularly informative and distinctive sub-set of a thing's necessary properties."[7] I think we should keep D7. There is nothing wrong with the implication that thought is God's only essential property. Descartes commits himself to this position in the *Principles*. Recall:

> There is *always one* principle property of substance which constitutes its nature and essence, and on which all the others depend. Thus extension in length, breadth and depth, constitutes the nature of corporeal substance; and thought constitutes the nature of thinking substance. [I, liii; AT VIII, 25; HR I, 240; my emphasis]

> I do not however observe more than *two ultimate classes* of real things—the one is intellectual things, or those of the intelligence, that is, pertaining to the mind or to thinking substance, the other is material things, or that pertaining to extended substance, i.e. to body. [I, xlviii; AT VIII, 23; HR I, 238; my emphasis]

No exception is made for God. When Descartes later considers God's place in the classification of substances, he divides the category of thinking substances into two subcategories on the basis of a difference in the necessary, but nonessential, properties of thinking substances. Some are necessarily created; others are necessarily uncreated:

> We may thus easily have two clear and distinct notions or ideas, the one of *created substance which thinks*, the other of corporeal substance, provided we carefully separate all the attributes of thought from those of extension. We can also have a clear and distinct idea of *an uncreated and independent thinking substance, that is to say of God.* [I, liv; AT VIII, 25–26; HR I, 241; my emphasis]

7. Williams, *Descartes*, p. 119.

The property of being uncreated, which defines the subcategory of thinking substances to which God belongs, is not, properly speaking, part of God's essence, any more than the property of being created, which defines the subcategory of thinking substances to which Descartes belongs, is part of Descartes's essence. God and Descartes are essentially thinking substances; the category of thinking substances is the ultimate category to which each belongs. They belong to different subcategories on the basis of their necessary, but nonessential, properties.

What, then, are we to make of the passages in which Descartes quite explicitly includes necessary and eternal existence and other properties in God's essence? If he does not intend to say that these properties are essential to God in the way thought is essential to God and to him, what does he intend to say? I think he intends to say two things.

The first is that being God entails having necessary and eternal existence, omniscience, and the like. It is logically impossible that something have the property of being God but lack these other properties; as Descartes usually puts it, his idea of God contains his idea of them. Look again at how Descartes states his position on God's nature:

> When mind afterwards considers the diverse conceptions which it has and when it there discovers the idea of a Being who is omniscient, omnipotent and absolutely perfect, which is far the most important of all; in it it recognises not merely a possible and contingent existence, as in all the other ideas it has of things which it clearly perceives, but one which is absolutely necessary and eternal. [*Principles*; I, xiv; AT VIII, 10; HR I, 224]

He does not report a discovery about that substance which is God; he reports a discovery about his idea of God. It contains the idea of necessary and eternal existence. In the *Meditations*, he writes:

> It is certain that I no less find the idea of God, that is to say, the idea of a supremely perfect Being, in me, than that of any figure or number whatever it is; and I do not know less clearly and distinctly that an eternal existence pertains to this nature than I know that all that which I am able to demonstrate of some figure or number truly pertains to the nature of this figure or number. [AT VII, 65; HR I, 180–181]

Descartes says that eternal existence "pertains" to his idea of God. I suggest he means that his idea of God contains his idea of eternal existence. This is clearly his position in the *Reply to the Second Objections:*

> Existence is contained in the idea or concept of everything, because we can conceive nothing except as existent, with this difference, that possible or contingent existence is contained in the concept of a limited thing, but necessary and perfect existence in the concept of a supremely perfect being. [AT VII, 166; HR II, 57]

Consider too the analogies by which Descartes develops his position:

> When I think of it with more attention, I clearly see that existence can no more be separated from the essence of God than can having its three angles equal to two right angles be separated from the essence of a triangle, or the idea of a mountain from the idea of a valley. [*Meditations*; AT VII, 66; HR I, 181]

(Necessary and eternal) existence is "essential" to God as having three angles equal to two right angles is "essential" to a triangle and being joined to a mountain is "essential" to a valley. How is having three angles equal to two right angles essential to a triangle and being joined to a mountain essential to a valley? Descartes surely does not think that those substances that are triangular in shape can only exist if they have three angles equal to two right angles. They can change, like the piece of wax of Meditation Two, and lose their triangular shape and their three angles equal to two right angles. The same is true of valleys. Descartes is concerned with the properties of being a triangle and being a valley, or, as he would put it, with his idea of triangle and his idea of a valley. The property of being a triangle contains that of having three angles equal to two right angles. The property of being a valley contains that of being joined with a mountain. The property of being God, by analogy, contains that of necessary and eternal existence.

The second part of Descartes's position comes out when he considers the disanalogy between his idea of God and his idea of a valley.

> From the fact that I cannot conceive of mountain without a valley, it does not follow that there is any mountain or any valley in existence, but only that the mountain and the valley, whether they exist or do not exist, cannot in any way be separated one from the other. While from the fact that I cannot conceive God without existence, it follows that

existence is inseparable from Him, and hence that He really exists; not that my thought can bring this to pass, or impose any necessity on things, but, on the contrary, because *the necessity which lies in the thing itself, the necessity of the existence of God, determines me to think in this way.* [*Meditations*; AT VII, 67; HR I, 181; my emphasis]

That the concept of a valley contains the concept of being joined to a mountain does not entail that a valley exists, but that the concept of God contains the concept of (necessary and eternal) existence entails that God exists. Most important of all, the concept of God contains the concept of (necessary and eternal) existence because (necessary and eternal) existence is "inseparable" from that substance that is God.

I do not quite understand the link Descartes finds between necessary and eternal existence being part of his concept of God and necessary and eternal existence being inseperable from God, but I doubt there is need even here to interpret Descartes as saying that necessary and eternal existence is essential to God in the way thought is essential to God and to himself. When Descartes says necessary and eternal existence is inseparable from God, he just means that it is necessary to God; God cannot exist without necessary and eternal existence. That property is inseparable from God just as contingent and temporary existence is inseparable from Descartes, and, as a result, it is part of the concept of God just as contingent and temporary existence is part of the concept of Descartes.[8]

In short, when Descartes says necessary and eternal existence is essential to God, he intends to say two things. First, the property of being God entails that of having necessary and eternal existence. Second, that substance that is God cannot exist without necessary and eternal existence. In each case, necessary and eternal existence is essential to God just as contingent and temporary existence is essential to Descartes; it is not essential to God in the way thought is essential to God and to Descartes. Descartes's views about God are consistent with D7.

Now let us use D7 to better appreciate C2 and C3. According to C2,

---

8. I do not claim that Descartes's argument for God's existence will be sound if we interpret him as I suggest. My claim is that my interpretation reflects Descartes's talk of how necessary and eternal existence is "essential" to God.

thought is essential to Descartes. He cannot exist without it, it is nontranscendental, and every nonnecessary, nonrelational property he has is a mode of it. According to C3, extension is not essential to Descartes. Either he can exist without it, or it is transcendental, or some nonnecessary, nonrelational property he has is not a mode of it. Descartes affirms the first disjunct:

> I am certain that God could have created me without putting me in possession of those other attributes of which I am unaware [extension and its modes]. Hence it was that those additional attributes were judged not to belong to the essence of the mind. [*Reply to the Fourth Objections*; AT VII, 219; HR II, 97]

He also affirms the last:

> The mind can be comprehended by us apart from the body, and, accordingly, is not a mode of the body. [*Notes against a Programme*; AT VIII-2, 350; HR I, 437]

His thought is not a mode of extension, so neither are the nonnecessary, nonrelational modes of his thought, such as doubt.

When does Descartes think he can gain metaphysical certainty of C2 and C3? In the *Discourse* he presents them, along with the rest of his theory of the self, in a way that suggests they are metaphysically certain for him as soon as he is metaphysically certain that he thinks and exists [AT VI, 33; HR I, 101]. When critics squawk, he reforms his position:

> The first objection is that it does not follow from the fact that the human mind reflecting on itself does not perceive itself to be other than a thing that thinks, that its nature or its essence consists solely in its being a thing that thinks, in the sense that this word *only* excludes all other things which might also be supposed to pertain to the nature of the soul. To this objection I reply that it was not my intention in that place to exclude these in accordance with the order that looks to the truth of the matter (as to which I was not then dealing), but only in accordance with the order of my thought; thus my meaning was that so far as I was aware, I knew nothing clearly as belonging to my essence, excepting that I was a thing that thinks, or a thing that has in itself the faculty of thinking. [*Meditations*; AT VII, 7–8; HR I, 137–138]

Descartes withdraws his claim that he is metaphysically certain of C_3 as soon as he is metaphysically certain he thinks and exists. His position about C_2 is less clear. He seems to imply that he is metaphysically certain of C_2 as soon as he is metaphysically certain he thinks and exists. Yet it is hard to see how one claim about his essence can be within the limits of his metaphysical certainty when the other is not.

Meditation Two contains the same frustrating mix of clarity and obscurity. Descartes as much as admits his metaphysical uncertainty of C_3:

> I shall exercise my imagination. I am not a collection of members which we call the human body: I am not a subtle air distributed through these members. . . . But perhaps it is true that these same things which I supposed were non-existent because they are unknown to me, are really not different from the self which I know. I am not sure about this, I shall not dispute it now; I can only give judgment on things that are known to me. [AT VII, 27; HR I, 152]

His remarks about C_2 are less straightforward:

> What of thinking? I find here that thought is an attribute that belongs to me; it alone cannot be separated from me. I am, I exist, that is certain. But how often? Just when I think; for it might possibly be the case if I ceased entirely to think, that I should likewise cease altogether to exist. [AT VII, 27; HR I, 151–152]

Descartes here says he cannot be deprived of thought. Does he intend to claim that thought is essential to him and to offer that claim as a metaphysical certainty? Does he just intend to say he is metaphysically certain that he thinks? Bernard Williams believes that Descartes does not intend to claim metaphysical certainty of C_2, because he merely says he *might* cease to exist if he ceases to think.[9] Margaret Wilson believes that Descartes intends to claim metaphysical certainty of C_2, because he entitles Meditation Two "Of the Nature of the Human Mind: that it is better known than body" (*De natura mentis humanae: quòd ipsa sit notior quàm corpus*) and regularly uses 'nature' ('*natura*') to refer to essences.[10]

9. Williams, *Descartes*, p. 103.
10. Margaret Wilson, *Descartes* (London: Routledge and Kegan Paul, 1978), p. 74.

I suggest Descartes's position is that C2, like C3, is metaphysically uncertain for him in Meditation Two. His metaphysical certainties are limited at that point to *cogitatio* propositions and the little he can infer from them with metaphysical certainty. C2 and C3 both contain too much information to be in that category; Descartes's best arguments for each use epistemological and metaphysical principles made doubtful by the Deceiver Hypothesis. This interpretation is consistent with Descartes's title for Meditation Two, which we can read as the statement that the qualities of the mind are better known in general than those of the body. Descartes sometimes uses 'nature' ('*natura*') to designate all of a thing's qualities:

> When we say that any attribute is contained in the nature [*naturâ*] or concept [*conceptu*] of anything, that is precisely the same as saying that it is true of that thing or can be affirmed of it [*Reply to the Second Objections*; AT VII, 162; HR II, 53]

That the mind's qualities—thinking, seeming to see light, and the like—are better known than those of the body is clearly a major theme of Meditation Two.

Descartes's Defense of C2 and C3: Past Interpretations

I want to develop my interpretation of Descartes's arguments for C2 and C3 in contrast to the two major misinterpretations of the past. The strengths of my interpretation are best appreciated against the backdrop of their weaknesses. The first is the Clear and Distinct Perception Interpretation and is inspired by Descartes's remarks in Meditation Six, when he defends C2 and C3 in the course of arguing for C6, that he and his body can exist apart. Let us first look at the whole passage and then concentrate on the parts that relate to C2 and C3 in particular.

Descartes begins:

> And first of all, because I know that all things which I understand clearly and distinctly can be created by God just as I understand them, it suffices that I am able to understand one thing apart from another clearly and distinctly in order to be certain that the one is different from

the other, since they can be made to exist in separation at least by the omnipotence of God; and it does not matter by what power this separation is made for me to judge them to be different. [AT VII, 78; HR I, 190*]

He presents a principle that can be roughly put

    i. Whatever I clearly and distinctly apprehend can be created by God just as I apprehend it.

and infers another:

    ii. If I clearly and distinctly apprehend one substance x apart from another one y, then x can exist apart from y.

He next presents his conception of himself and his body to show that he clearly and distinctly apprehends himself apart from his body; he defends C2 and C3 along the way:

Now just because I know certainly that I exist, and that meanwhile I do not remark that any other thing necessarily pertains to my nature or essence, except that I am a thinking thing, I rightly conclude that my essence consists solely in the fact that I am a thinking thing. And although possibly (or rather certainly, as I shall say in a moment) I possess a body with which I am very intimately conjoined, yet because, on the one side, I have a clear and distinct idea of myself inasmuch as I am only a thinking and unextended thing, and as, on the other, I possess a distinct idea of body, inasmuch as it is only an extended and unthinking thing, it is certain that I am really distinct from my body and can exist without it. [AT VII, 78; HR I, 190*]

Since he clearly and distinctly apprehends himself apart from his body, he can exist apart from his body.

Descartes's defense of C2 and C3 is contained in these lines:

Just because I know certainly that I exist, and that meanwhile I do not remark that any other thing necessarily pertains to my nature or essence, except that I am a thinking thing, I rightly conclude that my essence consists solely in the fact that I am a thinking thing. [AT VII, 78; HR I, 190]

What does Descartes mean by his premise that he is certain that he exists but does not "remark that any other thing pertains to [his] nature or essence except that [he is] a thinking thing?" How does he intend to get from this premise to C2 and C3? According to the Clear and Distinct Perception Interpretation, Descartes's initial premise is that he clearly and distinctly perceives he exists and thinks but does not clearly and distinctly perceive he has any other properties. He intends to get from this premise to C2 and C3 by the principle he states at the start of the passage: Whatever he clearly and distinctly perceives can be made by God just as he apprehends it. Stephen Schiffer puts the proposal this way: "Descartes means that it is possible for him to exist as just a thinking thing because he clearly and distinctly apprehends himself just as being a thinking thing—because, that is, he has a clear and distinct apprehension of himself as a thinking thing and that apprehension includes no apprehension of himself as being anything else."[11] Schiffer develops the proposal into an interesting argument for C3:

The Clear and Distinct Perception Defense of C3

1. If I clearly and distinctly perceive of x that it has P but I do not clearly and distinctly perceive of x that it has Q, then it is logically possible that x exists, has P, but lacks Q.
2. Every nontranscendental property R other than thought is such that I clearly and distinctly perceive of me that I exist and think but I do not clearly and distinctly perceive of me that I have R.
3. Every nontranscendental property R other than thought is such that it is logically possible that I exist and think but lack R.   [from 1 and 2]
4. Extension is a nontranscendental property other than thought.
5. It is logically possible that I exist and think but lack extension.   [from 3 and 4]
6. Therefore, extension is not essential to me.   [from 5 and D7][12]

11. Stephen Schiffer, "Descartes on His Essence," *Philosophical Review*, 85 (January 1976), p. 33. Other commentators who give versions of the Clear and Distinct Perception Interpretation are Bernard Williams, *Descartes*, Chapter 4, and Anthony Kenny, *Descartes: A Study of His Philosophy* (New York: Random House, 1968), pp. 89–90. Consider too James Van Cleve, "Conceivability and the Cartesian Argument for Dualism," *Pacific Philosophical Quarterly*, 64 (January 1983), pp. 35–45 for a related line of interpretation.

12. Schiffer, "Descartes on His Essence," p. 34. I have simplified Schiffer's argument so that it is directed at C3 instead of the more general conclusion that no property other than thought is essential to Descartes.

Schiffer also gives an interpretation of Descartes's argument for C2, but it is well criticized by Bernard Williams, who suggests a simpler, more plausible way to develop this part of the Clear and Distinct Perception Interpretation:[13]

The Clear and Distinct Perception Defense of C2

1. If I clearly and distinctly perceive of x that it has P but I do not clearly and distinctly perceive of x that it has Q, then it is logically possible that x exists, has P, but lacks Q.
2. Every nontranscendental property R other than thought is such that I clearly and distinctly perceive that I exist and think but I do not clearly and distintly perceive that I have R.
3. Every nontranscendental property R other than thought is such that it is logically possible that I exist and think but lack R.   [from 1 and 2]
4. No property other than thought is essential to me.   [from 3 and D7]
5. Some property is essential to me.
6. Therefore, I am essentially thinking.   [from 4 and 5]

The Clear and Distinct Perception Interpretation gives an explanation of how Descartes's experiences in Meditation Two prepare him to determine his essence in Meditation Six. At the start of Meditation Two, the second premise in the arguments for C2 and C3 is true of Descartes: He clearly and distinctly perceives that he exists and thinks without clearly and distinctly perceiving that he has any other properties. Yet he is metaphysically uncertain of this fact about his clear and distinct perception, as well as of the extra premises he needs to derive C2 and C3, especially the clear and distinct perception criterion for logical possibility (the first premise in each argument). The Deceiver Hypothesis (clear and distinct perception version) stands in his way. Once he rules out the Deceiver Hypothesis in Meditations Three, Four, and Five, he can use the arguments at hand to gain meta-physical certainty of C2 and C3.

---

13. Williams, *Descartes*, pp. 116–120; compare Schiffer, "Descartes on His Essence," pp. 34–36. It is worth noting that the second premise of this defense of C2 has an implication some may find objectionable. According to it, every nontranscendental property other than thought is such that Descartes clearly and distinctly perceives that he exists and thinks but does not clearly and distinctly perceive that he has it. Since Descartes's nontranscendental properties include doubting and seeming to see light, the second premise implies that he can have those properties without clearly and distinctly perceiving that he has them.

The problem with the Clear and Distinct Perception Interpretation is that it saddles Descartes with

CP: If I clearly and distinctly perceive of *x* that it has *P* but I do not clearly and distinctly perceive of *x* that it has *Q*, then it is logically possible that *x* exists and has *P* but lacks *Q*.

Descartes never presents this criterion for logical possibility. The closest he comes is the more vague and general principle, "All the things I apprehend clearly and distinctly can be created by God as I apprehend them." Descartes never says that he intends to use CP, or even the more vague and general principle, to defend C2 and C3; he may just intend to use the more vague and general principle to defend his final conclusion, C6, that he and his body can exist apart.[14] We are not

14. Some may object that Descartes's Meditation Six remarks clearly indicate an intention to defend his view on his essence by appeal to a clear and distinct perception criterion for logical possibility. Haldane and Ross translate Descartes's remarks so that they contain such an indication: "And first of all, because I know that all things which I apprehend clearly and distinctly can be created by God as I apprehend them, it suffices that I am able to apprehend one thing apart from another clearly and distinctly in order to be certain that the one is different from the other, since they may be made to exist in separation at least by the omnipotence of God; and it does not signify by what power this separation is made in order to compel me to judge them to be different: *and therefore*, just because I know certainly that I exist, and that meanwhile I do not remark that any other thing necessarily pertains to my nature or essence, excepting that I am a thinking thing, I rightly conclude that my essence consists solely in the fact that I am a thinking thing" [*Meditations*; HR I, 190; my emphasis]. The emphasized phrase 'and therefore' indicates that Descartes intends to derive his conclusion about his essence from the general principle about clear and distinct perception he has just presented. Haldane and Ross's translation is another example of their often-noted preference for the French translation of the *Meditations* over the Latin original. The relevant section of the French text reads: "*Et partant*, de cela même que je connais avec certitude que j'existe, et que cependant je ne remarque point qu'il appartienne nécessairement aucune autre chose à ma nature ou à mon essence, sinon que je suis une chose qui pense, je conclus fort bien que mon essence consiste en cela seul, que je suis une chose qui pense" [AT IX, 62; my emphasis]. The primary meaning of '*et partant*' in seventeenth-century French is 'and therefore.' The Latin original reads "*ac proinde*, ex hoc ipso quòd sciam me existere, quòdque interim nihil plane aliud ad naturam sive essentiam meam pertinere animadvertam, præter hoc solum quòd sim res cogitans, recte concludo meam essentiam in hoc uno consistere, quòd sim res cogitans" [AT VII, 78; my emphasis]. The phrase '*ac proinde*' can be used to express the logical relation between premises and a conclusion that we express by 'therefore,' but, like 'therefore' and 'then,' it also has a continuitive or exhortative sense used to convey transitions in thought and best expressed in English by 'now' or 'and.' I give '*ac proinde*' its continuitive sense in my translation of the passage. Other

justified in attributing CP to Descartes to fill the gaps in his argument, for CP is indefensible, and Descartes cannot adopt it without contradicting some of his most plausible claims. What can Descartes tell a materialist who asks for a defense of CP? He might appeal to the psychological aspects of clear and distinct perception and argue: "If we clearly and distinctly perceive of x that it has P but do not clearly and distinctly perceive of x that it has Q, we are psychologically certain that x has P but not psychologically certain that it has Q; in that case, we can conceive of x existing with P but without Q, and, since whatever we can conceive is possible, x can exist with P but without Q." Any materialist worth his stuff will question the moves from psychological certainty and uncertainty to conceivability and from conceivability to logical possibility. To borrow and simplify an example of Arnauld's [*Fourth Objections*; AT VII, 201–202; HR II, 83], suppose a student clearly and distinctly perceives of an object before him that it is a triangle but does not clearly and distinctly perceive of it that it has three angles equal to two right angles. He is psychologically certain of the object that it is a triangle and not psychologically certain of it that it has three angles equal to two right angles. Are we to say he can conceive of the object that it exists, is a triangle, and lacks three angles equal to two right angles, and that it is, therefore logically possible for the object to exist, be a triangle, and not have angles equal to two right angles? No. Either the inference from psychological certainty and uncertainty to conceivability or the inference from conceivability to logical possibility is mistaken.

Descartes might appeal to God: "Since God can do anything, when we clearly and distinctly perceive of x that it has P but do not clearly and distinctly perceive of x that it has Q, God can make it the case that x has P but not Q; whatever God can do is possible, so our clear and distinct perception implies that x can have P but lack Q." It is important to note that the soundness of this argument is unaffected if we replace the

---

commentators do so, too; consider Bernard Williams, *Descartes*, p. 104, and Elizabeth Anscombe and Peter Geach, *Descartes: Philosophical Writings* (New York: Bobbs-Merrill, 1954), p. 114. Laurence Lafleur seems to give the expression its merely continuitive sense, since he ignores it in his translation, *Descartes: Meditations on First Philosophy* (New York: Bobbs-Merrill, 1951), p. 74. The text does not, therefore, clearly indicate that Descartes intends to derive his position on his essence from a clear and distinct perception criterion for logical possibility.

references to clear and distinct perception by ones to another intentional attitude, say belief, doubt, or desire. The argument does not establish any special connection between clear and distinct perception *per se* and logical possiblity. A materialist will give Descartes a choice: Is God bound by the law of contradiction or not? If God is not bound, as Descartes believes, then the fact that God can create *x* with *P* but not *Q* does not entail that it is logically possible that *x* can have *P* but not *Q*. If God is bound by the law of contradiction, God can only do what is logically possible, and, before Descartes appeals to God's power, he must show that it is logically possible that *x* has *P* but lacks *Q*, which is just what he appeals to God's power to show.

Descartes can always define clear and distinct perception to make it true by definition that we cannot clearly and distinctly perceive that *x* has *P* unless we clearly and distinctly perceive *x* to have every property necessary for its existence or entailed by *P*. A materialist will then accept CP and reject as question begging Descartes's claim to perceive clearly and distinctly that he thinks without clearly and distinctly perceiving that he is extended; thought is just a mode of extension, according to the materialist.

Descartes will contradict himself if he accepts CP. Early in Meditation Two, before he asks what he is, he clearly and distinctly perceives that he exists but does not clearly and distinctly perceive that he is a substance [AT VII, 25; HR I, 150]. Nonetheless, he correctly believes he cannot exist without being a substance. At the start of Meditation Three, he clearly and distinctly perceives that he exists, thinks, and is a substance [AT VII, 35; HR I, 158], but he does not clearly and distinctly perceive that he is created until later [AT VII, 48–49; HR I, 168]. Nonetheless, he cannot exist, think, and be a substance without being created.

Anthony Kenny trades these problems for new ones in a modified version of the Clear and Distinct Perception Interpretation. He suggests that Descartes defends C2 and C3 by

CP(a): If I clearly and distinctly perceive of *x* that it has *P* and lacks *Q*, then it is logically possible that *x* exists with *P* but without *Q*.[15]

15. Kenny, *Descartes*, pp. 89–90.

CP(a) is an improvement on CP, since Descartes can derive CP(a) from EP3 (that all clear and distinct perceptions are true) and he can adopt it without contradicting himself. The problem is that Descartes cannot use CP(a) to defend C2 and C3 without claiming to perceive clearly and distinctly that he is not extended. How can Descartes get that clear and distinct perception? He must deduce that he is not extended from direct clear and distinct perceptions, but he never explicitly develops such a deduction, and the best deduction available to him uses C3 itself as a premise (consider my discussion in Chapter 7 of the deductions available).

The Clear and Distinct Perception Interpretation saddles Descartes with a very poor defense of C2 and C3. We owe it to him and to ourselves to look for something better.

The second familiar interpretation of Descartes's defense of C2 and C3, the Epistemic Criterion Interpretation, is inspired by passages in the *Discourse:*

> And then, examining attentively that which I was, I saw that I could conceive that I had no body, and that there was no world nor place where I might be; but yet that I could not for all that conceive that I was not. On the contrary, I saw from the very fact that I thought of doubting the truth of other things, it very evidently and certainly followed that I was; on the other hand, if I had only ceased from thinking, even if all the rest of what I had ever imagined had really existed, I should have no reason for thinking I had existed. From that I knew that I was a substance the whole essence or nature of which is to think. [AT VI, 32–33; HR I, 101]

Descartes takes note of his metaphysical uncertainty that he has a body and his metaphysical certainty that he exists; he observes that he gains his metaphysical certainty that he exists from his metaphysical certainty that he thinks and that his beliefs about his mental state may well be the only evidence capable of making him metaphysically certain he exists. He concludes that thought is his only essential property. We are again left wondering exactly what his premises are and how he gets from them to his conclusion. According to the Epistemic Criterion Interpretation, his premises concern what evidence he must have to be metaphysically certain that he exists. He must be metaphysically certain that he thinks; he does not need to be metaphysically certain he has other properties, like extension. Descartes gets from these premises to his conclusion by an epistemic criterion for essential properties: His essential properties are those he must be metaphysically certain he has in order to be metaphysically certain he exists.

The details and problems of this approach are best shown by an example, and the best example is given by Anthony Kenny.

> One principle that would enable Descartes to derive his conclusion from his premises might run as follows. Those properties constitute the essence of a thing that are severally necessary and jointly sufficient to establish the existence of that thing with certainty. This principle, coupled with the premise that the single property of thinking is both necessary and sufficient to establish with certainty my own existence, will yield the conclusion that my essence is constituted by thinking.[16]

I think Kenny is suggesting this argument:

The Epistemic Criterion Defense of C2 and C3

1. P belongs to the essence of x if and only if (1) no one can be metaphysically certain of x that it exists unless his evidence includes the metaphysical certainty of x that it has P, and (2) anyone metaphysically certain of x that it has P is metaphysically certain of x that it exists.
2. No one can be metaphysically certain of me that I exist unless his evidence includes the metaphysical certainty of me that I think.
3. Anyone who is metaphysically certain of me that I think is metaphysically certain of me that I exist.
4. I am metaphysically certain of me that I exist without being metaphysically certain of me that I am extended.
5. Therefore, I am essentially thinking.   [from 1, 2, and 3]
6. Therefore, I am not essentially extended.   [from 1 and 4]

The Epistemic Criterion Interpretation explains why Descartes is metaphysically uncertain of C2 and C3 in Meditation Two. If he reflects at that point on the justification relations that hold between his beliefs, he will make the discoveries recorded in the second, third, and

---

16. Kenny, *Descartes*, p. 83. Norman Malcolm gives a more complex version of the Epistemic Criterion Interpretation in "Descartes's Proof that His Essence Is Thinking," *Philosophical Review*, 74 (July 1965), pp. 315–338. Kenny criticizes Malcolm's interpretation, as does Schiffer in "Descartes on His Essence," pp. 29–31.

fourth premises, but those discoveries will at best be moral certainties for him. They and his epistemic criterion for essential properties will be metaphysically uncertain until he rules out his reasons to doubt clear and distinct perceptions. Once he does, he can gain metaphysically certainty of C_2 and C_3 by the argument at hand.

Like the Clear and Distinct Perception Interpretation, the Epistemic Criterion Interpretation is a suggestion about how Descartes *would* defend C_2 and C_3. Descartes never states the criterion for essences given in the interpretation; it is Kenny's suggestion about what Descartes would say if we asked for more information. We should evaluate the Epistemic Criterion Interpretation by the same standards we applied to the Clear and Distinct Perception Interpretation. Does it give Descartes a strong argument for C_2 and C_3? Is it consistent with what he says elsewhere?

Kenny does not suggest any argument Descartes can give for the epistemic criterion for essences. Descartes cannot derive it from the definition of an essential property, since that definition contains no even implicit epistemic conditions. In the absence of an argument, the criterion is just an *ad hoc* principle designed to get Descartes the results he wants, and any appeal to it has all the advantages of fiat over finesse.

The interpretation conflicts with Descartes's own description of how he determines his essence. When Arnauld challenges Descartes's exclusion of extension and its modes from his essence, Descartes acknowledges:

> [I must explain] how, *from the fact that I knew that nothing belongs to my essence* (i.e. to the essence of the mind alone) *beyond the fact that I am a thinking being, it follows that in actual truth nothing else does belong to it.* [*Reply to the Fourth Objections*; AT VII, 219; HR II, 96]

He then says:

> For although much exists in me of which I am not yet conscious (for example, in that passage I did, as a fact, assume that I was not yet aware that my mind had the power of moving the body, and that it was substantially united with it), yet since that which I do perceive is adequate to allow of my existing with it as my sole possession, I am certain that God could have created me without putting me in possession of those attributes of which I was unaware. Hence, it was that those

additional attributes were judged not to belong to the essence of the mind.

For in my opinion nothing without which a thing can still exist is comprised in its essence. [*Reply to the Fourth Objections*; AT VII, 219; HR II, 97]

Descartes explains that he moves from premises describing his metaphysical uncertainty whether he has extension and its modes to the intermediate conclusion that he can exist without those properties and from there to the ultimate conclusion that they are not essential to him. His argument has three stages: a description of his epistemic state, an intermediate conclusion about what properties he can exist without, and a final conclusion about what properties are not essential to him. The Epistemic Criterion Interpretation tries to replace the second stage by an *ad hoc* criterion for essential properties.

Commentators who adopt either the Clear and Distinct Perception Interpretation or the Epistemic Criterion Interpretation often think poorly of Descartes's defense of C2 and C3. It is no wonder; the arguments they attribute to him are weak and inconsistent with his stated claims and intentions. Things do not have to be this way, though. We can interpret Descartes so that he has strong arguments consistent with his other views.

Descartes's Gambit and C3

If Descartes does not intend to derive his conclusions about his essence from premises about his clear and distinct perceptions or about what he must know to know that he exists, where does he intend to start? I suggest he starts with P1, P2, and P3, that he is metaphysically certain he thinks and exists but metaphysically uncertain he has a body. He makes an oblique reference to each at the start of his argument in the *Discourse:*

And then, examining attentively that which I was, I saw that I could conceive that I had no body, and that there was no world nor place where I might be [P3]; but yet I could not for all that conceive that I was not [P2]. On the contrary, I saw from the very fact that I thought of doubting the truth of other things, it very evidently and certainly fol-

lowed that I was [P1 and P2]; on the other hand if I had only ceased
from thinking, even if all the rest of what I had ever imagined had really
existed, I should have no reason for thinking that I had existed. From
that I knew that I was a substance the whole essence or nature of which
is to think [C2 and C3]. [AT VI, 32–33; HR I, 101]

Consider again his argument in Meditation Six:

> Now just because I know certainly that I exist, and that meanwhile I do
> not remark that any other thing necessarily pertains to my nature or
> essence, except that I am a thinking thing, I rightly conclude that my
> essence consists solely in the fact that I am a thinking thing. [AT VII,
> 78; HR I, 190*]

He infers C2 and C3 ("I rightly conclude that my essence consists
solely in the fact that I am a thinking thing") from two premises: He
knows certainly that he exists, and he "does not remark that any other
thing necessarily pertains to [his] nature or essence except that [he is] a
thinking thing." The first premise is obviously P2, that he is metaphysically certain he exists. I think the second premise is a confused
description of what properties he finds in himself with metaphysical
certainty; when he says he does not remark that anything except
thought necessarily pertains to his nature or essence, he basically
means he is metaphysically certain that he thinks (P1) and metaphysically uncertain that he has other properties, like having a body
(P3). It is surely as reasonable to read his second premise this way as it
is to read it as a confused reference to what he clearly and distinctly
perceives or to what he must know to know he exists.

How can Descartes get from P1, P2, and P3 to his conclusions about
his essence? Let us start with C3, that he is not essentially extended.

The Gambit Defense of C3

1. That I think and that I exist are metaphysically certain for me; that I
   have a body is morally, but not metaphysically, certain for me as
   long as all my evidence for it ultimately consists of sensation reports.

The metaphysical certainty criterion (EP1) and the definition of a
reason for doubt (D3) let Descartes infer:

2. I have a reason to doubt that I have a body as long as all my

evidence for that proposition ultimately consists of sensation reports. [from 1 and EP1]

3. Some hypothesis indicates how my *de se* belief that I have a body might be false despite my evidence for it or how an essential part of my evidence might be false despite my evidence for that essential part as long as all my evidence ultimately consists of sensation reports. [from 2 and D3]

Descartes's research in Meditation One enables him to explain his reason to doubt his belief in his body more precisely:

4. The sensation version of the Deceiver Hypothesis indicates how my *de se* belief that I have a body might be false despite my evidence for it as long as all my evidence ultimately consists of sensation reports.

This is stage one of the Gambit defense of C3.

Descartes must now derive some intermediate conclusions about what is logically possible from this initial information about his epistemic state. He must show, in particular, that he can exist without the property of being extended. The principles that explain how reasons for doubt indicate that a belief might be false contain what he needs.

Recall EP13: *q* indicates to *S* how *S*'s morally certain belief *p* might be false despite *S*'s evidence for *p* only if either (1) it is logically necessary that *p* or (2) it is logically possible that *q* is true and *p* is false. It is not logically necessary that Descartes has a body:

5. The content of my *de se* belief that I have a body is not a logically necessary truth.

Since the sensation version of the Deceiver Hypothesis indicates how Descartes's morally certain belief in his body might be false, it is logically possible that that hypothesis is true and his belief false:

6. The sensation version of the Deceiver Hypothesis and the content of my *de se* belief that I have a body are such that it is logically possible that the former is true and the latter is false. [from 4, 5, and EP13]

EP15 says: *q* indicates to *S* how *S*'s morally certain belief *p* might be false despite *S*'s evidence for *p* only if (1) *q* entails that proposition that is the content of S's *de se* belief that S exists and (2) q entails that proposition that is the content of S's *de se* belief that S thinks. This enables Descartes to infer:

> 7. The sensation version of the Deceiver Hypothesis entails the content of my *de se* beliefs that I think and exist.   [from 4 and EP15]

Descartes may combine steps (6) and (7) to get

> 8. The sensation version of the Deceiver Hypothesis, the content of my *de se* belief that I think, the content of my *de se* belief that I exist, and the content of my *de se* belief that I have a body are such that it is logically possible that the first three (the sensation version of the Deceiver Hypothesis, the content of my *de se* belief that I think, the content of my *de se* belief that I exist) are true and the fourth (the content of my *de se* belief that I have a body) is false.   [from 6 and 7]

Descartes is now ready to draw some metaphysical conclusions about his nature. All he needs is a way to switch from talking about the logical possibility of particular combinations of propositions about himself to talking about the logical possibility of his existing in particular ways. I argue in Chapter 3 that Descartes's views on the content of *de se* attitudes are naturally and plausibly captured by the Self-Identity Theory. That theory implies that the contents of his *de se* attitudes are necessarily about him; more exactly:

> 9. The sensation version of the Deceiver Hypothesis, the content of my *de se* belief that I think, the content of my *de se* belief that I exist, and I are such that it is logically necessary that if they are true, then I exist and they are true of me.
> 10. The content of my *de se* belief that I exist, the content of my *de se* belief that I have a body, and I are such that it is logically necessary that if the first is true and the second is false, then I exist, the first is true of me, and the second is false of me.

Steps (8), (9), and (10) entail:

> 11. I am such that it is logically possible that I exist, think, have sensations, but do not have a body (am neither extended nor related to an extended thing which is my body).   [from 8, 9, and 10]

The definition of an essential property (D7) enables Descartes to at last conclude:

12. Therefore, I am not essentially extended.   [from 11 and D7]

Steps (1–4) are the epistemic stage of the argument. In steps (5–8) the epistemic principles that explain Descartes's concept of indication generate intermediate conclusions to the effect that particular combinations of propositions about him are logically possible. Steps (9–12) complete the argument by using the insight that the contents of Descartes's *de se* attitudes are necessarily about him to infer the logical possibility of his existing without being extended and the definition of an essential property to infer that he is not essentially extended.

The Gambit Defense of C3 gives Descartes an argument for attribute dualism. Line (10) says he can exist, think, and have sensations without being extended. If, as Descartes surely does, we define the concept of a physical property so that every physical property entails extension, line (10) implies that neither thought, in general, nor sensation, in particular, is a physical property. At least some mental properties are not physical.

Some virtues of the interpretation on which the Gambit Defense is based are easy to see. It explains the relation between Meditations Two and Six just as well as the Clear and Distinct Perception Interpretation and the Epistemic Criterion Interpretation do. In Meditation Two, Descartes is in the epistemic state described in the first stage of the argument. He may be morally certain that he is in that state, but he is not metaphysically certain of it, and he is not metaphysically certain of 'the premises he needs to construct the second and third stages of the argument. Things presumably change in Meditation Six. He rules out his reasons to doubt his clear and distinct perceptions; he is able to gain metaphysical certainty of the description of his epistemic state and the premises he needs to derive C3.

The Gambit Interpretation avoids the major textual problem in the Epistemic Criterion Interpretation. It captures Descartes's intention to move from premises about his epistemic state to conclusions about his essence by intermediate results about what is logically possible. It also displays clearly the central role that Descartes's position on the nature and content of certainty plays in his argument. The epistemic principles that spell out his conception of metaphysical certainty enable him to move from his initial epistemic premises to intermediate conclusions about the logical possibility of particular propositions about himself. EP1, EP13, and EP15, which we have already found behind his claims to metaphysical uncertainty about his body and metaphysical certainty about his thought and existence, play especially important roles. Descartes's position on the content of his *de se* metaphysical certainty and uncertainty is also central to his argument. It enables him to move from his intermediate conclusions about the logical possibility of particular propositions about himself to his final conclusion about the logical possibility of his existing in particular ways.

The most impressive feature of the Gambit Interpretation is that it gives Descartes a strong argument for C3. The best way to see this is to consider how the Gambit Defense resists the two strongest objections traditionally raised against Descartes's position.

Objections to the Gambit Defense of C3

I mentioned at the start of this chapter that some commentators object that Descartes defends his theory of the self by question begging or *ad hoc* principles. They are right with regard to the defenses based on the Clear and Distinct Perception and Epistemic Criterion interpretations. The former uses an indefensible criterion for logical possibility; the latter an *ad hoc* criterion for essential properties. These critics are wrong with regard to the Gambit Defense.

The Gambit Defense opens with premises about Descartes's self-knowledge backed by his theory of certainty and the Deceiver Argument of Meditation One. Those who criticize Descartes's theory of the self, and C3 in particular, are often willing to accept his views on self-knowledge; some, like Hobbes, seem to think that his views on self-knowledge are obvious (consider Hobbes's remarks in the *Third Objections and Replies* [AT VII, 171–174; HR II, 60–62] and Arnauld's in the *Fourth Objections* [AT VII, 197–198; HR II, 80–81]).

The second stage of the Gambit Defense uses two epistemic principles based on attractive insights. EP13 rests on the idea that, at least where contingent moral certainties are concerned, we do not indicate how someone's belief might be false by citing a hypothesis that log-ically entails that belief. EP15 is based on the idea that a hypothesis indicates how our beliefs might be false only if it assumes we exist and think. The strength of each principle is shown by the role it plays in explaining Descartes's metaphysical certainty that he exists and thinks.

The argument's third stage uses the definition of an essential proper-ty—specifically, the condition that all essential properties are neces-sary—and the premise that the contents of our *de se* attitudes are necessarily about us. That all essential properties are necessary is un-objectionable; I present the attractive features of the Self-Identity The-ory of *de se* attitudes in Chapter 3.

The Gambit Defense of C3 is not, then, question begging or *ad hoc*. Descartes's critics must work harder to avoid his conclusion that he is not essentially extended, and their best strategy is to fall back to their second standard objection: His argument proves too much; the princi-ples he uses to derive C3 can be used to construct analogous arguments for clearly false conclusions. Arnauld sets the trend here. He interprets Descartes as giving the Clear and Distinct Perception Defense for C3 and objects in this way:

> Let us assume that a certain man is quite sure that the angle in a
> semicircle is a right angle and that hence the triangle made by this angle
> and the diameter is right-angled; but suppose he questions and has not
> yet firmly apprehended, nay, let us imagine that, misled by some fallacy,
> he denies that the square on its base is equal to the square on the sides of
> the right-angled triangle. Now, according to our author's reasoning, he
> will see himself confirmed in his false belief. For, he will argue, while I
> clearly and distinctly perceive that this triangle is right-angled, I yet
> doubt whether the square on its base is equal to the square on its sides.
> Hence the equality of the square on the base to those on the sides does
> not belong to its essence. [*Fourth Objections*; AT VII, 201–202; HR II,
> 83]

If Descartes may reason, "I clearly and distinctly perceive that I think without clearly and distinctly perceiving that I am extended, hence I can exist, think, and be unextended," a novice geometer may reason, "I clearly and distinctly perceive that this triangle is right-angled with-out clearly and distinctly perceiving that the square on its base is equal to the square on its sides, hence, it can exist, be right-angled, and be such that the square on its base does not equal the square on its sides."

Arnauld has shot a decoy instead of the duck. Descartes does not give the Clear and Distinct Perception Defense for C3. He adopts the Gambit Defense, and it can withstand this attack. A novice geometer might give either of two "gambit-type" arguments; Descartes may reject the first without surrendering his argument for C3, and he may accept the second. The first goes as follows:

1. I am morally, but not metaphysically, certain that every right triangle's base has a square equal to the square on its sides.
2. Some hypothesis gives me a reason to doubt that every right triangle's base has a square equal to the square on its sides.   [from 1 and EP1]
3. Some hypothesis indicates how my belief (that every right triangle's base has a square equal to the square on its sides) might be false despite my evidence for it.
4. That every right triangle's base has a square equal to the square on its sides is not a logically necessary truth.
5. The hypothesis that indicates how my belief might be false despite my evidence and the proposition that is the content of my belief are such that it is logically possible that the former is true and the latter is false.   [from 3, 4, and EP13]
6. Therefore, it is logically possible that some right triangle's base has a square unequal to the square on its sides.   [from 5]

Descartes does not have to give up the Gambit Defense of C3 to explain what is wrong. Premise (4) is false. It is logically necessary that every right triangle's base has a square equal to the square on its sides. The corresponding premise in the Gambit Defense of C3 is that it is not logically necessary that Descartes has a body, which is true, since, at the very least, Descartes might not exist. What if a geometer contemplates a piece of paper the shape of a right triangle and gives the following argument?

1. I am morally, but not metaphysically, certain that this substance is a right triangle and its base has a square equal to the square on its sides.
2. Some hypothesis gives me a reason to doubt that this substance is a right triangle and its base has a square equal to the square on its sides.   [from 1 and EP1]
3. Some hypothesis indicates how my belief (that this substance is a right triangle and its base has a square equal to the square on its sides) might be false despite my evidence for it.

4. That this substance is a right triangle and its base has a square equal to the square on its sides is not a logically necessary truth.
5. That hypothesis that indicates how my belief might be false despite my evidence and that proposition that is the content of my belief are such that it is logically possible that the former is true and the latter is false. [from 3, 4, and EP13]
6. Therefore, it is logically possible that it is not the case that this substance is a right triangle and its base has a square equal to the square on its sides. [from 5]

Descartes does not have to find a way to reject this argument. The novice geometer is right. Suppose the substance he considers ceases to exist or loses its triangular shape the way the piece of wax loses its shape in Meditation Two; then it is not the case that the substance is a right triangle and its base has a square equal to the square on its sides.[17]

Michael Hooker also thinks that Descartes's defense of C3 proves too much.[18] He suggests that Descartes might derive C3 from epistemic premises by this argument:

1. It is epistemically (metaphysically) possible for me that I exist and no bodies exist.
2. If it is epistemically (metaphysically) possible for me that p, then it is logically possible that p.
3. It is logically possible that I exist and no bodies exist. [from 1 and 2]
4. If I am essentially extended, then it is not logically possible that I exist and no bodies exist.
5. Therefore, I am not essentially extended. [from 3 and 4]

Hooker notes that just as it is metaphysically possible for Descartes in Meditation Two that he exists and there are no bodies, it is also

17. Descartes does not respond to Arnauld's objection as I have; in fact, he makes only some confused remarks [*Reply to the Fourth Objections*; AT VII, 223–225; HR II, 100–101]. I think the source of his confusion is that he conflates Arnauld's objection to his argument for C3 with a second objection Arnauld gives three paragraphs later, one that uses the same example but is directed at his argument for C6, that he and his body can exist apart. Descartes tries to answer both objections at once and ends up without a clear reply to the first and with a partially clear and successful reply to the second, which I consider in Chapter 7.

18. Michael Hooker, "Descartes's Denial of Mind–Body Identity," in *Descartes: Critical and Interpretative Essays*, ed. Michael Hooker (Baltimore: Johns Hopkins Press, 1978), pp. 171–185, especially pp. 180–183.

metaphysically possible for him that he exists and every mind is a body. If Descartes gives the above argument for C3, then, he must also accept the following:

1. It is epistemically (metaphysically) possible for me that I exist and no mind not identical with a body exists.
2. If it is epistemically (metaphysically) possible for me that *p*, then it is logically possible that *p*.
3. It is logically possible that I exist and no mind not identical with a body exists.   [from 1 and 2]
4. If I am essentially unextended, it is not logically possible that I exist and no mind not identical with a body exists.
5. Therefore, I am not essentially unextended.   [from 3 and 4]

Descartes cannot accept this argument, according to Hooker. Its conclusion combines with the principle that whatever is unextended is essentially unextended to imply that Descartes is extended. Hooker, however, misrepresents Descartes's defense of C3. Surely Descartes does not intend to bridge the gap between his epistemic premises and his intermediate conclusions about what is logically possible by saying that whatever is metaphysically possible for him is logically possible. That is equivalent to saying that whatever is logically necessary is metaphysically certain for him, and, even on his worst days, Descartes never says that.[19]

A revised form of Hooker's objection poses a serious challenge to Descartes. In Chapter 7, I consider Descartes's argument for C4, that he is unextended. Suppose an atheist runs through that argument, clearly and distinctly perceiving each step. His clear and distinct perceptions give him moral certainty—EP14 says all clear and distinct perceptions are morally certain—but he lacks metaphysical certainty since he has not ruled out the clear and distinct perception version of the Deceiver Hypothesis. The atheist is morally, but not metaphysically, certain that he is unextended, just as Descartes, in Medita-

---

19. Hooker also assumes Descartes believes that whatever is unextended is essentially unextended. Not so. Descartes believes that being unextended is one of his *necessary*, but *nonessential* properties. Remember that he limits his essence to thought. We can fix this aspect of Hooker's counterexample argument by replacing his references to Descartes's essential properties by ones to Descartes's necessary properties.

tion Two, is morally, but not metaphysically, certain that he has a body. The atheist may now mimic the Gambit Defense of C3:

1. I am morally, but not metaphysically, certain that I am unextended.
2. Some hypothesis gives me a reason to doubt that I am unextended.   [from 1 and EP1]
3. Some hypothesis indicates how my *de se* belief that I am unextended might be false despite my evidence for it or how an essential part of my evidence might be false despite my evidence for that essential part.   [from 2 and D3]
4. The clear and distinct perception version of the Deceiver Hypothesis indicates how my *de se* belief that I am unextended might be false despite my evidence for it.
5. The content of my *de se* belief that I am unextended is not a logically necessary truth.
6. The clear and distinct perception version of the Deceiver Hypothesis and the content of my *de se* belief that I am unextended are such that it is logically possible that the former is true and the latter is false.   [from 4, 5, and EP13]
7. The clear and distinct perception version of the Deceiver Hypothesis entails the content of my *de se* beliefs that I think and exist.   [from 4 and EP15]
8. The clear and distinct perception version of the Deceiver Hypothesis, the content of my *de se* belief that I think, the content of my *de se* belief that I exist, and the content of my *de se* belief that I am unextended are such that it is logically possible that the first three are true and the fourth is false.   [from 6 and 7]
9. The clear and distinct perception version of the Deceiver Hypothesis, the content of my *de se* belief that I think, the content of my *de se* belief that I exist, and I are such that it is logically necessary that if they are true, then I exist and they are all true of me.
10. The content of my *de se* belief that I exist, the content of my *de se* belief that I am unextended, and I are such that if the first is true and the second is false, then I exist and the first is true of me and the second is false of me.
11. Therefore, I am such that it is logically possible that I exist, think, and am extended.   [from 8, 9, and 10]

Descartes cannot accept this conclusion. He believes himself to be a noncomposite substance and denies that such entities can think and be extended. Only a complex combination of two substances, a mind and a body, can both think and occupy space [*Notes against a Programme*; AT VIII-2, 350–351; HR I, 437].

Can Descartes consistently reject the atheist's argument without rejecting his own? I think so. Compare the fourth step in Descartes's argument:

> 4. The sensation version of the Deceiver Hypothesis indicates how my *de se* belief that I have a body might be false despite my evidence for it as long as all my evidence ultimately consists of sensation reports.

with the fourth step of the atheist's analogue:

> 4. The clear and distinct perception version of the Deceiver Hypothesis indicates how my *de se* belief that I am unextended might be false despite my evidence for it.

Neither premise follows directly from the ones before it. The preceding premises entail only that *either some unspecified* hypothesis indicates how the belief at hand might be false despite the evidence for it *or some unspecified* hypothesis indicates how an essential part of the evidence might be false despite the evidence for that essential part. The fourth premise in the Gambit Defense is based on Descartes's Meditation One analysis of his metaphysical uncertainty about having a body when sensation is his only source of evidence. The fourth premise in the atheist's argument is based on the atheist's analysis of his metaphysical uncertainty about being unextended when he clearly and distinctly perceives an argument to show that he is unextended. Descartes may say that his own analysis and fourth premise are correct whereas the atheist's analysis and fourth premise are incorrect.

Concentrate on Descartes's fourth premise. In Meditation One, he inductively bases his belief in his body on sensation reports. The sensation version of the Deceiver Hypothesis slides into the inductive gap between his belief and his evidence to indicate how his belief might be false despite his sensory evidence. He may have been created so that, while all his sensation reports are true, he is neither extended nor related to an extended thing that serves as his body. Now consider the atheist's fourth premise. The atheist deduces his belief that he is unextended by considering the argument Descartes ultimately provides for that conclusion. The argument consists of first-person claims about his epistemic state, epistemological principles, and metaphysical principles; he clearly and distinctly perceives them all, and they do in fact entail that he is unextended. Yet the clear and distinct perception version of the Deceiver Hypothesis does not cast doubt on the atheist's conclusion by sliding into an inductive gap between his conclusion and his premises to indicate how his conclusion might be false despite them. There is no inductive gap. The clear and distinct perception version of the Deceiver Hypothesis casts doubt on the atheist's conclusion by sliding into the gap between his direct clear and distinct perception of his supposedly self-evident epistemological and metaphysical principles and the principles themselves to indicate how they might be false despite his direct clear and distinct perception of them. The atheist's fourth premise is false. It should be

> 4(a). The clear and distinct perception version of the Deceiver Hypothesis indicates how some epistemological and metaphysical principles that are an essential part of my evidence for my *de se* belief that I am unextended might be false despite my evidence for them (my direct clear and distinct perception of them).

This premise does not enable the atheist to show that he can exist, think, and be extended.

If the atheist inductively bases his belief that he is unextended on sensation reports, will not his epistemic state with regard to that belief be analogous to Descartes's with regard to his belief that he has a body? No. Sensation can only give the atheist evidence to support his belief he *is extended*. The atheist will not be *morally certain* that he is unextended and will not, therefore, be able to infer by EP1 that he has reason to doubt that he is unextended: according to EP1, p is a metaphysical certainty for S if and only if p is a moral certainty for S and S has no reason to doubt p. To get from this to the conclusion that we have a reason to doubt p, we need the premise that we are morally, but not metaphysically, certain that p. The only way the atheist can gain moral certainty that he is unextended is to deduce that conclusion from sophisticated epistemological and metaphysical principles made morally certain by direct clear and distinct perception, in which case hypotheses give him a reason to doubt his morally certain belief that he is unextended by indicating how those principles might be false despite his clear and distinct perception of them.[20]

Descartes's Gambit and C2

Descartes says so little to defend his claim that he is essentially thinking (C2), that it is tempting to believe he awards it the same self-evident status he gives his belief that he thinks. C2 is not self-evident, however. Descartes needs an argument for it, and the question is whether his Gambit strategy can provide one.

We might generalize the argument for C3 to get an argument for the conclusion that no property other than thought is essential to him, add the assumption that some property is essential to him, and conclude that he is essentially thinking. The argument in outline form will run as follows:

  i. That I think and that I exist are metaphysically certain for me; every property I have other than thought is such that I am morally, but not metaphysically, certain that I have it as long as sensation is my only source of evidence.
 ii. If P is a property I have other than thought, I am such that it is logically possible that I exist, think, and lack P.   [from i]
iii. No property other than thought is essential to me.   [from ii]
 iv. Some property is essential to me.
  v. Therefore, I am essentially thinking.   [from iii and iv]

This is no way to interpret Descartes. The first premise is clearly false; Descartes has many properties of which his sensations do not make him morally certain; he will say that being unextended is one. The second premise is false, since Descartes cannot exist without the properties of being unextended and being created.

There is a better way. To show thought is essential to him, Descartes just has to show it meets three conditions: (1) it is necessary to him, (2) all his nonnecessary, nontranscendental properties are modes of it, and (3) it is nontranscendental. He does not need to worry about the third

---

20. Descartes would, I think, respond in a similar way to attempts to construct arguments analogous to his Gambit Defense of C3 to support other claims he rejects, such as that he is not necessarily created.

condition; it is obvious that something can exist without thinking. He needs only to make a few metaphysical assumptions to show the first and second conditions are met. The most controversial assumptions he needs are that some property is essential to him and that thought is a mode of extension if it is a mode of any property. These are not obviously true, and materialists need not accept them. Nonetheless they do not beg the question against materialists, and they are endorsed by any materialist who claims that extension is essential to Descartes and thought is only one of its modes.

Here is how Descartes can use these assumptions to show thought is essential to him.

The Gambit Defense of C2

1. I am such that it is logically possible that I exist, think, have sensations, and am not extended. [from P1, P2, and P3 in the Gambit Defense of C3]
2. I think.
3. Thought is a nonrelational property.
4. Some property is essential to me.
5. Thought is a mode of extension if it is a mode of any property.

Descartes's initial premise that he can think without being extended implies

6. Thought is not a mode of extension. [from 1]

Lines (5) and (6) entail

7. Thought is not a mode of any property. [from 5 and 6]

Since, by the definition of an essential property (D7), each of Descartes's nonnecessary, nonrelational properties is a mode of each of his essential properties, and since he is assuming that thought is a nonrelational property, he may infer

8. If I am such that I can exist but not think, then thought is a mode of whatever property is essential to me. [from 2, 3, 4, and D7]

Lines (4), (7), and (8) entail

9. I cannot exist without thinking. [from 4, 7, and 8]

Thought is necessary to Descartes.

Descartes still has to show that all his nonnecessary, nonrelational properties are modes of thought. He may say:

10. Doubt is one of my nonnecessary, nonrelational properties.

Since he is assuming that he has an essence, he may adopt

11. Doubt is a mode of whatever property is essential to me.   [from 4, 10, and D7]

It is also true that

12. If doubt is a mode of a particular property, then that property is thought, a mode of thought, or such that thought is a mode of it.

He has shown that thought is not a mode of any property, which combines with line (12) to entail

13. If doubt is a mode of a particular property, then that property is thought or a mode of thought.   [from 7 and 12]

Lines (11) and (13) entail

14. Whatever property is essential to me is thought or a mode of thought.   [from 11 and 13]

Since, by the definition of an essential property (D7), every nonnecessary, nonrelational property is a mode of whatever property is essential to Descartes, and the relation of being a mode is transitive, Descartes may conclude from (14) that

15. Every nonnecessary, nonrelational property I have is a mode of thought.   [from 14 and D7]

Thought clearly meets the third condition for being essential to Descartes:

16. Thought is a nontranscendental property.

Descartes may conclude:

17. Therefore, I am essentially thinking. [from 9, 15, 16, and D7]

The first stage of the argument (lines 1–9) shows that thought is necessary to Descartes; the second stage (lines 10–15) shows that all his nonnecessary, nonrelational properties are modes of thought. It is assumed in line (16) that thought is a nontranscendental property. That Descartes is essentially thinking follows by the definition of an essential property (D7).

It is important to appreciate the role played by the first premise, that Descartes can exist, think, even have sensations, without being extended. Descartes uses this premise, along with the assumption that if thought is a mode of any property it is a mode of extension, to rule out the possibility that thought is just a mode of some property that is essential to him. He gets his first premise from P1, P2, and P3 in the Gambit Defense of C3. His defense of C2 thus stems from his defense of C3. It is ultimately based on his three initial premises about self-knowledge and depends on his position on the nature and content of certainty.

I do not, of course, claim that Descartes actually develops this argument for C2. He never develops any argument for C2. My claim is that this argument is available to him, and if we take it to be an argument he would give, we can better appreciate several parts of his position. We can see why Descartes cannot gain metaphysical certainty of C2 in Meditation Two. The Gambit Defense of C2 uses a host of premises that are metaphysically uncertain for him until he rules out his clear and distinct perception version of the Deceiver Hypothesis. Descartes admits in Meditation Two that he is metaphysically uncertain of the first premise, that he can think without being extended [AT VII, 27; HR I, 152; & AT VII, 7–8; HR I, 137–138]. We can extend the Gambit Defense of C2 to obtain Descartes's further conclusion that thought is his only essential property. Line (14) of the argument says each of his essential properties is thought or a mode of thought. Just by adding the premise that no essential property is a mode of another, it follows that thought alone is Descartes's essence. Most important of all, the Gambit Defense of C2 shows how Descartes can

derive C2 from his initial premises about self-knowledge. The deriva-
tion makes use of metaphysical assumptions, especially that some
property is essential to him and that thought is a mode of extension if it
is a mode of any property, which clearly need some argument. Yet
these assumptions do not beg the question against materialists and are
in fact accepted by any materialist who says extension is essential to
Descartes and thought is one of its modes. At the very least, Descartes
can confront materialists with a challenging argument for C2 to go
with his powerful argument for C3.

Descartes's defense of the first part of his theory of the self is much
stronger than is often thought. Once we understand the major concepts he uses, such as those of substance and an essential property,
ignore the dead ends suggested by remarks that seem to imply use of
the Clear and Distinct Perception and Epistemic Criterion defenses
and take his references to his Gambit strategy seriously, we can see that
he establishes the weak version of C1, that he is a substance, with
metaphysical certainty in Meditation Two, has a powerful argument
for C3, that he is not essentially extended, and can parlay his defense
of C3 into challenging arguments for attribute dualism and C2, that he
is essentially thinking. Descartes's arguments contain controversial
premises—what else would we expect?—but he never begs the question by simply assuming what any materialist would deny.

Chapter 7

BODY AND SOUL

Scratch a radical, and you will often find a moderate brave enough to go where the laws of logic and a few seductive assumptions lead. Berkeley derives his idealism from his rejection of scepticism, Hume his scepticism from his empiricism, and Mill his libertarianism from his utilitarianism. In the second part of his theory of the self, Descartes derives his substance dualism—minds are not bodies—from his views on his essence, which he has just derived from his almost commonsensical theory of self-knowledge.

Three Theses

Descartes gives us three radical theses to consider. He presents the thesis that he is numerically distinct from his body implicitly in

C4: I am not extended.

and explicitly in

C5: I am not numerically identical with my body.

He also separates himself and his body in another way.

Two substances are said to be really distinct, when each of them can exist apart from the other. [*Reply to the Second Objections*; AT VII, 162; HR II, 53]

Descartes presents the thesis that he is "really distinct" from his body in C6:

C6:   My body and I are such that each can exist without the other (it is logically possible that it exists but I do not, and it is logically possible that I exist and it does not.)[1]

The third thesis is Descartes's claim to be a substance in the strong sense defined by D6b.

C1b: I have a real attribute, and there is no *y* such that *y* has a real attribute, *y* is numerically distinct from me, *y* exists contingently, and it is logically impossible that I exist and *y* does not exist.

Other commentators interpret Descartes's claim to be really distinct from his body differently than I do. Edwin Curley reads it as the claim that Descartes is numerically distinct from his body; Bernard Williams reads it as the claim that Descartes is necessarily numerically distinct from his body.[2] They are both wrong. Descartes's definition of real distinction in the *Reply to the Second Objections*, which I have just quoted, makes it quite clear that to say substances are really distinct is not to say they are numerically distinct or even necessarily numerically distinct; it is to say that they can exist without each other.

The Numerical Distinction Thesis does not entail the Real Distinction Thesis. Substances, in the generous D6a sense of 'substance,' can be numerically distinct even though at least one of them can not exist without the other. God and Descartes are numerically diverse, but Descartes cannot exist without God. Descartes is numerically diverse from the substance composed of himself and his body, but that sub-

---

1. I read C6 *de re*. A *de dicto* reading implies that it is logically possible that something is my body and I do not exist. This is obviously false. It is impossible that something is *my* body and I do not exist (although it is logically possible that something, which was by body when I existed, now exists and I do not).

2. Edwin Curley, *Descartes against the Skeptics* (Cambridge: Harvard University Press, 1978), pp. 197–199; Bernard Williams, *Descartes: The Project of Pure Inquiry* (New York: Penguin Books, 1978), p. 117.

stance cannot exist without him. The Real Distinction Thesis entails the Numerical Distinction Thesis, however. If *x* and *y* are really distinct, each can exist without the other, and if each can exist without the other, they are not necessarily numerically identical; if they are not necessarily numerically identical, they are not numerically identical, period.

Some may object that substances can be numerically identical without being necessarily so. Curley notes: "The morning star is identical with the evening star, but this identity statement is a contingent one, whose truth had to be learned by empirical investigation."[3] It all depends on what we take the identity statement to be. There is the *de dicto* claim: "The morning star is numerically identical with the evening star, and it is logically possible that the morning star is not numerically identical with the evening star." This claim is true, but it does not contradict my *de re* claim that *x* and *y* are numerically identical only if they are necessarily numerically identical. There is the *de re* claim: "The morning star is numerically identical with the evening star, and these things are themselves such that it is logically possible that they are numerically diverse." This is false. One and the same thing is both the morning star and the evening star, and that thing cannot be other than itself.

Descartes only needs to establish the Numerical Distinction Thesis to establish substance dualism, so why is he interested in the stronger Real Distinction Thesis? Indeed, why does he give it so much attention? He argues for it in a special supplement to the *Reply to the Second Objections* [AT VII, 160–170; HR II, 52–59] and entitles Meditation Six, "Of the Existence of Material Things, and the Real Distinction between the Soul and Body of Man."

Descartes wants to establish the Real Distinction Thesis to accomplish the second "official" task he announces in the letter of dedication to the *Meditations*. His first official task is to prove God's existence [*Meditations*; AT VII, 1–3; HR I, 133–134]; his second concerns the immortality of the soul:

> And as regards the soul, although many have considered that it is not easy to know its nature, and some have even dared to say that human

3. Curley, *Descartes against the Skeptics*, p. 202.

reasons have convinced us that it would perish with the body, and that
faith alone could believe the contrary, nevertheless, inasmuch as the
Lateran Council held under Leo X (in the eighth session) condemns
these tenents, and as Leo expressly ordains Christian philosophers to
refute their arguments and to employ all their powers in making known
the truth, I have ventured in this treatise to undertake the same task.
[*Meditations*; AT VII, 2–3; HR I, 134]

Descartes does not try to show that the soul continues to exist after the
body is destroyed, since

the premises from which the immortality of the soul may be deduced
depend on an elucidation of a complete system of Physics. [*Meditations*;
AT VII, 13–14; HR I, 141]

He settles for showing that

the extinction of the mind *does not follow* from the corruption of the
body. [*Meditations*; AT VII, 13; HR I, 141; my emphasis]

He does this by showing that he is really distinct from his body; he *can*
exist even if it does not.

Let me clarify his position a bit. There are several ways to play the
devil's advocate and argue for personal mortality. One could argue as
follows:

  i. I am necessarily such that if nothing exists as my body, then I do not
     exist.
 ii. If my body experiences death and the accompanying physical cor-
     ruption, then nothing will exist as my body.
iii. Therefore, if my body experiences death and the accompanying
     physical corruption, I will no longer exist.

Descartes does not need the Real Distinction Thesis to block this
argument. The Gambit Defense of C3, that he is not essentially extended, contains a strong argument to show that the first premise is
false; he can exist, think, even have sensations, without having a body.
Descartes could not use the Real Distinction Thesis to stop this argument if he wanted to do so. The argument is based on the premise that
he cannot exist unless *something* is his body, and the Real Distinction

Thesis says only that he can exist without *that particular substance which is his body.*

I think Descartes wants to use the Real Distinction Thesis to answer a different argument:

i. My body and I are necessarily such that if my body does not exist, then I do not exist.
ii. If my body experiences death and the accompanying physical corruption, then it will cease to exist.
iii. Therefore, if my body experiences death and the accompanying physical corruption, I will cease to exist.

Read the first premise *de re:* Descartes and his body are such that he cannot exist unless it does. According to the second premise Descartes's body ceases to exist when it experiences death. Descartes rejects both premises, but he is only ready to refute the first in the *Meditations*. His argument against the second involves showing that the substance that is his body is not destroyed in death, and, as he points out [*Meditations*; AT VII, 13–14; HR I, 141], he cannot show this without venturing far beyond the scope of the *Meditations* to develop his physics. To refute the first premise, Descartes must show he can exist even if that substance that is his body does not. This is just what the Real Distinction Thesis says.

The Numerical Distinction Thesis: Non-Gambit Interpretations

Some commentators think that Descartes derives the Numerical Distinction Thesis (C4 and C5) from the Real Distinction Thesis or a variation on it.[4] Two things encourage this view. The Real Distinction Thesis entails the Numerical Distinction Thesis, and it is initially hard, especially if we think of substance dualism as the highpoint of Descartes's theory of the self, to see how the Real Distinction Thesis

---

4. Curley interprets Descartes as attempting to derive the thesis that he is numerically distinct from his body from the claim that each mind exists independently of each body and each body exists independently of each mind; *Descartes against the Skeptics*, pp. 197–199.

can be important except as a stepping stone to the Numerical Distinction Thesis.

Nonetheless, we have just seen that the Real Distinction Thesis has an important role of its own in Descartes's philosophy, and, when we consider the text, we find that he never explicitly uses it as a lemma to show that he is numerically distinct from his body. Descartes does not even mention numerical distinction when he discusses the real distinction between himself and his body in the *Reply to the Second Objections*:

> God can effect whatever we clearly perceive just as we perceive it (preceding Corollary). But we clearly perceive the mind, i.e. a thinking substance, apart from the body, i.e. apart from any extended substance (Post. II); and vice versa we can (as all admit) perceive body apart from mind. Hence, at least through the instrumentality of the Divine power, mind can exist apart from body, and body apart from mind.
>
> But now, substances that can exist apart from each other, are really distinct (Def. X). But mind and body are substances (Deff. V, VI and VII), that can exist apart from each other (just proved). Hence there is a real distinction between mind and body. [AT VII, 169–170; HR II, 59]

He does not present the Numerical Distinction Thesis when he presents the Real Distinction Thesis in Meditation Six:

> And although possibly (or rather certainly, as I shall say in a moment) I possess a body with which I am very intimately conjoined, yet because, on the one side, I have a clear and distinct idea of myself inasmuch as I am only a thinking and unextended thing, and as, on the other, I possess a distinct idea of body, inasmuch as it is only an extended and unthinking thing, it is certain that I am really distinct from my body and can exist without it. [AT VII, 78; HR I, 190*][5]

5. Haldane and Ross translate Descartes's conclusion in a way that is closer to the French text. They give us "It is certain that this I (that is to say, my soul by which I am what I am), is entirely and absolutely distinct from my body, and can exist without it" [HR I, 190]. The French text is "Il est certain que ce moi, c'est-à-dire mon âme, par laquelle je suis ce que je suis, est entièrement & véritablement distincte de mon corps, & qu'elle peut être ou exister sans lui" [AT IX, 62]. The Latin text is: "Certum est me a corpore meo revera esse distinctum, & absque illo posse existere" [AT VII, 78]. Even if we read Descartes as they do and take his conclusion to contain both the Numerical Distinction Thesis and the Real Distinction Thesis, this passage does not give us any textual warrant for believing he wants to derive the former from the latter.

In the *Discourse*, Descartes reflects on his self-knowledge and reports:

> From that I knew that I was a substance the whole essence or nature of which is to think, and that for its existence there is no need of any place, nor does it depend on any material thing; so that this 'me,' that is to say, the soul by which I am what I am, is entirely distinct from body, and is even more easy to know than is the latter; and even if body were not, the soul would not cease to be what it is. [AT VI, 33; HR I, 101]

Even if we read Descartes's claim to be "entirely" distinct from his body as a reference to both real and numerical distinctness, there is no indication here that he derives the latter from the former.

There is another popular misconception about how Descartes argues for the Numerical Distinction Thesis. In *The Search after Truth*, he has Polyander say:

> And more than that, I do not even know that I have a body, since you have shown me that I might doubt it. In addition to this I may add that I cannot even absolutely deny that I have a body. Yet, while entirely setting aside all these suppositions, this will not prevent my being certain that I exist. On the contrary, they confirm me yet more in the certainty that I exist and that I am not a body; otherwise, doubting of my body, I should at the same time doubt of myself, and this I cannot do; for I am absolutely convinced that I exist, and I am so much convinced of it, that I can in no wise doubt of it. [AT X, 518; HR I, 319; consider too: *Discourse*; AT VI, 33; HR I, 101]

Many incorrectly believe Descartes is inferring the Numerical Distinction Thesis from the fact that he can doubt his body's existence but not his own.

Anthony Kenny suggests that Descartes is giving this argument:[6]

1. I can feign that my body does not exist.
2. I cannot feign that I do not exist.
3. Therefore, I am not numerically identical with my body.   [from 1 and 2]

Kenny points out the argument's flaw. To get from the premises to the conclusion, we need the principle of the indiscernibility of identicals:

6. Anthony Kenny, *Descartes: A Study of His Philosophy* (New York: Random House, 1968), p. 79. I have slightly modified Kenny's statement of the argument.

"For any things x and y, if x is numerically identical with y, then for all properties P, x has P if and only if y has P." This principle is not applicable to intensional contexts, and that is just what we have in the first two premises, which are to be read *de dicto*.[7]

Michael Hooker presents a different version of the argument from doubt with a different logical flaw:[8]

1. I can doubt that my body exists.
2. I cannot doubt that I exist.
3. My body has the property of being possibly doubted by me to exist. [from 1]
4. I do not have the property of being possibly doubted by me to exist. [from 2]
5. For all things x and y, if x is numerically identical with y, then for all properties P, x has P if and only if y has P.
6. If I am numerically identical with my body, then my body has the property of being possibly doubted by me to exist if and only if I have the property of being possibly doubted by me to exist. [from 5]
7. My body, but not I, has the property of being possibly doubted by me to exist. [from 3 and 4]
8. Therefore, I am not numerically identical with my body. [from 6 and 7]

This argument correctly applies the principle of the indiscernibility of identicals to the extensional contexts provided by premises (3) and (4), which are to be read *de re*. The new error in the argument is that (3) and (4) do not follow from the first two *de dicto* premises. Hooker tells us:

> There is something wrong with the inference from (1) and (2) to [3] and [4], from *de dicto* propositions to their *de re* counterparts. To see that the inference is amiss, suppose that I am attempting to discover whether John is Tom's father. I reason as follows. I can doubt that John has ever fathered a son, so John has the property of being possibly doubted by me to have ever fathered a son. I cannot doubt that Tom's father has ever fathered a son, so Tom's father does not have the property of being

7. Kenny, *Descartes*, p. 80.
8. Michael Hooker, "Descartes's Denial of Mind–Body Identity," in *Descartes: Critical and Interpretive Essays*, ed. Michael Hooker (Baltimore: Johns Hopkins University Press, 1978), pp. 172–173.

possibly doubted by me to have ever fathered a son. Since John has a property not had by Tom's father, the two are distinct.[9]

The problem with both Kenny's and Hooker's interpretations is just that there is a more charitable and more interesting way to interpret Descartes. We may read his remarks in *The Search after Truth* and elsewhere so that, instead of containing sophomoric logical blunders, they contain a cogent attempt to extend his Gambit strategy to the defense of the Numerical Distinction Thesis.

Descartes's Gambit and C4 and C5

I believe that Descartes intends to derive C4, that he is not extended, and C5, that he is numerically distinct from his body, from his claims about his essence, which are in turn derived from his views on self-knowledge. Descartes's reasoning is impeccable. His mistakes lie in the metaphysical assumptions by which he links the Numerical Distinction Thesis to his position on his essence, and even those are attractive when viewed in themselves rather than with an eye to where they ultimately lead in the context of his philosophy.

Take another look at the passage in *The Search after Truth*:

> And more than that, I do not even know [*scio*] that I have a body, since you have shown me that I might doubt of it. In addition to this I may add that I cannot even absolutely deny that I have a body. Yet, while entirely setting aside all these suppositions, this will not prevent my being certain that I exist. On the contrary, they confirm me yet more in the certainty that I exist and I am not a body; otherwise, doubting of my body, I should at the same time doubt of myself, and this I cannot do; for I am absolutely convinced [*persuasus*] that I exist, and I am so much convinced [*persuasus*] of it that I can in no wise doubt of it. [AT X, 518; HR I, 319]

Descartes concludes, "I am not a body"; I think that it is best to read his statement as C4, that he is not extended. C5, that he is numerically distinct from his body, ultimately follows from C4 by the uncontrover-

---

9. Hooker, "Descartes's Denial of Mind–Body Identity," pp. 173–174; I have modified the numerical references in Hooker's statement so that they correctly refer to premises (3) and (4) in the argument at hand.

sial assumption that his body is extended. Descartes's premises seem to concern what he *can* doubt, especially in the last sentence of the passage, but he is actually concerned with what is metaphysically certain for him. Consider his talk about what he *knows* right at the start of the passage. He confuses psychological certainty with metaphysical certainty as he goes on, but we have seen him fall into this mistake before and should be able to see through it by now. His intended strategy is to derive C4 and, ultimately, C5 from premises about his self-knowledge.

Descartes's argument in the *Discourse* accepts a similar interpretation. He opens with his premises about self-knowledge:

> And then, examining attentively that which I was, I saw that I could conceive that I had no body, and that there was no world nor place where I might be [P3]; but yet that I could not for all that conceive that I was not [P2]. On the contrary, I saw from the very fact that I thought of doubting the truth of other things, it very evidently and certainly followed that I was [P1 and P2]; on the other hand if I had only ceased from thinking, even if all the rest of what I had ever imagined had really existed, I should have no reason for thinking that I had existed. [AT VI, 32–33; HR I, 101]

He goes on to infer, first, that he is a substance the whole essence of which is to think (C1, C2, and C3), then, that he is not extended (C4) and, finally, that he is numerically and really distinct from his body (C5 and C6):

> From that I knew that I was a substance the whole essence or nature of which is to think, [C1, C2, and C3] and that for its existence there is no need of any place [C4], nor does it depend on any material thing; so that this 'me,' that is to say, the soul by which I am what I am, is entirely distinct from body [C5 and C6], and is even more easy to know than is the latter, and even if body were not, the soul would not cease to be what it is. [AT VI, 32–33; HR I, 101]

How can Descartes get from his premises about self-knowledge to C4 and C5? The most direct available route is this:

The Gambit Defense of C4 and C5

1. That I think and that I exist are metaphysically certain for me; that I

have a body is morally, but not metaphysically, certain for me as long as all my evidence consists of sensation reports.

2. I can exist, think, have sensations, but lack a body.   [from 1 by the moves used in the Gambit Defense of C3, that Descartes is not essentially extended]
3. If I am extended, I am necessarily extended.
4. I am not extended.   [from 2 and 3]
5. That substance which is my body is extended.
6. For all things x and y, if x is numerically identical with y, then for all properties P, x has P if and only if y has P.
7. Therefore, I am not numerically identical with my body.   [from 4, 5, and 6]

The argument opens with the successful moves used in the Gambit Defense of C3 to show that Descartes can exist without a body. C4 follows on the assumption that all extended things are necessarily extended, which Descartes clearly accepts. C5 follows by the principle of the indiscernibility of identicals and the assumption that Descartes's body is extended, which he also accepts.

The Gambit Defense of C4 and C5 displays the roots of Descartes's substance dualism. His substance dualism is an extension of his essentialism, which he derives from his premises about self-knowledge with the aid of his position on the nature and content of certainty.

The Gambit Defense of C4 and C5 helps us appreciate Descartes's view that he cannot establish C4 and C5 with metaphysical certainty until Meditation Six. He is in the epistemic state described by the first premise as early as Meditation Two, but he is not metaphysically certain that he is in that state or of the rest of his argument until he rules out the clear and distinct perception version of the Deceiver Hypothesis by the arguments of Meditations Three, Four, and Five.

The Gambit Defense is innocent of the logical blunders in the arguments from doubt suggested by Kenny and Hooker. There is no misuse of the principle of the indiscernibility of identicals here; no faulty inference from *de dicto* propositions to their *de re* counterparts. The principle of the indiscernibility of identicals is applied to the extensional contexts supplied by lines (4) and (5). Line (4), that Descartes is not extended, is validly deduced from previous steps in the argument. Line (5), that Descartes's body is extended, is uncontroversial. There is only one potentially controversial and undefended step in the argument: the premise that if Descartes is extended he is necessarily extended. This premise does not beg the question against materialists—some even accept it—but it needs justification. Why not say Descartes is only contingently extended and bail out of his Gambit, before it lands us in substance dualism?

Descartes never tries to show that if he is extended he is necessarily extended, but it is worth considering how he might do so. His essentialism is, I think, the key. He accepts:

1. I have an essential property.

The definition of an essential property (D7) implies:

2. If I am contingently extended, then either extension is a relational property or it is a mode of every property essential to me.

He believes:

3. Extension is not a mode of any other property.
4. Extension is a nonrelational property.

Descartes affirms the fourth premise in the *Principles*, where he identifies a thing's extension with its "internal place" rather than with its "external place" [II, xv; AT VIII, 48; HR I, 261] and says the difference between internal and external place is that external place is "magnitude, figure, and situation *as regards other bodies*" [II, xiii; AT VIII, 47; HR I, 260; my emphasis], while internal place is not. These premises entail:

5. Therefore, if I am extended, I am necessarily extended.

Perhaps Descartes would reason in this way and so move from the assumption that he has an essence to the view that he is extended only if he is necessarily extended, and from there, by the Gambit Defense of C4 and C5, to the Numerical Distinction Thesis and substance dualism. The basic metaphysical assumption in his argument would then be that he has an essence, some necessary property of which every one of his contingent nonrelational properties is a mode. We may not want to join him in this assumption, especially after seeing how easily it can lead to substance dualism, but we must admit that it is not question begging or wildly implausible.[10]

Descartes's Gambit and C6

Does Descartes do equally well in his defense of the even stronger Real Distinction Thesis? It is hard to tell. First, we have to plane away several apparent inconsistencies and ambiguities to give his argument a definite shape; then we can consider some major objections that have been made to it.

Consider, once again, the Meditation Six version of Descartes's argument:

> And first of all, because I know that all things which I understand clearly and distinctly can be created by God just as I understand them, it suffices that I am able to understand one thing apart from another clearly and distinctly in order to be certain that the one is different from the other, since they may be made to exist in separation at least by the omnipotence of God; and it does not matter by what power this separation is made for me to judge them to be different. . . . and although possibly (or rather certainly, as I shall say in a moment) I possess a body with which I am very intimately conjoined, yet because, on the one side, I have a clear and distinct idea of myself inasmuch as I am only a thinking and unextended thing, and as, on the other, I possess a distinct idea of body, inasmuch as it is only an extended and unthinking thing, it is certain that I am really distinct from my body and can exist without it. [AT VII, 78; HR I, 190*]

Descartes argues in a similar way in *Reply to the Second Objections:*

> God can effect whatever we clearly perceive just as we perceive it (preceding Corollary). But we clearly perceive the mind, i.e. a thinking substance, apart from the body, i.e. apart from any extended substance (Post. II); and *vice versa* we can (as all admit) perceive the body apart from the mind. Hence, at least through the instrumentality of the Divine power, mind can exist apart from body, and body apart from mind.

10. That Descartes has an essence is also a crucial assumption in the Gambit Defense of C2, that he is essentially thinking. Consider my discussion of that argument in Chapter 6.

But now, substances that can exist apart from each other, are really distinct (Def. X). But mind and body are substances (Deff. V, VI and VII) that can exist apart from each other (just proved). Hence, there is a real distinction between mind and body. [AT VII, 169–170; HR II, 59]

Descartes never indicates that these passages contain different arguments, and the differences between them seem to be ones of style rather than substance: Descartes, for example, writes of himself and his body in Meditation Six and of the mind and the body in *Reply to the Second Objections*. I treat the passages as containing the same argument.[11] That argument goes roughly like this:

The Gambit Defense of C6: First Version

1. Whatever I clearly and distinctly understand can be made by God just as I understand it.
2. If I clearly and distinctly understand x apart from y and y apart from x, then x and y are such that God can cause x to exist while y does not exist, and y to exist while x does not exist.   [from 1]
3. If x and y are such that God can cause x to exist while y does not exist, and y to exist while x does not exist, then x and y are such that it is logically possible that x exists while y does not exist, and it is logically possible that y exists while x does not exist (x and y are really distinct).
4. If I clearly and distinctly understand x apart from y and y apart from x, then x and y are really distinct.   [from 2 and 3]
5. I clearly and distinctly understand x apart from y and y apart from x if there is a property P and a property Q such that I clearly and distinctly understand that x has P but lacks Q, and I clearly and distinctly understand that y has Q but lacks P.
6. I clearly and distinctly understand that I have thought but lack extension, and I clearly and distinctly understand that my body has extension but lacks thought.
7. Therefore, my body and I are really distinct.   [from 4, 5, and 6]

Descartes starts with the general principle that whatever he clearly and distinctly understands can be created by God as he understands it. He infers the more specific principle that if he clearly and distinctly under-

---

11. What of the *Discourse* [AT VI, 33; HR I, 101]? Does Descartes defend the Real Distinction Thesis in a similar way there? Descartes does not develop an argument for the Real Distinction Thesis in the *Discourse*, although he surely has it and the Numerical Distinction Thesis in mind in his conclusion: "This 'me,' that is to say, the soul by which I am what I am, is entirely distinct from body."

stands one thing apart from another, God can make each exist apart from the other. He refines this principle into a criterion for real distinctness, which he applies to himself and his body by claiming to understand clearly and distinctly that he thinks but is not extended and that his body is extended but does not think.

How important is God's role in the argument? Would Descartes accept an argument just like this one, except that the references to what God can do are replaced by ones to what is logically possible and premise three, which links God's abilities to what is logically possible, is gone? Sometimes the answer seems to be no:

> In order to prove that one thing is really distinct from another, nothing less can be said, than that the divine power can separate one from the other. [*Reply to the Fourth Objections*; AT VII, 227; HR II, 102]

Sometimes the answer seems to be yes:

> It does not matter by what power this separation is made for me to judge them [my mind and my body] to be different. [*Meditations*; AT VII, 78; HR I, 190*]

> Here it must be noted that I employed the Divine power as a means, not because any extraordinary power was needed to effect the separation of mind and body, but because, treating as I did of God alone in what precedes, there was nothing else for me to use. But our knowledge of the real distinctness of two things is unaffected by any question as to the power that disunites them. [*Reply to the Second Objections*; AT VII, 170; HR II, 59]

It is at least clear what Descartes's position *should* be. His use of God as a link between what he clearly and distinctly understands and what is logically possible is inconsistent with his general position on God's abilities. Premise (3) assumes God can only do what is logically possible, but Descartes thinks God is not limited by the laws of logic; all things possible and impossible are within God's power. It is best to interpret Descartes's argument so that it does not rely on God:

The Gambit Defense of C6: Second Version

1. If I clearly and distinctly understand x apart from y and y apart from x, then x and y are such that it is logically possible that x exists while y does not exist, and it is logically possible that y exists while x does not exist (x and y are really distinct).

2. I clearly and distinctly understand *x* apart from *y* and *y* apart from *x* if there is a property *P* and a property *Q* such that I clearly and distinctly understand that *x* has *P* but lacks *Q*, and I clearly and distinctly understand that *y* has *Q* but lacks *P*.

3. I clearly and distinctly understand that I have thought but lack extension, and I clearly and distinctly understand that my body has extension but lacks thought.

4. Therefore, my body and I are really distinct.   [from 1, 2, and 3]

We now face two tough questions about Descartes's talk of what he clearly and distinctly understands. First, is Descartes concerned with what he clearly and distinctly *perceives* or with what he clearly and distinctly *conceives?* The difference is important. It is tantamount to that between what he knows to be the case and what he can conceive to be the case. Descartes's clear and distinct perceptions are limited to what is true, psychologically certain, and, at this point in the *Meditations*, metaphysically certain for him. His clear and distinct conceptions presumably—Descartes never explains what it is for a conception to be clear and distinct—extend, like conception in general, to what is false, dubitable, and even unreasonable to believe. Descartes can clearly and distinctly conceive of something's being the case when it actually is not—when he can doubt that it is and when it is unreasonable for him to believe that it is. If his clear and distinct conceptions are limited at all, they are, I suppose, limited to what is logically possible.[12] Second, is Descartes concerned with what he clearly and distinctly understands *de dicto* or with what he clearly and distinctly understands *de re?* We may read his second premise *de dicto:*

2a. I clearly and distinctly understand *x* apart from *y* and *y* apart from *x* if there is a proposition *p* to the effect that *x* has a property *P* but lacks a property *Q*, a proposition *q* to the effect that *y* has *Q* but lacks *P*, and I clearly and distinctly understand that *p* and that *q*.

We may also read it *de re:*

2b. I clearly and distinctly understand *x* apart from *y* and *y* apart from *x* if there is a property *P* and a property *Q* such that I clearly and

12. Edwin Curley seems to think that Descartes is concerned with what he clearly and distinctly *conceives; Descartes against the Skeptics*, pp. 193–199. Margaret Wilson seems to think that Descartes is concerned with what he clearly and distinctly *perceives; Descartes* (London: Routledge and Kegan Paul, 1978), pp. 185–198.

distinctly understand of *x* that it has *P* but lacks *Q*, and I clearly and distinctly understand of *y* that it has *Q* but lacks *P*.

Although (2a) and (2b) are equivalent on some accounts of the distinction between *de dicto* and *de re* attitudes, they are not equivalent on others.

The text requires us to interpret Descartes as concerned with what he clearly and distinctly perceives. Although, when he presents his argument in Meditation Six, Descartes writes vaguely of what he "understands,"[13] he writes quite clearly of what he perceives in *Replies to the Second Objections*.[14] He again writes of what he perceives in his response to Arnauld's objections:

> But mind can be perceived [*percipi*] distinctly and completely, or sufficiently so to let it be considered to be a complete thing without any of those forms or attributes by which we recognize that body is a substance, as I think I have sufficiently shown in the Second Meditation; and body is understood [*intelligitur*] distinctly and as a complete thing apart from the attributes attaching to the mind. [*Reply to the Fourth Objections*; AT VII, 223; HR II, 99–100*][15]

There is also strong philosophical support for taking Descartes to be concerned with his clear and distinct perceptions rather than his clear

13. Et primò, quoniam scio omnia quæ clare & distincte intelligo, talia a Deo fieri posse qualia illa intelligo, satis est quòd possim unam rem absque alterâ clare & distincte intelligere, ut certus sim unam ab alterâ esse diversam, quia potest saltem a Deo seorsim poni [AT VII, 78; consider too: *Principles*, I, lx; AT VIII, 28; HR I, 243].

14. Quidquid clare percipimus, a Deo fieri potest, prout illud percipimus (per. coroll. præcedens). Sed clare percipimus mentem, hoc est, substantiam cogitantem, absque corpore, hoc est, absque substantiâ aliquâ extensa (per. post. 2); & vice versâ corpus absque mente (ut facilè omnes concedunt) [AT VII, 169–170].

15. Some passages in the French text may seem to support the view that Descartes is concerned with what he clearly and distinctly conceives: "Tout ce que nous concevons clairement peut être fait par Dieu en la manière que nous le concevons" [*Reply to the Second Objections*; AT IX, 131]; "Il suffit que je puisse concevoir clairement et distinctement une chose sans une autre, pour être certain que l'une est distincte ou différente de l'autre" [*Meditations*; AT IX, 62]. Yet Descartes uses the very same talk of 'conception' to describe what he clearly and distinctly *perceives*. Here is how the principle that all clear and distinct perceptions are true is presented in Meditation 4: "Parce que toute conception claire et distincte est sans doute quelque chose de réel et de positif, et partant ne peut tirer son origine du néant, mais doit nécessairement avoir Dieu pour son auteur, Dieu, dis-je, qui,étant souverainement parfait, ne peut être cause d'aucune erreur; & par conséquent il faut conclure qu'une telle conception ou un tel jugement est véritable" [AT IX, 49–50].

and distinct conceptions. His first two premises will be false if they are about what he clearly and distinctly conceives; it does not matter whether we read them *de dicto* or *de re*.

Take Descartes's first two premises to be about what he clearly and distinctly conceives *de dicto*. They claim that if he clearly and distinctly conceives a proposition to the effect that x has P but lacks Q, and he clearly and distinctly conceives a proposition to the effect that y has Q but lacks P, then he clearly and distinctly conceives each substance apart from the other, and they are really distinct. Not so. Descartes is not really distinct from Descartes, but if he is Elizabeth's favorite substance and does not realize it, he may clearly and distinctly conceive the propositions he would express by "I think but am not extended" and "Elizabeth's favorite substance is extended but does not think"; the first is a proposition to the effect that he thinks but is not extended, and the second a proposition to the effect that he is extended but does not think.[16]

What if Descartes's first two premises are about his *de re* clear and distinct conceptions? They then claim that if Descartes clearly and distinctly conceives of x that it has P but lacks Q and clearly and distinctly conceives of y that it has Q but lacks P, then he clearly and distinctly conceives each substance apart from the other, and they are really distinct. Descartes does not develop a full account of *de re* attitudes. The most I have extracted from his remarks is the necessary condition:

EP8: S is metaphysically certain (believes, doubts, conceives, etc.) *de re* of x that it is F only if there is a proposition p such that (1) S is metaphysically certain (believes, doubts, conceives, etc.) *de dicto* that p, and (2) p is a proposition to the effect that x is F.

To conceive *de re* of a substance that it has one property but not another, one must conceive *de dicto* a proposition to the effect that the substance has the one property but not the other. What else, if anything, is required? If we answer this question for Descartes by either of

---

16. Descartes can clearly and distinctly conceive these propositions separately and he can clearly and distinctly conceive their conjunction, which he would express by "I think but am not extended, and Elizabeth's favorite substance is extended but does not think."

the two standard approaches now taken to *de re* attitudes, his premises—interpreted as premises about *de re* clear and distinct conception—turn out to be false.[17]

The latitudinarian approach is to make the condition in EP8 both
necessary and sufficient for *de re* attitudes. The *de re* versions of
Descartes's premises then have the same problem as the *de dicto* ones.
They can be used to show that he is really distinct from himself.

The classical approach is to make the condition in EP8 necessary,
but not sufficient, for a *de re* attitude. Having a *de re* attitude to a
substance requires both having a corresponding *de dicto* attitude to a
proposition about the substance and identifying, in some appropriate
way, the substance as the subject of the proposition. When Descartes
clearly and distinctly conceives that Elizabeth's favorite substance is
extended but unthinking, he does not have a *de re* conception about
himself, unless he both is Elizabeth's favorite substance and identifies
himself as such. If we take this approach, Descartes's first two premises
are still false.[18] Suppose there is a vase and a dish before Descartes and
he is blindfolded. He touches the vase and says, "I conceive clearly
and distinctly that this is the most valuable object in the world but not
the most desired." He conceives a proposition to the effect that the vase
has one property but not another, and, according to any standard
account of "identification," he identifies the vase as the subject of the
proposition. He clearly and distinctly conceives *de re* of the vase that it
is the most valuable object but not the most desired. He next touches
the vase with his other hand, and believing he is touching something
else, says, "I conceive clearly and distinctly that this is the most desired
object in the world but not the most valuable." He clearly and distinctly conceives a proposition to the effect that the vase is the most
desired but not the most valuable, and he identifies the vase as the

17. The literature on *de re* attitudes is too extensive to list here. Those unacquainted with the topic might consider Roderick Chisholm, *Person and Object* (London: George Allen and Unwin, 1976); Roderick Chisholm, "Knowledge and Belief:
'De Dicto' and 'De Re,'" *Philosophical Studies*, 29 (1976), pp. 1–20; Ernest Sosa,
"Propositional Attitudes *De Dicto* and *De Re*," *Journal of Philosophy*, 67 (1970), pp.
883–896; Richard Feldman, "Actions and *De Re* Belief," *Canadian Journal of Philosophy*, 8 (1978), pp. 577–582; and Lynne Rudder Baker, "*De Re* Belief in Action,"
Philosophical Review, 91 (July 1982), pp. 363–387.

18. The following example is inspired by Lynne Rudder Baker's discussion of the
classical approach in "*De Re* Belief in Action."

subject of that proposition. He conceives clearly and distinctly of the vase that it is the most desired and not the most valuable. Descartes thus gains two clear and distinct conceptions of the vase: First, it is the most valuable, but not the most desired, object; second, it is the most desired, but not the most valuable, object. His first two premises in his argument for C6 thus imply that he clearly and distinctly conceives the vase apart from itself so that the vase is really distinct from itself.

There is another problem with the view that Descartes relies on classical *de re* conceptions: He does not have a classical *de re* conception of his body as extended but not thinking in Meditation Six. He may conceive *de dicto* the proposition he would express by "My body is extended but does not think," yet to move from this to the corresponding classical *de re* conception of his body, he must identify the particular substance that is his body as his body, that is, as the subject of the proposition he conceives. A close reading of Meditation Six reveals that Descartes never makes such an identification. He argues that there are bodies and that he has one, but he does not identify a particular body as his.

In all, we run into serious textual and philosophical problems if we interpret Descartes's talk about what he clearly and distinctly understands as talk about what he clearly and distinctly conceives. The problems are there whether we pick *de dicto* or *de re* clear and distinct conception.

We avoid all these problems if we decide Descartes is interested in what he clearly and distinctly perceives *de dicto*. His argument becomes

The Gambit Defense of C6: Third Version

1. If I clearly and distinctly perceive x apart from y and y apart from x, then x and y are such that it is logically possible that x exists while y does not exist, and logically possible that y exists while x does not exist (x and y are really distinct).
2. I clearly and distinctly perceive x apart from y and y apart from x if there is a proposition p to the effect that x has a property P but lacks a property Q, there is a proposition q to the effect that y has Q but lacks P, and I clearly and distinctly perceive that p and that q.
3. My body and I are such that there is a proposition to the effect that I think but am not extended, there is a proposition to the effect that my body is extended but does not think, and I clearly and distinctly perceive each proposition.
4. Therefore, my body and I are really distinct. [from 1, 2, and 3]

Consider the advantages of understanding Descartes's argument in this way. We capture the passages in which Descartes appeals to his clear and distinct perceptions about himself and his body to show that they are really distinct. We skirt the issue, as Descartes does, of the necessary and sufficient conditions for *de re* attitudes. We do not require Descartes to identify a particular substance as his body; he just has to perceive clearly and distinctly that his body, whatever substance it may be, is extended but does not think. The argument's first two premises cannot be used to show that Descartes is really distinct from himself: Descartes cannot clearly and distinctly perceive the propositions he would express by "I think but am not extended" and "Elizabeth's favorite substance is extended but does not think," when both are about him; if both are about him, one of them is false and cannot be perceived clearly and distinctly.

There is just one major flaw in this interpretation of Descartes's argument for the Real Distinction Thesis. It is out of step with his progress in Meditation Six. It has him appeal to his clear and distinct perception that his body is extended and does not think, but he actually argues for the Real Distinction Thesis before he clearly and distinctly perceives that he has a body.

> And although possibly (or rather certainly, as I shall say in a moment) I possess a body with which I am very intimately conjoined, yet because, on the one side, I have a clear and distinct idea of myself inasmuch as I am only a thinking and unextended thing, and as, on the other, I possess a distinct idea of body inasmuch as it is only an extended and unthinking thing, it is certain that I am really distinct from my body and can exist without it. [*Meditations*; AT VII, 78; HR I, 190*]

The flaw is easily removed. When Descartes argues for the Real Distinction Thesis, he appeals to his clear and distinct perception of conditionals about what his body is like, if it exists. He says he has a clear and distinct idea of his body as extended and thinking; he means he clearly and distinctly perceives the conditional he would express by "If my body exists, then it is extended but does not think." We should interpret his argument for the Real Distinction Thesis accordingly:

The Gambit Defense of C6: Fourth Version

1. If I clearly and distinctly perceive x apart from y and y apart from x, then x and y are such that it is logically possible that x exists while y

does not exist and logically possible that *y* exists while *x* does not exist (*x* and *y* are really distinct).

2. I clearly and distinctly perceive *x* apart from *y* and *y* apart from *x* if there is a proposition *p* to the effect that if *x* exists, *x* has a property *P* but lacks a property *Q*, there is a proposition *q* to the effect that if *y* exists, *y* has *Q* but lacks *P*, and I clearly and distinctly perceive that *p* and that *q*.

3. There is a proposition to the effect that if I exist, I think but am not extended; there is a proposition to the effect that if my body exists, it is extended but does not think; and I clearly and distinctly perceive both propositions.

4. Therefore, if my body exists, my body and I are really distinct.   [from 1, 2, and 3]

This is Descartes's argument for the Real Distinction Thesis, except for a few minor changes that are inspired by the objections of his contemporaries. Note that I call the argument a "Gambit Defense," even though it does not use P1, P2, and P3 as premises. Descartes relies on P1, P2, and P3 in an indirect way. He uses them to construct his argument for C4, that he is not extended, and C5, that he is not identical with his body, and his examination of those arguments is part of the process by which he perceives clearly and distinctly that if he exists, he thinks but is not extended and that if his body exists, it is extended but does not think. He derives C6 from the fact that he has these clear and distinct perceptions. Descartes uses his premises about self-knowledge to construct the arguments he follows to get his mind in a particular state, and he deduces the Real Distinction Thesis from the fact that his mind is in that state.[19]

It is important to appreciate the initial plausibility of Descartes's criterion for real distinctness. Suppose he clearly and distinctly perceives that if *x* exists, it has *P* but lacks *Q*, and that if *y* exists, it has *Q* but lacks *P*. Two things seem to follow if *x* and *y* exist. First, they are

19. Descartes thus indirectly uses the Numerical Distinction Thesis to defend the Real Distinction Thesis, rather than vice versa. His argument for the Numerical Distinction Thesis is one of the arguments he must examine to gain the clear and distinct perceptions he cites in his defense of the Real Distinction Thesis.

My interpretation of Descartes's argument for the Real Distinction Thesis captures his view that he cannot gain metaphysical certainty of the thesis until he rules out the clear and distinct perception version of the Deceiver Hypothesis. That hypothesis gives him a reason to doubt each premise of the Gambit Defense of C6.

numerically diverse. Second, neither is a complex substance of which the other is a part; one substance contains another as a part only if it has all the real attributes of the other; for example, the union of Descartes's mind and body both thinks and is extended. So *x* and *y* are numerically distinct and neither is a complex substance of which the other is a part. That should be enough to make them capable of existing apart.

The Criterion for Real Distinctness: Objections and Adjustments

Caterus criticizes Descartes's criterion for real distinctness in the *First Objections*. Arnauld attacks it in the *Fourth Objections*. Their objections and Descartes's replies can help us better appreciate the criterion and, so, the Gambit Defense of C6.

Caterus appeals to Duns Scotus:

> In so far as one thing can be conceived as distinct and separate from another, the adequate distinction to draw between them is what he [Scotus] calls a *formal* and *objective* one, which is intermediate between a *real* distinction and a distinction of *reason. It is thus that he* [Scotus] *distinguishes between Divine justice and Divine pity.* They have, *he says,* concepts formally diverse prior to any operation of the understanding, so that, even then, the one is not the other; yet it does not follow that, because God's justice can be conceived apart from his pity, they can also exist apart. [AT VII, 100; HR II, 8][20]

Arnauld makes a similar point in a different way. Suppose a man reasons:

> Since I know that all things I clearly and distinctly understand can be created by God just as I understand them to exist, it is sufficient for me, in order to be sure that one thing is distinct from another, to be able to understand the one clearly and distinctly apart from the other, because it can be isolated by God. *But I clearly and distinctly understand that*

20. Note how Caterus's example demonstrates our need to distinguish between numerical distinctness and real distinctness. That God is just and that God has pity are numerically distinct states of affairs, but they are not really distinct (neither can exist without the other).

this triangle is right-angled, without comprehending that the square on its base is equal to the squares on its sides. Hence God at least can create a right-angled triangle, the square on the base of which is not equal to the squares on its sides. [AT VII, 202; HR II, 83*]

As long as we accept Descartes's criterion for real distinctness, we must, according to Arnauld, give the unacceptable *ad hoc* reply that

the man in question does not perceive clearly and distinctly that the triangle is right-angled. [AT VII, 202; HR II, 83–84*]

Neither Caterus nor Arnauld has a firm grip on Descartes's criterion for real distinctness. Caterus objects to a criterion formulated in terms of what we clearly and distinctly *conceive*. It is hard to tell what sort of criterion Arnauld finds objectionable; he initially seems interested in the principle that if we clearly and distinctly perceive a proposition about *x* without clearly and distinctly perceiving one about *y*, then *x* and *y* are really distinct, but he gives a counterexample to the principle that if we clearly and distinctly perceive a thing to have one quality without clearly and distinctly perceiving it to have another, then the thing can have the first quality without the second. None of these principles is part of the Gambit Defense of C6, which uses

EP19′: If *x* and *y* are such that (1) there is a proposition *p* to the effect that if *x* exists, then *x* has a property *P* but lacks a property *Q*, (2) there is a proposition *q* to the effect that if *y* exists, then y has *Q* but lacks *P*, and (3) *S* clearly and distinctly perceives that *p* and that *q*, then *x* and *y* are really distinct.

We might object to this principle by modifying Caterus's example: God's justice cannot exist apart from God's pity, even though Descartes or someone else clearly and distinctly perceives that if God's justice exists, it is an instance of justice, not pity, and if God's pity exists, it is an instance of pity, not justice. Descartes's replies to Caterus and Arnauld suggest an appropriate response. He throws out Caterus's counterexample because it is not a case of someone who clearly and distinctly perceives one thing apart from another in such a way that each is perceived to be an "entity in itself," a substance.

In the matter of the formal distinction which the learned Theologian claims to draw from Scotus, my reply is briefly to the effect that this distinction in no way differs from a modal one, and applies only to incomplete entities, which I have accurately demarcated from complete beings. This is sufficient to cause one thing to be conceived separately and as distinct from another by the abstracting action of the mind when it conceives the thing inadequately, without sufficing to cause two things to be thought of so distinctly and separately that we understand each to be an entity in itself and diverse from every other; in order that we may do this a real distinction is absolutely necessary. [*Reply to the First Objections*; AT VII, 120; HR II, 22]

Arnauld's counterexample has a similar defect:

For firstly, although perhaps a triangle may be taken in the concrete as a substance possessing a triangular shape, certainly the property of having the square on the base equal to the squares on the sides is not a substance; so too, neither can either of these two things be understood to be a complete thing in the sense in which *Mind and Body* are. [*Reply to the Fourth Objections*; AT VII, 224; HR II, 100]

Descartes may say the same about my modified version of Caterus's objection. It does not involve someone who clearly and distinctly perceives one thing apart from another in such a way that each is clearly and distinctly perceived to be a substance. If God's justice and God'd pity are entities in the world, they are qualities or, perhaps, states of affairs—not substances.

Descartes criterion for real distinctness now looks like this:

EP19″: If x and y are such that (1) there is a proposition p to the effect that if x exists, then x *is a substance* with a property P but without a property Q, (2) there is a proposition q to the effect that if y exists, then y *is a substance* with Q but without P, and (3) S clearly and distinctly perceives that p and that q, then x and y are really distinct.

His claim to satisfy the criterion relative to his body must be changed accordingly. Recall that Descartes has a weak and a strong definition of what a substance is:

D6a: x is a substance $=_{df.}$ x has a real attribute.
D6b: x is a substance $=_{df.}$ (1) x has a real attribute, and (2) there is no y such that y has a real attribute, y is not numerically identical to x, y exists contingently, and it is logically impossible that x exists and y does not.

His defense of the Real Distinction Thesis (C6) will beg the question if he uses the strong concept of a substance in his real distinctness criterion: he cannot clearly and distinctly perceive that, if he exists, he is a substance in the strong sense, unless he is a substance in the strong sense, and he is not a substance in the strong sense unless he can exist without his body, which is what he is trying to show. Descartes only needs to use the weak notion of a substance in his criterion: God's justice and pity do not have real attributes (extension, thought, and their modes); the same goes for the properties of the triangle cited by Arnauld.

Some commentators believe that Descartes restricts his criterion for real distinctness to essential properties.[21] I do not know of any passage in which he explictly makes this move, but it can get him around another difficult case. Suppose he clearly and distinctly perceives that he is a simple, rather than a complex, substance, but his union with his body is a complex, rather than a simple, one (he is not composed of any other entity with real attributes, although his union with his body is). He can avoid the false conclusion that he is really distinct from his union with his body if he changes his criterion to

> EP19‴: If x and y are such that (1) there is a proposition p to the effect that if x exists, then x is a substance and has a property P but not a property Q *essentially*, (2) there is a proposition q to the effect that if y exists, then y is a substance and has Q but not P *essentially*, and (3) S clearly and distinctly perceives that p and that q, then x and y are really distinct.

Descartes cannot clearly and distinctly perceive that if his union with his body exists, it is an essentially complex, not an essentially simple, substance. His union with his body has no essential property—no necessary, nontranscendental property of which all its nonnecessary, nonrelational properties are modes. Some of its nonnecessary, nonrelational properties are modes of thought; others are modes of extension.

21. Margaret Wilson, *Descartes*, pp. 185–198, interprets Descartes's premises in support of the Real Distinction Thesis so that they concern essential properties. That, as we have seen, Descartes argues for his claims about his essence in the middle of arguing for his Real Distinction Thesis in Meditation Six provides some support for this interpretation.

One difficult case remains for Descartes's criterion for real distinctness: God. No substance is really distinct from God, since none can exist unless God exists, yet Descartes can clearly and distinctly perceive that if his body exists, it is a substance that is essentially extended but not essentially thinking, and he can clearly and distinctly perceive that if God exists, God is a substance that is essentially thinking but not essentially extended. His criterion of real distinctness implies that his body is really distinct from God. Descartes deals with a similar problem when he presents his strong definition of substance in the *Principles* [I, li–lii; AT VIII, 24–25; HR I, 239–240]. He defines a substance as an entity that exists independently of any other, decides that only God meets this definition, and weakens it: A substance is an entity that exists independently of any other entity that is contingent. This strategy has an arbitrary air, but Descartes might use it again and change his criterion for real distinctness to

> EP19: If x and y are such that (1) there is a proposition p to the effect that if x exists, then x is a *contingent* substance and has a property P but not a property Q essentially, (2) there is a proposition q to the effect that if y exists, then y is a *contingent* substance and has Q but not P essentially, and (3) S clearly and distinctly perceives that p and that q, then x and y are really distinct.

Descartes cannot clearly and distinctly perceive a proposition to the effect that if God exists, God is a contingent substance, essentially thinking but not essentially extended.

Descartes's criterion is now true. Suppose we clearly and distinctly perceive that if x exists, x is a contingent substance with one property as its essence, and if y exists, y is a contingent substance with another property as its essence. Two things follow if x and y exist: (1) x and y are numerically diverse contingent substances and (2) neither is a complex substance with the other as one of its parts. Each should be able, then, to exist without the other. Neither is tied to the other by identity or by a part–whole relation; it is possible that either exist without the other.

Descartes just needs the requisite clear and distinct perceptions about himself and his body to show they are really distinct. This is where his argument fails. He must use his arguments for the rest of his theory of the self, including C4, that he is not extended, and C5, that he is numerically distinct from his body, to gain those clear and distinct perceptions. The arguments are not question begging or logically invalid, but with the exception of his argument for C1a, that he is a substance in the weak sense, they are not deductions from self-evident premises and so cannot generate the clear and distinct perceptions he needs.

Descartes's Gambit and C1b

We have come to the end of the line: Descartes's claim to be a substance in the strong sense of 'substance.'

> C1b: I have a real attribute, and there is no y such that y has a real attribute, y is numerically distinct from me, y exists contingently, and it is logically impossible that I exist and y does not.

The closest Descartes comes to arguing for C1b is

> For in accordance with the knowledge which we have of God, we are certain that He can carry into effect all that of which we have a distinct idea. That is why from the fact that we now have, e.g. the idea of an extended or corporeal substance, although we do not yet know certainly whether such really exists at all, we may yet conclude that it may exist; and if it does exist, any one portion of it which we can demarcate in our thought must be distinct from every other part of the same substance. Similarly because each one of us is conscious that he thinks, and that in thinking he can shut off from himself all other substance, either thinking or extended, we may conclude that each of us, similarly regarded, is really distinct from every other thinking substance and from every corporeal substance. [*Principles*, I, lx; AT VIII, 28; HR I, 243–244]

Descartes seems to be trying to "generalize" his argument for the claim that he is really distinct from his body to show that he is really distinct from every other substance. He is incautious, to say the least. He is not really distinct from every other substance. He cannot exist without God; the union of him and his body cannot exist without him. The most Descartes may claim by his own metaphysics is that he—and, by extension, each of us—can exist without every other contingent substance (C1b); none of us is a complex substance of which some other contingent substance is a necessary part.

If we take a nip here and a tuck there, we can get an interesting defense of C1b out of Descartes's remarks in the *Principles*:

The Gambit Defense of C1b

1. If x and y are contingent substances (have real attributes) and I can demarcate x from y in thought, then it is logically possible that x exists while y does not exist.
2. I am a contingent substance.
3. If y is a contingent substance other than me, I can demarcate myself from y in thought.
4. Therefore, I have a real attribute, and there is no y such that y has a real attribute, y is numerically diverse from me, y exists contingently, and it is logically impossible that I exist and y does not.   [from 1, 2, and 3]

The question is what does Descartes have in mind when he writes of demarcating one substance from another in thought. We can reject two extreme answers right away:

D9′: S demarcates x from y in thought = $_{df.}$ there is a proposition p to the effect that x has some property P, a proposition q to the effect that y lacks P, and S clearly and distinctly perceives that p and that q.

This definition equates demarcating one substance from another with clearly and distinctly perceiving a difference in their properties. It is too generous. Descartes can clearly and distinctly perceive that his union with his body is extended, while he is not, but he correctly maintains that his union with his body cannot exist without him. A second alternative is

D9″: S demarcates x from y in thought = $_{df.}$ there is a proposition p to the effect that x has a property P essentially, a proposition q to the effect that y does not have P essentially, and S clearly and distinctly perceives that p and that q.

On this definition, demarcating one substance from another amounts to perceiving clearly and distinctly a difference in their essential properties. This definition does not let Descartes demarcate himself from any other thinking substance. The best interpretation lies between the extremes:

D9: *S demarcates x from y in thought* = $_{df}$ there is a proposition *p* to the effect that *x* has a property *P* as a mode of its essence, a proposition *q* to the effect that *y* lacks *P* as a mode of its essence, and *S* clearly and distinctly perceives that *p* and that *q*.

Descartes can demarcate himself from each extended substance by clearly and distinctly perceiving that he doubts as a mode of his essence while it does not doubt at all. He can demarcate himself from his union with his body by clearly and distinctly perceiving that, while he doubts as a mode of his essence, that complex substance has no essence. He can demarcate himself from every other thinking substance by clearly and distinctly perceiving a difference between his modes of thought and those of the other substances. As Descartes puts it, "in thinking he can shut off from himself all other substance, either thinking or extended."

D9 lets us see how the argument for C1b is a "Gambit Defense." Descartes uses his claims to self-knowledge to construct his argument for C2, that he is essentially thinking; by examining that argument, he gains a clear and distinct perception that he is essentially thinking, and that clear and distinct perception is part of what makes his third premise here, that he can demarcate himself from every other contingent substance, true. The argument for C1b is a "Gambit Defense" in the same way the argument for the Real Distinction Thesis is. In each, Descartes relies on earlier arguments constructed from his premises about self-knowledge to gain clear and distinct perceptions and then appeals to the fact that he has those clear and distinct perceptions to establish his conclusion.

D9 leaves Descartes holding some tough problems, even though it is the best way to understand his talk of demarcating one substance from another. Two especially deserve mention. First, how is it Descartes can clearly and distinctly perceive a difference between his modes of thought and those of any other thinking substance? Descartes might say he can clearly and distinctly perceive that, as a mode of his thought, he affirms the proposition he would express by "I think" and, for any other thinking substance, he can clearly and distinctly perceive that it does not affirm *that very same proposition* as a mode of its thought. How, though, can Descartes gain these clear and distinct perceptions? Second, we need some reason to accept the premise that if Descartes can demarcate one thing from another, it is possible for the one to exist without the other. What if Descartes is just a bundle of perceptions? Could he not demarcate himself—the whole bundle—from any proper subset of himself by clearly and distinctly perceiving that he has a particular mode of thought the subset lacks? It would not follow that Descartes—the whole bundle—can exist when the subset does not.

Conclusion

The second part of Descartes's theory of the self (that he is not extended, is numerically distinct from his body, and capable of existing apart from every other contingent substance) is more radical than the first (that he is a substance, essentially thinking but not essentially extended) and far more radical than his views on self-knowledge (that he is metaphysically certain that he thinks and exists but metaphysically uncertain that he has a body). Nonetheless, Descartes derives the second part from the first part, and the first part from his theory of self-knowledge. He does so without the blunders so often attributed to him. He does not beg the question, misapply the principle of the indiscernibility of identicals, or incorrectly infer *de re* propositions from their *de dicto* counterparts. His reasoning is impeccable; his assumptions are not outrageous, especially when considered in themselves rather than with an eye to where they ultimately lead in the context of the rest of his philosophy. Descartes's development of his theory of the self is a fine example of how a moderate, at base almost commonsensical, philosophical position can be radicalized.

SUMMARY

That Descartes uses his theory of self-knowledge to support his theory of the self is common knowledge. How he does so is common ignorance. Indeed, if people clearly explain what they clearly understand, even Descartes is unsure of the details.

I have presented the details of Descartes's Gambit. I have explained his views on self-knowledge against the background of his theory of the nature and content of certainty. I have developed the arguments that run from his premises about self-knowledge, by way of his position on the nature and content of certainty, to his conclusions about his nature and his relation to his body.

I have shown how Descartes's theory of certainty is the central element in his Gambit strategy. It is the basis of his defense of his premises about self-knowledge (P_1, P_2, and P_3). It provides the principles that enable him to move from those premises to intermediate conclusions about the logical possibility of his existing in some ways and not others, from which he derives his theory of the self (C_1–C_6).

I have shown that Descartes does not just assume his versions of attribute and substance dualism or fall into them by a logical blunder. He reasons his way to them by an insightful strategy that frequently generates strong arguments. His arguments give us good reason to consider more carefully how a correct account of self-knowledge may commit us to substantive conclusions about our nature.

Appendix

PREMISES, CONCLUSIONS, DEFINITIONS, AND EPISTEMIC PRINCIPLES

Premises about Self-knowledge

P1: I am certain that I think.
P2: I am certain that I exist.
P3: I am uncertain that I have a body.

Conclusions about the Self

C1:   I am a substance.
C1a: I have a real attribute.
C1b: I have a real attribute and there is no y such that y has a real attribute, y is numerically distinct from me, y exists contingently, and it is logically impossible that I exist and y does not exist.
C2:   I am essentially thinking.
C3:   I am not essentially extended.
C4:   I am not extended.
C5:   I am not numerically identical with my body.
C6:   My body and I are such that each can exist without the other.

Definitions

D1: p is a moral certainty for $S =$ df. (1) believing p is more reasonable for S from the standard epistemic perspective than denying p or

271

doubting p (neither believing nor denying p), and (2) believing some proposition q is more reasonable for S from the standard perspective than believing p only if q is a metaphysical certainty for S.

D2: p is a metaphysical certainty for S $=$ df. (1) believing p is more reasonable for S from the standard epistemic perspective than doubting or denying p, and (2) it could never be more reasonable for S to believe some proposition q than it is at present for S to believe p.

D3: q gives S a reason to doubt S's morally certain belief p if and only if (1) q is a metaphysical possibility for S, and (2) either q indicates to S how p might be false despite S's evidence for p, or q indicates to S how an essential part of S's evidence for p might be false despite S's evidence for that essential part.

D4: p is a psychological certainty for S $=$ df. S believes p and S is unable to doubt or deny p.

D5: S's knowledge that p with degree of certainty C is permanent $=$ df. (1) S knows that p with degree of certainty C and (2) there is no proposition q such that (a) q is true, (b) S is not certain of q or of not-q to degree C, and (c) if S were to become certain of q to degree C, while retaining his evidence for p, S would cease to be certain of p to degree C.

D6a: x is a substance $=$ df. x has a real attribute.

D6b: x is a substance $=$ df. (1) x has a real attribute, and (2) there is no y such that y has a real attribute, y is numerically distinct from x, y exists contingently, but it is logically impossible that x exists and y does not.

D7: A property P is essential to a substance x $=$ df. (1) it is necessary that if x exists, then x has P, (2) P is a nontranscendental property, and (3) every nonrelational, nonnecessary property of x is a mode of P.

D8: P is a nontranscendental property $=$ df. it is logically possible that some substance lacks P.

D9: S demarcates x from y in thought $=$ df. there is a proposition p to the effect that x has a property P as a mode of its essence, a proposition q to the effect that y lacks P as a mode of its essence, and S clearly and distinctly perceives that p and that q.

Epistemic Principles

EP1: p is a metaphysical certainty for S if and only if p is a moral certainty for S and S has no reason to doubt p.

EP2: A human S is metaphysically certain that *p* only if S clearly and distinctly perceives that *p*.

EP3: A human S clearly and distinctly perceives that *p* only if *p* is true.

EP4: A human S clearly and distinctly perceives that *p* only if S is psychologically certain that *p*.

EP5: If S knows that *p* with moral, but not metaphysical, certainty, then S's knowledge that *p* is impermanent.

EP6: If S knows that *p* with metaphysical certainty, S's knowledge that *p* is permanent.

EP7: S is metaphysically certain (believes, doubts, conceives, etc.) *de se* that he himself is F only if there is a proposition *p* such that (1) S is metaphysically certain (believes, doubts, conceives, etc.) *de dicto* that *p*, and (2) *p* is a proposition to the effect that S is F.

EP8: S is metaphysically certain (believes, doubts, conceives, etc.) *de re* of *x* that it is F only if there is a proposition *p* such that (1) S is metaphysically certain (believes, doubts, conceives, etc.) *de dicto* that *p*, and (2) *p* is a proposition to the effect that *x* is F.

EP9: S is metaphysically certain (believes, doubts, conceives, etc.) *de se* that he himself is F only if S is metaphysically certain (believes, doubts, conceives, etc.) *de re* of S that it is F.

EP10: S apprehends *x* only if there is some proposition *p* such that (1) S considers *de dicto* that *p*, and (2) *p* is a proposition to the effect that *x* has (lacks) some property.

EP11: S apprehends *x* only if there is some property C such that (1) C is an individual concept of *x* (*x* has C and it is impossible that more than one thing has C), and (2) S conceives C.

EP12: If S conceives *de se* that he himself is F and *p* is the propositional content of S's conception, then no one other than S can conceive that *p*.

EP13: *q* indicates to S how S's morally certain belief *p* might be false despite S's evidence for *p* only if either (1) it is logically necessary that *p*, or (2) it is logically possible that *q* is true and *p* is false.

EP14: If S clearly and distinctly perceives that *p*, then S is morally certain that *p*.

EP15: *q* indicates to S how S's morally certain belief *p* might be false despite S evidence for *p* only if (1) *q* entails that proposition that is the content of S's *de se* belief that S exists, and (2) *q* entails that proposition that is the content of S's *de se* belief that S thinks.

EP16: *q* indicates to S how S's morally certain belief *p* might be false despite S's evidence for *p* only if either (1) it is logically necessary that p, or (2) it is logically possible that q is true, S believes p, and p is false.

EP17: S clearly and distinctly perceives that p directly if and only if either (1) S noninferentially considers p and it is naturally necessary that if S noninferentially considers p, then S believes p, or (2) S noninferentially considers p, p is true, and it is naturally necessary that if S noninferentially considers p and p is true, then S believes p.

EP18: (1) If S considers the deduction of p from premises each of which S clearly and distinctly perceives directly and it is naturally necessary that S believes p when S considers that deduction and clearly and distinctly perceives its premises directly, then S clearly and distinctly perceives p deductively; and
(2) If S considers the deduction of p from premises each of which S clearly and distinctly perceives directly or deductively, and it is naturally necessary that S believes p when S considers that deduction and clearly and distinctly perceives its premises, then S clearly and distinctly perceives p deductively; and
(3) S clearly and distinctly perceives p deductively only if S satisfies the conditions in (1) or (2) relative to p.

EP19: If x and y are such that (1) there is a proposition p to the effect that if x exists, then x is a contingent substance and has a property P but not a property Q essentially, and (2) there is a proposition q to the effect that if y exists, then y is a contingent substance and has Q but not P essentially, and (3) S clearly and distinctly perceives that p and that q, then x and y are really distinct.

INDEX

Library of Congress Cataloging-in-Publication Data

Markie, Peter J., 1950–
 Descartes's gambit.

 Includes index.
  1. Descartes, René, 1596–1650. I. Title.
B1875.M345 1986   194   86-6241
ISBN 0-8014-1906-9 (alk. paper)